How to be a historian

How to be a historian

Scholarly personae in historical studies,
1800–2000

Edited by Herman Paul

Manchester University Press

Copyright © Manchester University Press 2019

While copyright in the volume as a whole is vested in Manchester University Press, copyright in individual chapters belongs to their respective authors, and no chapter may be reproduced wholly or in part without the express permission in writing of both author and publisher.

Published by Manchester University Press
Oxford Road, Manchester M13 9PL
www.manchesteruniversitypress.co.uk

British Library Cataloguing-in-Publication Data
A catalogue record for this book is available from the British Library

ISBN 978 1 5261 3280 2 hardback
ISBN 978 1 5261 5603 7 paperback

First published 2019

Paperback published 2021

The publisher has no responsibility for the persistence or accuracy of URLs for any external or third-party internet websites referred to in this book, and does not guarantee that any content on such websites is, or will remain, accurate or appropriate.

Typeset in Adobe Garamond Pro by
Servis Filmsetting Ltd, Stockport, Cheshire

Contents

Notes on contributors   vii

    Introduction. Scholarly personae: what they are and why they matter – *Herman Paul*   1

1 The contested persona of the historian: on the origins of a permanent conflict – *Ian Hunter*   15

2 Ranke vs Schlosser: pairs of personae in nineteenth-century German historiography – *Herman Paul*   36

3 Fixing genius: the Romantic man of letters in the university era – *Travis E. Ross*   53

4 Generational continuities and composite personae: French historiography from the 1870s to the 1950s – *Camille Creyghton*   72

5 Pasha and his historic harem: Edward A. Freeman, Edith Thompson and the gendered personae of late-Victorian historians – *Elise Garritzen*   89

6 Interpretative and investigative: the emergence and characteristics of modern scholarly personae in China, 1900–30 – *Q. Edward Wang*   107

7 Coalescence and conflict: historians and their personae in the Portuguese New State – *António da Silva Rêgo*   130

8 The emergence of the English Marxist historian's scholarly persona: the English Revolution debate of 1940–41 – *Sina Talachian*   146

CONTENTS

9 Of communism, compromise and Central Europe: the scholarly persona under authoritarianism – *Monika Baár*   164

10 What is an African historian? Negotiating scholarly personae in UNESCO's *General History of Africa* – *Larissa Schulte Nordholt*   182

11 The finitude of personae: Bryce Lyon, François Louis Ganshof and the biography of Pirenne – *Henning Trüper*   201

Index   219

Notes on contributors

Monika Baár is Professor by Special Appointment in Central European Studies at the Institute for History at Leiden University. She is author of *Historians and Nationalism: East-Central Europe in the Nineteenth Century* (2010) and co-author of *A History of Modern Political Thought in East-Central Europe* (2 vols, 2016–18).

Camille Creyghton is a lecturer in history and cultural studies at the University of Amsterdam and a postdoctoral fellow at the Centre for the History of Political Thought at Queen Mary University, London. She wrote a PhD thesis on the afterlife of Jules Michelet in French historiography and politics (2016). Her current research is about intellectual exiles in Paris, Brussels and London (1830–48).

Elise Garritzen is a senior research fellow at the University of Helsinki. She has published articles on nineteenth-century historiography in *History of Humanities, Clio* and *Storia della Storiografia*. Her current project explores the use of paratexts for professional self-fashioning in late-Victorian history books.

Ian Hunter is Emeritus Professor in the Institute for Advanced Studies in the Humanities at the University of Queensland. He is the author of various studies in the history of political thought and the history of historiography, including *Rival Enlightenments* (2001), *The Secularisation of the Confessional State* (2007) and 'About the dialectical historiography of international law' (2016).

Herman Paul is Professor of the History of the Humanities at Leiden University. He also holds a special chair in secularization studies at the University of Groningen. The author of *Key Issues in Historical Theory*

(2015) and *Hayden White: The Historical Imagination* (2011), he is currently at work on a book on virtues and vices in nineteenth-century German historical studies.

António da Silva Rêgo holds a MA (Research) in History from Leiden University and is a PhD student at Birkbeck, University of London. He is writing a PhD thesis on the development of history as an academic discipline in Portugal during the Estado Novo regime (1926–74).

Travis E. Ross is a lecturer in the Department of History at Yale University. He is currently working on a book project focused on Hubert Howe Bancroft's History Company and the long history of knowledge capitalism in the United States.

Larissa Schulte Nordholt is a PhD candidate at the Institute for History at Leiden University. She works on the historiography of UNESCO's *General History of Africa/l'Histoire générale de l'Afrique*.

Sina Talachian is a PhD student in History at the University of Cambridge, specializing in intellectual history and working on a dissertation on the invention of the Marxist historian.

Henning Trüper is Core Fellow at the Helsinki Collegium for Advanced Studies. He is the author of *Topography of a Method: François Louis Ganshof and the Writing of History* (2014) and co-editor of *Historical Teleologies in the Modern World* (2015). He is currently finishing a book about the history of orientalist philologies and setting out on a new project about the organized saving of lives from shipwreck on the shores of modern Europe.

Q. Edward Wang is Professor of History at Rowan University and Changjiang Professor at Peking University. He has published extensively in comparative history and historiography and Chinese cultural and intellectual history, including co-authoring *A Global History of Modern Historiography* (2008; 2017), which has appeared in Chinese, German, Greek and Russian.

INTRODUCTION

Scholarly personae: what they are and why they matter

Herman Paul

Introduction

'What kind of a historian do I want to be?' For American history students in the late 1960s, pursuing their degrees while the Vietnam War was escalating and students' protests were spreading from campus to campus, this question imposed itself with singular strength. Back in the 1950s, it had seemed as if American historians had been able to reach consensus on what historical professionalism entailed. Most notably, this had included a marked distancing from 'overdeveloped commitment' to present-day concerns such as displayed by a previous generation of 'progressive' historians. During the 1960s, however, this counterprogressive consensus, as Peter Novick calls it, was called into question – initially in learned articles, but quickly also in classrooms and scholarly gatherings. Symbolic in this regard was the 1969 meeting of the American Historical Association in Washington, DC, where the profession turned out to be deeply divided, not only over the Vietnam War, but also over the legitimacy of new, 'radical' branches of history that aimed to give voice to underrepresented cultures, races and sexes.[1]

One of those so-called radicals was Howard Zinn at Boston University. Teaching in a movie theatre because no lecture hall was large enough to accommodate his class, Zinn encouraged his students to combine historical scholarship with social activism, for instance by having them write papers on their involvement in local community organizations. This implied a rejection of scholarly objectivity as traditionally understood. '[I]n a world where children are still not safe from starvation or bombs', Zinn asked rhetorically, 'should not the historian thrust himself and his writing into history, on behalf of goals in which he deeply believes?' Although the Boston University administration answered this question with an unambiguous 'no', Zinn's radicalism fascinated younger scholars at the Left, just as did his defence of scholarly activism in *The Politics of History* (1970).[2]

Related to Zinn's activism was the emancipatory agenda behind women's history. Historians heard Gerda Lerner criticize the American Historical Association during its 1968 annual meeting for being an old boys' network. They read her fulminations against 'the competitiveness which is structured into our institutional and professional life' and heard women's historians address each other as 'sister' so as to emphasize an ideal of non-competitive female collegiality. As a participant in the first Berkshire Conference on the History of Women (1973) remembers, it was a time of 'great excitement and expectation'. Would the hegemony of the white, male, middle-aged history professor soon be a thing of the past?[3]

None of this went uncontested, of course. In *The American Historical Review*, Irwin Unger got ample opportunity to explain that the young Turks in American historical studies 'often [fail] to play the scholarly game by the most elementary rules of fair play', 'allow the tone and rhetoric of the picket line and the handbill to invade their professional work' and display a 'contempt for pure history'.[4] In universities and colleges throughout the USA, faculty members warned their students not to take classes with young radicals – a heterogeneous group that also included Hayden White, the soon-to-be-famous historical theorist whose manifesto 'The burden of history' (1966) had just been published. Like Zinn and Lerner, though, White captivated numerous students with his 'belligerent style' of thinking, writing and teaching. Was it possible, students wondered, to be a historian like White: politically engaged, seemingly indifferent to disciplinary standards, more interested in pop art than in methodology books and celebrating creativity instead of insisting on accuracy?[5]

At stake, then, was the professional identity of the historian or, more specifically, the advantages and drawbacks of competing models of how to be a historian. If this volume draws attention to such models, or *scholarly personae*, it does so because the question 'what kind of a historian do I want to be?' is one well suited for positioning American historians in the late 1960s – or, for that matter, any other group of historians at any other time – on a larger historiographical canvas. Precisely to the extent that the question 'what kind of a historian do I want to be?' is a recurring one, travelling in different guises through time and space, it allows for comparisons across schools, traditions, countries and periods for which existing historiographical literature does not typically allow.

Scholarly personae: micro and macro approaches

What exactly are *scholarly personae*?[6] For the sake of terminological clarification, let me distinguish three different ways in which the term is currently being used.[7] One locates scholarly personae at the *micro level* – scholars' individual biographies; another engages in *macro-level* analysis by equating personae with broadly shared templates of what it means to be a scholar; while a third approach – the one adopted in this volume – defines scholarly personae as time- and place-specific models, characterized by specific habits, virtues, skills or competencies and circulating at a *meso level*, in between the micro and macro perspectives privileged in the first two approaches.

The first approach is advocated most prominently by the journal *Persona Studies*. Drawing on a tradition in literary studies that understands the term 'persona' to denote how literary characters appear in novels or other fictional texts, *Persona Studies* encourages research on how people 'produce', 'perform', 'enact', 'inhabit', 'negotiate' and 'manage' their selves. In this approach, 'persona' is a concept related to Erving Goffman's 'presentation of self' and Stephen Greenblatt's 'self-fashioning'. All three terms refer to how people orchestrate their public appearance, at specific points in time and place, with particular goals and audiences in mind. A recent special of *Persona Studies*, edited by Mineke Bosch, Kirsti Niskanen and Kaat Wils, applies this to the history of science by examining through various case studies how scholars present themselves to their colleagues and the outer world – not only in the language they speak, but also in the moustaches or the high heels they wear.[8]

Identifying personae with modes of public self-presentation is not exactly what Lorraine Daston and H. Otto Sibum had in mind when, in 2003, they introduced the concept in the history of science. On the contrary: whereas Bosch and others emphasize the 'I' in 'what kind of a historian do *I* want to be?', Daston and Sibum – main representatives of the second approach – underline 'what *kind* of a historian'. They are interested in broadly shared templates that defined, often for several generations, what it meant to be a scholar. Concretely, Daston and Sibum think of the 'scientist' that emerged in early-Victorian England as an alternative to the early-modern natural philosopher (and its equivalents in continental Europe: the *scientifique* as distinguished from the *savant* and the *Wissenschaftler* as opposed to the *Gelehrter*). Personae in this second sense of the word are 'types of person' that broadly define the kind of person that a scholar has to be in order to be recognizable as a scholar. Personae, then, are like species or classes: collective entities that allow for great variety, but are held together by some common features, such as commitment to experimentation or, in the case of the twentieth-century technocrat, a desire to transform knowledge into intellectual capital.[9]

Although Daston and Sibum acknowledge that individuals can add personal touches to existing personae, they emphasize that personae are logically prior to persons developing their selves:

> To understand personae in this sense is to reject a social ontology that treats only flesh-and-blood individuals as real, and dismisses all collective entities as mere aggregates, parasitic upon individuals. Personae are as real or more real than biological individuals, in that they create the possibilities of being in the human world, schooling the mind, body, and soul in distinctive and indelible ways.[10]

All this implies that scholarly personae in Daston's and Sibum's sense of the word are slowly changing entities. They allow for *longue durée* histories, focused not on biographical *événements*, but on broadly shared and slowly evolving templates that defined what it meant to be a 'man of learning' or a 'man of science'.

The importance of both approaches becomes apparent if we apply them to the case with which we started: American historical studies in the 1960s. What is fascinating about the first approach is that it sheds light on the means that historians use in trying to get attention or to claim authority – demanding a right to speak as a woman in an overwhelmingly male world, for instance. It is no coincidence that one of Gerda Lerner's admirers, referring to her provocation at the 1968 convention of the American Historical Association, characterized her 'formidable speaking skills', 'graceful German accent' and 'matronly sexuality' as 'potent weapons'.[11] Also, this research line helpfully reminds us that scholarly identities are always embodied, negotiated and performed by individuals in real-life situations.

In addition, Daston's and Sibum's approach allows us to see how, in 1960s America, the scholar as an academic knowledge-seeker was challenged by a new or, rather, revitalized model of the scholar as critic or activist. As Jonathan Weiner has argued, many controversies in 1960s American historical studies revolved around the question 'who is a historian and who is not?'[12] What was at stake for Zinn, Lerner, White and their critics was the identity of the scholar – his or her responsibilities and, specifically, the kind of conduct appropriate for an academic historian, in and outside of the classroom. In broad strokes, one might say that the 'scholar' was contrasted with the 'critic' and that these were regarded as incompatible models, not because one was more openly political than the other, but because the 'objectivity' ascribed to the former was interpreted as a conservative defence of the status quo that was irreconcilable with the progressive values advocated by the latter.

Studying 1960s historiography from this perspective has the advantage of highlighting parallels, similarities and mutual influences between movements that are too often analysed separately. A scholarly personae perspective as developed by Daston and Sibum can help explain why social history, women's history and black history were closely intertwined and why, for instance, Zinn could draw on the example of emerging black studies programmes in American higher education in advocating his own version of radical history:

> These multiplying Black Studies programs do not pretend to just introduce another subject for academic inquiry. They have the specific intention of so affecting the consciousness of black and white people in this country as to diminish for both groups the pervasive American belief in black inferiority. This deliberate attempt to foster racial equality should be joined, I am suggesting, by similar efforts for national and class equality.[13]

Yet both approaches also have their limitations. As a historiographical strategy, zooming in on micro-level self-presentation comes at a price. Biographical case studies, fascinating as they may be, are not particularly well suited for analysing patterns, trends, analogies and differences. Continuities over time, similarities across borders and transfers between historiographical traditions tend to remain invisible, or appear as marginal only. Also, micro-level analysis runs a risk of confusing the individual with the social, for instance by attributing Zinn's activist mode of scholarship more to his unique personality than to the template of the 'critic' that circulated widely in the 1960s humanities. Consequently, by focusing on how historians and historiographical schools distinguished themselves from each other, historians of historiography leave something out of the picture. As Peter Galison puts it, '[e]xamine one particular laboratory with too much magnification and you won't see the building up of ways of being a scientist – the scientific persona, changing over time, is not an individual's invention'.[14]

Daston's and Sibum's approach is well suited for addressing this concern. Yet by engaging in macro-level analysis, it also leaves something out of the picture. It is not, for instance, sufficient to observe that various forms of emancipatory historiography in the 1960s all worked with a highly charged contrast between the 'scholar' and the 'critic'. Historians also want to know why such an outspoken critic of consensus historiography as John Higham was perceived by Zinn as a conservative establishment figure, why the 'moral critic' that Higham called for in the 1960s differed significantly from the 'social critic' as envisioned by a younger generation and why a Marxist historian like Christopher Lasch could not stand 'people's history' as practiced by Zinn.[15] Even if a narcissism of small differences accounts for some (or much) of the animosity between and within the protest movements in 1960s historical studies, it is relevant to observe that contemporaries cared about differences that were more finely grained than those between the 'scholar' and the 'critic'. In other words, a macro-level analysis leaves too little room for acknowledging that contemporaries sometimes preferred to draw more finely grained distinctions between 'types' of historians or intellectuals.[16]

So, whereas Galison rightly argues that historians limiting themselves to micro-level analysis run a risk of ignoring the extent to which persons exist by virtue of personae, historians focusing too much on macro-level comparisons face the reverse problem: they run of risk of undervaluing contextual variation. Capturing the fine texture of academic life requires attentiveness to resemblances, parallels and recurring patterns as well as to individuals who navigate, combine or alternate existing templates. Scholarly personae, therefore, should not be studied exclusively from macro and/or micro perspectives. The interplay between the archetypical and the individual comes into view especially at a *meso level*, intermediate between the macro and the micro.[17]

Scholarly personae: an intermediate perspective

This volume therefore locates scholarly personae at an intermediate level, where scholars relate (positively or negatively) to models (real or imaginary) that they believe to embody habits, virtues, skills or competencies required for being a good scholar. On one hand, these models typically draw on broader templates – the *Naturforscher*, the *femme savant* and the technocrat at Daston's and Sibum's macro level. On the other hand, they are constantly being discussed and negotiated by individuals in specific cultural situations, at the micro level of the historical domain typical of the *Persona Studies* approach. So, if scholarly personae are 'regulative ideals made flesh', as Gadi Algazi helpfully puts it, or 'models of scholarly selfhood' that specify the 'abilities, attitudes, and dispositions that are regarded as crucial for the pursuit of scholarly study', a history of historiography focusing on personae can be attentive to constant interaction between repertoires and performances, models and users, ideals and realities.[18]

Concretely, this means that *hermeneutic questions*, revolving around the uses, meanings and significance of scholarly personae in actual historical practice, are of central importance to the approach adopted here. Its guiding question is how scholars draw on repertoires of scholarly personae, appropriate them in specific historical circumstances and adapt them to the needs of the moment. So, in the case of Gerda Lerner, the feminist critic of patriarchal structures in American historical studies, the question central to the third approach is not how Lerner supported her message with gestures, voice and facial expressions (the first approach) or drew on the time-honoured persona of the scholar as critic (approach number two). Instead, the key question is how Lerner put the scholar-as-critic persona to work by adapting it to 1960s feminist culture, contrasting it with competitive personae, justifying its legitimacy, emphasizing its importance and bringing it to life by socializing her students into an activist ethos, characterized by feminist pride, solidarity, upfront criticism of the academic status quo and lots of grass-roots mobilizing.[19]

In developing this third approach to scholarly personae, I have so far relied mostly on nineteenth-century German examples.[20] One reason for doing so is a historiographical one. Given that the world of Leopold von Ranke and his pupils has been relatively well studied, the added value of a personae perspective (on which more below) can be demonstrated by comparing it in considerable detail to existing historiographical studies. A second, more peculiar reason for selecting nineteenth-century Germany as a first case study is that at the time German historians had the habit of invoking models that very much resembled scholarly personae. This happened most notably in debates over 'the virtues of the historian', among which nineteenth-century authors usually listed impartiality, accuracy, honesty, industry, patriotism and loyalty. Although historians hardly disagreed about the importance of these virtues as such, they quarrelled frequently about their relative weight. Was love of country more important than impartiality or vice versa? Was objectivity the undisputed number one virtue or did honesty require historians to admit that objectivity was an unattainable ideal?

Interestingly, historians did not discuss these questions in the abstract, but associated them with high-profile figures such as Ranke, Georg Waitz and Heinrich von Treitschke. The point was not that these historians represented different virtues, as one might be tempted to infer from phrases like 'Rankean objectivity'. What mattered was rather that their names – proper names turned into generic ones – stood for different hierarchies of virtue. In stereotypical manner, they represented different orders of virtue – hierarchies headed by accuracy and precision in the case of Waitz and by patriotism in the case of Treitschke. Circulating widely in nineteenth-century German historical studies, these images, 'intermediate between the individual biography and the social institution', served as models of scholarly selfhood in that they shaped 'the individual in body and mind'.[21] Yet, at the same time, these codified images of the virtuous historian were considerably more specific than Daston's and Sibum's personae. They represented different ways in which historians in nineteenth-century Germany envisioned and enacted their scholarly identity. They were models of identification that showed in vivid detail what a virtuous historian might look like.

If this shows how fruitful it is to examine nineteenth-century German historical studies through the prism of scholarly personae, it also illustrates the limitations of the case. While German historians never adopted a single persona – they always navigated between multiple ones – this might have been different in countries where historical studies were less 'professionalized' than in Wilhelmine Germany. In late-Victorian Britain, for instance, the battles fought out between James Anthony Froude and Edward Augustus Freeman revolved, not around the pros and cons of different historiographical models, but around a highly charged contrast between 'professionals' and 'amateurs'. Also, while historians in the French Third Republic resembled their colleagues on the other side of the Rhine in habitually criticizing each other on religious, moral and political grounds, they were less inclined to map their discipline with the help of clearly delineated personae.[22] Consequently, what is needed for further developing the persona approach (the third that I defined) is comparative historiographical research, attentive to national and regional variation.

The need for such comparative research becomes even more apparent if we realize that *persona* was originally a Roman concept, with strong connotations of a public role identity (e.g. actors wearing a mask to convey that they are playing a role; politicians conforming to the image of a 'public man', distinguished from their personal selves).[23] In order to find out to what degree scholarly personae as defined in this volume are indebted to this classic European heritage and to what extent they can be applied in historiographical research on, say, Meiji Japan or late-Qing dynasty China, we have to expand our geographical horizon and include case studies from across the world. Only comparative historiographical research can make clear what are the strengths and the limitations of the personae concept.

This volume

Precisely this is what the current volume aims to do. Specialists on various historiographical traditions have been invited to apply, test and refine the personae concept (third approach) in case studies ranging from China to the United States and from Africa to Eastern Europe. All authors have subsequently been granted a relatively large degree of freedom to highlight what they consider most distinctive about their case studies, or most important in the light of existing scholarship. Consequently, the chapters do not follow a strict format, but identify a broad range of issues relevant to the study of scholarly personae.[24]

Thus, while Chapters 1 and 2 show, on the base of German examples, that personae were contested because they represented different ways of 'schooling the mind, body, and soul', Chapters 3 and 4, on the antebellum United States and the French Third Republic, draw attention to relatively stable patterns underlying such variety, such as the Romantic notion of the author as an individual. Chapter 5, on Edward A. Freeman and his female assistants, shows to what extent this individual was male-gendered: 'historian' was not a role identity that women could easily claim. Interpreting controversies among early-twentieth-century Chinese historians through the prism of scholarly personae, Chapter 6 makes a case for the concept being applicable outside the Western world, if only because Chinese historians also cared about habits, virtues and other dispositions needed for engaging in historical studies.

Whereas scholarly personae have so far been studied almost exclusively in relatively 'open' societies, Chapters 7, 8 and 9 try out the concept in contexts marked by various forms of political pressure: the Portuguese New State under António de Oliveira Salazar, the Communist Party of Great Britain and the Hungarian People's Republic. Different as these cases are, they all show that personae were not always models that historians adopted voluntarily: they could be imposed through state-sponsored institutions and enforced through legal and political mechanisms (which shows in passing that personae could be important enough to gain political attention). Chapter 10, on UNESCO's *General History of Africa* project, discusses another highly politicized case: the attempt to create a truly 'African historian', distinct from the 'Western historian' associated with colonial regimes. Ironically, this 'decolonization' of scholarly personae was not very successful, partly because European historians were needed to facilitate cross-language communication between French- and English-speaking Africans. This, finally, raises the question with which the volume closes: can personae come to an end? Drawing on Belgian examples, Chapter 11 firmly answers this question in the affirmative.

Although all chapters can be read individually, they have in common that they apply, test and refine scholarly personae as models circulating in what Fernand Braudel would have called a *temps intermédiaire* between the slowly evolving rhythms of *longue durée* history and the rapidly changing situations captured in *histoires événementielles*.[25] It is precisely at this intermediate level, characteristic of the third approach identified above, that scholarly personae can make a difference in the history of historiography. To conclude this introduction, I would like to mention five of these differences – that is, five possible advantages of scholarly personae as a historiographical prism.

Why personae matter

First of all, a personae perspective allows us to write the 'self' back into the history of historiography – that is, not the biographical self, but the scholarly self as it is moulded and shaped in accordance with prevailing models of habit, virtue, skill or competence. Various chapters in this volume show how discipline formation in historical studies went hand in hand with a disciplining of the historian's body and mind through educational practices, social expectations or political pressures. Examining historical studies with an eye to personae that schematically embodied the features characterizing a true historian at a given time and place therefore draws attention to the 'psychagogical' dimension of academic life: the socializing of young men and women into an ethos deemed appropriate for students of history.[26]

Secondly, a topography of personae in historical studies may yield new insight into the unity or disunity of fields that participants and later historians alike have often mapped in terms of competing 'approaches'. A classic example of this interpretative strategy can be found in Gerald Grob's and George Athan Billias's influential *Interpretations of American History* (4th edn, 1982), a book that offers a kaleidoscopic overview of a steadily growing number of 'approaches' to the American past. By emphasizing difference or even 'fragmentation' – a trope in the history of post-World War II American historiography – such typologies of approaches often have a dispersive effect of a kind illustrated in the following passage on New Left historians in the 1960s:[27]

> A strict taxonomy might demarcate differences between the self-consciously Marxist work of an early wave, whose members included current or former Communists, Trotskyists, and Schachtmanites, and that of a younger cohort who listed toward anarchism and the counterculture. It might also distinguish between the earlier work of figures such as James Weinstein and Christopher Lasch, which focused on politics with a strong anti-liberal bent, and the 'new social history' of the early 1970s, which tended to avoid or downplay politics except in the loosest sense.[28]

As a remedy against exaggerated 'fragmentation' narratives, a personae perspective allows for renewed appreciation of family resemblances among the emancipatory elements in 1960s American historiography, just as it draws attention to gravitational forces between 'investigative' and 'interpretative' personae in China around 1900 and to similarities between the models of virtue that circulated in nineteenth-century German historical studies.

Thirdly, a personae perspective allows for rich comparisons across time, space and fields of study. Was the German historian Hans-Ulrich Wehler a 'Treitschke *redivivus*', as his colleague Thomas Nipperdey once claimed – not in the sense that Wehler's political views resembled Treitschke's, but because both historians represented a type of scholar strongly committed to furthering a political cause? Or was Wehler a 'Habermas of history' – an analogy that invoked Habermas as a persona rather than a person, just as Ranke did when he compared himself to Cook and Columbus, busy discovering 'unknown islands of world history'? In this respect, our volume joins an emerging body of scholarship that compares how scholarly selfhood was construed across fields that are usually studied in isolation from each other.[29]

More ambitiously, scholarly personae can serve as a connecting thread between scholarly *biographies* (individual life stories), *institutions* (universities, archives, professional organizations), *methodologies* (codified in volumes like Ernst Bernheim's *Lehrbuch der historischen Methode*) and *religious-political conflict* of a kind visible in German historical studies shortly after the *Kulturkampf* and the establishment of the German Empire. At the intersection between biographies, institutions, methods and religious-political conflict lay the issue of scholarly personae: models of how to be a historian that were upheld to aspiring historians (especially in educational contexts), codified in methodology manuals (with 'methods' sometimes being near-synonymous to 'virtues'), institutionally propagated by, for instance, source-editing projects that helped define the marks of a good historian by hiring only philologically virtuous historians, and often fiercely debated on moral, political and/or religious grounds (as much by Jews, Catholics, Socialists, and women who felt excluded from it, as by an overwhelmingly male, liberal, bourgeois, Protestant community of scholars).[30]

And this is not yet all. In the fifth and final place, studying historians through the prism of scholarly personae is also an exercise in professional self-reflection. Historians studying what it means to be a historian cannot avoid the question as to what their own selves look like, what virtues or dispositions guide their own conduct and what are the models of virtue on which they orient themselves. These are pressing questions, especially in the light of two important developments in contemporary academia. One is a still-growing concern about academic diversity in terms of gender, ethnicity and sexual orientation, which is fuelled in part by postcolonial efforts at 'provincializing Europe' and 'decolonizing academia'.[31] As a result of this, scholarly personae embedded in white, male privilege have become increasingly suspect, even if alternatives are still being sought. Secondly, in academic regimes that critics sometimes brand as 'neo-liberal', historians around the world find themselves under pressure to attract external research money, despite the fact that less than half a century ago many historians in particular saw competitive research funding as a corrupting force. In terms of personae, this means that they are being pushed in the direction of an 'entrepreneurial self' that Hubert Howe Bancroft, the protagonist of Travis Ross's chapter, would have had little trouble recognizing. So, in contemporary contexts, too, historians cannot avoid the question 'what kind of a historian do I want to be?'[32]

It is with an eye to these issues that we, editor and authors, offer this volume to our readers – as an exploration of scholarly personae in the history of historiography, but also as a mirror that invites present-day historians to reflect on what it means to be a historian in the early-twenty-first century.[33]

Notes

1 John Higham with Leonard Krieger and Felix Gilbert, *History* (Englewood Cliffs, NJ: Prentice-Hall, 1965), p. 134; Peter Novick, *That Noble Dream: The 'Objectivity Question' and the American Historical Profession* (Cambridge: Cambridge University Press, 1988), p. 332; John Higham, 'The cult of "American consensus": homogenizing our history', *Commentary*, 27 (1959), 93–100; Carl Mitta, 'Forty years on: looking back at the 1969 Annual Meeting', *Perspectives on History*, 48 (2010), 14–15.
2 Howard Zinn, *The Politics of History* (Boston, MA: Beacon Press, 1970), p. 1; Davis D. Joyce, *Howard Zinn: A Radical American Vision* (Amherst, NY: Prometheus, 2003), pp 17, 83–9; Martin Duberman, *Howard Zinn: A Life on the Left* (New York: New Press, 2012), pp 169–70, 182, 192–4.
3 Kathryn Kish Sklar, 'Remembering Gerda Lerner: "for the future of women's past"', *Journal of Women's History*, 26 (2014), 12–15, at 14; Gerda Lerner, *The Majority Finds Its Past: Placing Women in History* (Oxford: Oxford University Press, 1979), p. vii; Lise Vogel, 'Telling tales: historians of our own lives', *Journal of Women's History*, 2 (1991), 89–101, at 91.
4 Irwin Unger, 'The "New Left" and American history: some recent trends in United States historiography', *The American Historical Review*, 72 (1967), 1237–63, at 1262.
5 Hayden V. White, 'The burden of history', *History and Theory*, 5 (1966), 111–34; Hans Kellner, 'Introduction', in Frank Ankersmit, Ewa Domańska and Hans Kellner (eds), *Re-Figuring Hayden White* (Stanford, CA: Stanford University Press, 2009), pp 1–8, at p. 2; Sidney M. Bolkosky, 'From the book to the survivor', in Samuel Totten (ed.), *Working to Make a Difference: The Personal and Pedagogical Stories of Holocaust Educators Across the Globe* (Lanham, MD: Lexington, 2003), pp 1–30, at p. 2.
6 In replacing 'scientific personae' with 'scholarly personae', I seek to emphasize that personae can be found throughout the academic spectrum, not only in what is nowadays known as 'science'.
7 My distinctions correspond to Gadi Algazi's typology in '*Exemplum* and *Wundertier*: three concepts of the scholarly persona', *Low Countries Historical Review*, 131:4 (2016), 8–32.
8 Erving Goffman, *The Presentation of Self in Everyday Life* (Garden City, NY: Doubleday, 1959); Stephen Greenblatt, *Renaissance Self-Fashioning: From More to Shakespeare*

(Chicago: University of Chicago Press, 1980); P. David Marshall and Kim Barbour, 'Making intellectual room for persona studies: a new consciousness and a shifted perspective', *Persona Studies*, 1:1 (2015), 1–12; Kirsti Niskanen, Mineke Bosch and Kaat Wils, 'Scientific personas in theory and practice: ways of creating scientific, scholarly, and artistic identities', *Persona Studies*, 4:1 (2018), 1–5. On moustaches and high heels, see also Mineke Bosch, 'Scholarly personae and twentieth-century historians: explorations of a concept', *Low Countries Historical Review*, 131:4 (2016), 33–54, at 43.

9   Lorraine Daston and H. Otto Sibum, 'Introduction: scientific personae and their histories', *Science in Context*, 16 (2003), 1–8.
10 Ibid., 3–4.
11 Sklar, 'Remembering Gerda Lerner', 13, 14.
12 Jonathan M. Wiener, 'Radical historians and the crisis in American history, 1959–1980', *The Journal of American History*, 76 (1989), 399–434, at 399.
13 Zinn, *Politics*, p. 36.
14 Paula Findlen, 'The two cultures of scholarship?' *Isis*, 96 (2005), 230–7; Steven Shapin, 'Hyperprofessionalism and the crisis of readership in the history of science', *Isis*, 96 (2005), 238–43; Robert E. Kohler and Kathryn M. Olesko, 'Introduction: Clio meets science', *Osiris*, 27 (2012), 1–16; Peter Galison, 'Ten problems in history and philosophy of science', *Isis*, 99 (2008), 111–24, at 122.
15 Novick, *Noble Dream*, p. 377; Joyce, *Howard Zinn*, pp 118, 121–2.
16 See, e.g., Christopher Lasch, *The New Radicalism in America (1889–1963): The Intellectual as a Social Type* (New York: Alfred A. Knopf, 1965).
17 Herman Paul, 'Sources of the self: scholarly personae as repertoires of scholarly selfhood', *Low Countries Historical Review*, 131: 4 (2016), 135–54.
18 Daston and Sibum, 'Introduction', 7–8; Algazi, '*Exemplum* and *Wundertier*', 11; Herman Paul, 'What is a scholarly persona? Ten theses on virtues, skills, and desires', *History and Theory*, 53 (2014), 348–71, at 353.
19 Sklar, 'Remembering Gerda Lerner'; Joyce Antler, 'Remembering Gerda Lerner: the "mother" of women's history' (3 January 2013), online at https://jwa.org/blog/remembering-gerda-lerner-mother-of-womens-history (consulted 20 September 2018).
20 Herman Paul, 'Distance and self-distanciation: intellectual virtue and historical method around 1900', *History and Theory* 50:4 (2011), 104–16; 'The heroic study of records: the contested persona of the archival historian', *History of the Human Sciences* 26:4 (2013), 67–83; 'The virtues and vices of Albert Naudé: toward a history of scholarly personae', *History of Humanities*, 1 (2016), 327–38; 'The virtues of a good historian in early Imperial Germany: Georg Waitz's contested example', *Modern Intellectual History*, 15 (2018), 681–709.
21 Daston and Sibum, 'Introduction', 2.
22 Ian Hesketh, 'Diagnosing Froude's disease: boundary work and the discipline of history in late-Victorian Britain', *History and Theory*, 47 (2008), 373–95; Camille Creyghton *et al.*, 'Virtue language in historical scholarship: the cases of Georg Waitz, Gabriel Monod and Henri Pirenne', *History of European Ideas*, 42 (2016), 924–36, at 929–32.
23 Hannah Arendt forcefully made this point in her *On Revolution* (New York: Viking Press, 1963), pp 112–13. See also Richard Sennett, *The Fall of Public Man* (Cambridge: Cambridge University Press, 1977), especially pp 286–92.
24 In doing this, the present volume supplements a contributed volume on scholarly personae in oriental studies: Christiaan Engberts and Herman Paul (eds), *Scholarly Personae in the History of Orientalism, 1870–1930* (Leiden: Brill, forthcoming).
25 Fernand Braudel, 'Histoire et sciences sociales: la longue durée', *Annales*, 13 (1958), 725–53.
26 I borrow this term from Ian Hunter, 'The history of philosophy and the persona of the philosopher', *Modern Intellectual History*, 4 (2007), 571–600; 'Hayden White's philosophical history', *New Literary History*, 45 (2014), 331–58.
27 Gerald N. Grob and George Athan Billias, *Interpretations of American History: Patterns*

and Perspectives, 4th edn, vol. 2 (New York: Free Press, 1982), p. 17; Novick, *Noble Dream*, pp 573–629; Eric Foner, 'Introduction', in Foner (ed.), *The New American History* (Philadelphia, PA: Temple University Press, 1990), pp vii–xi; Richard T. Vann, 'No king in Israel? Individuals and schools in American historiography', in Rolf Torstendahl (ed.), *An Assessment of Twentieth-Century Historiography: Professionalism, Methodologies, Writings* (Stockholm: Almqvist & Wiksell, 2000), pp 175–94.

28 David Greenberg, 'Agit-prof: Howard Zinn's influential mutilations of American History', *The New Republic* (19 March 2013), online at https://newrepublic.com/article/112574/howard-zinns-influential-mutilations-american-history (consulted 20 September 2018).

29 Thomas Nipperdey, 'Wehlers "Kaiserreich": Eine kritische Auseinandersetzung', *Geschichte und Gesellschaft*, 1 (1975), 539–60, at 542; Paul Nolte, *Hans-Ulrich Wehler: Historiker und Zeitgenosse* (Munich: C. H. Beck, 2015), p. 9; Leopold von Ranke, *Das Briefwerk*, ed. Walther Peter Fuchs (Hamburg: Hoffmann und Campe, 1949), pp 123, 126; Jeroen van Dongen and Herman Paul, 'Introduction: epistemic virtues in the sciences and the humanities', in Van Dongen and Paul (eds), *Epistemic Virtues in the Sciences and the Humanities* (Cham: Springer, 2017), pp 1–10 (and the literature mentioned there).

30 I develop this argument in a book manuscript provisionally entitled 'The Historian's Self: Virtues and Vices in German Historical Studies, 1871–1914'.

31 See, e.g., A. C. L[ichtenstein], 'Decolonizing the *AHR*', *The American Historical Review*, 123 (2018), xiv–xvii. Dipesh Chakrabarty, *Provincializing Europe: Postcolonial Thought and Historical Difference* (Princeton, NJ: Princeton University Press, 2000) remains, of course, the *locus classicus*.

32 Everett Carll Ladd, Jr and Seymour Martin Lipset, *The Divided Academy: Professors and Politics* (New York: McGraw-Hill, 1975), p. 360; Ulrich Bröckling, *The Entrepreneurial Self: Fabricating a New Type of Subject* (Los Angeles: SAGE, 2016).

33 This volume emerges out of a workshop on 'The Persona of the Historian: Repertoires and Performances', held on 26–7 January 2017 at Leiden University. I organized this workshop in the context of a project on 'The Scholarly Self: Character, Habit, and Virtue in the Humanities, 1860–1930', funded by the Netherlands Organisation for Scientific Research (NWO). I wish to thank all contributors for their stimulating thoughts and insights, student assistant Marieke Dwarswaard for practical help, John Firth for his meticulous copy-editing, and the staff at Manchester University Press for managing the publication process with great efficiency.

CHAPTER 1

The contested persona of the historian: on the origins of a permanent conflict

Ian Hunter

Introduction

In the 1820s, the universities of Protestant Germany witnessed an unprecedented conflict over the nature of historical writing and what it meant to be a historian. That this conflict remains as unresolved today as it did when the first academic salvoes were fired is one of its several remarkable features. Standing on one side of this conflict, the source-critical empirical historiography of Leopold von Ranke and his school reached back into seventeenth-century ecclesiastical history and eighteenth-century constitutional history. From these sources the Ranke school borrowed historical *topoi*, objectifying methods and a detached intellectual outlook. Emerging in opposition to Rankean empirical historiography, the dialectical philosophical history of G. W. F. Hegel and his followers was no older than the Kantian philosophical revolution of the 1790s, even if its roots lay in the history of Protestant metaphysics. Hegelian philosophical history attacked empirical historiography from an unprecedented vantage point. It viewed history as a process in which human reason or a 'world spirit' struggled to become conscious of itself by treating the 'positive' or 'empirical' institutions of church and state as the 'estranged' forms of the spirit itself, thereby promising the latter's emancipation through the dialectical overcoming of this estrangement.

This chapter provides an account of the conflict between Rankean empirical history and Hegelian philosophical history by approaching them as radically opposed and mutually hostile intellectual cultures, from which issued two completely different ways of modelling the intellectual comportment or persona of the historian. In approaching the conflict in this way, the author pays homage to an unsurpassed study from the 1920s, by the German-Jewish historian Ernst Simon.[1]

Cultural and political context

To the extent that they were focused in history writing, then the conflicts surrounding Hegel and his followers at Berlin University in the 1820s were sharpened by a clash between two radically opposed historical outlooks and comportments of the historian. On one hand, Leopold von Ranke and his students viewed history as a technical discipline for providing an 'impartial' account of past events – centrally the events of German ecclesiastical and political-constitutional history – by using source-critical methods to validate and contextualize the documentary records of these events. On the other hand, Hegel and his followers viewed history as a philosophical discipline for providing a hermeneutic interpretation of world history. This was achieved by using the dialectical exercise to view institutions and events as symbols of the degree to which reason or spirit had retrieved self-consciousness and freedom from its own estranged forms.[2] Before describing the Berlin academic conflicts in more detail, and in order to come to terms with their extraordinary depth and vehemence, it is necessary to sketch the circumstances of German cultural and political history from which they emerged.

As far as the long-term circumstances are concerned, Rankean empirical and Hegelian philosophical historiographies may be regarded as the tips of large cultural-political icebergs, carried and shaped by historical currents that were fundamentally religious and political. If Rankean history-writing was a document-based empirical account of German constitutional and ecclesiastical history, that was in part because German constitutional and ecclesiastical institutions themselves operated through the generation and interpretation of documents. But it was also because the disciplines of constitutional and ecclesiastical history had developed methods for viewing these documents as records of purely human activities – of war- and peace-making, of religious rivalry and reform – rather than as expressions of transcendental justice or religious truth. By excluding irreconcilably opposed theologies and philosophies from their negotiation and administration, the public law treaties that formed the pillars of the German constitution – the Treaty of Augsburg of 1555 and the Westphalian treaties of 1648 – made the suspension of theological and philosophical 'foundations' into a condition of the juridification of religious and political conflict. Since the objective of this juridification was not to rationalize or secularize the confessional religions, but to preserve them from internecine destruction by recognizing and entrenching them in a multi-confessional religious constitution, the resulting constitutional order wore a distinctive Janus face: it consisted of a relativistic (and in this limited sense) 'secular' juridical framework, inside which plural religions were free to teach their confessions as absolute truths.[3]

By excluding theological and philosophical truths from the constitutional framework, the disciplines and institutions of public law gave rise to a remarkable, unintended consequence. They permitted the development of an empirical, documentary, constitutional historiography, in which the constitution was historicized through the trail of treaty documents, regardless of political-philosophical or natural-law norms.[4] In its turn, the development of this document-based empirical method permitted constitutional historiography to intersect with empirical ecclesiastical history and biblical criticism. For, in developing the methods of humanist erudition, these latter disciplines had also suspended theological and metaphysical truths in order to view the documents deposited by the church and its theologians 'impartially'; that is, regardless of their claims to transcendent truth, as records of purely human activities, interests and motives.[5] In this way, erudite or scholarly ecclesiastical history had developed a view of the imperial churches as a plurality of historical institutions teaching rival absolute truths, which directly intersected the public-law constitutional view of them. From these developments emerged a remarkable historical nexus between the methods and outlook of constitutional and ecclesiastical historiographies and those of Ranke's source-critical, empirical historiography. If the former historiographies tracked their objects by following the documentary trails deposited by the institutions of public and church law, then Ranke synthesized these historiographies and their documentary records at a more abstract level, using them to write a history of the 'German nation' and its search for a proper state-form.

While they were intertwined with those from which Rankean empirical historiography had emerged, the lineages of religious, philosophical and political history that issued in Hegelian philosophical historiography assumed a very different and finally oppositional form. After Lutheran fideism had excluded it from Protestant universities during the sixteenth century, the academic metaphysics that would eventually issue in Kantian and Hegelian philosophies returned at the beginning of the seventeenth. This was principally in order to supply a philosophical explication and defence of the official Lutheran confession – the Formula of Concord of 1577 – against its Calvinist and Catholic rivals.[6] It was at this point that the double-sided philosophical anthropology that would pass into Kantian and Hegelian philosophies was first elaborated. This occurred initially in accounts of the relation between the two natures of Christ – his immaterial, active, divine intellectual nature, and his corporeal, passive, human sensibility – which showed how spiritual being could be present in humanity and in the Eucharistic host.[7] In defending the absolute truth of a particular religious doctrine, academic metaphysics of this kind operated under the umbrella of the Janus-faced Augsburg-Westphalian constitution, the role of which was to provide legal protection for a plurality of such truths. Yet such academic metaphysics was fundamentally hostile to this relativistic constitutional framework, insisting that the realization of the kingdom of God on earth requires that the constitutional order itself be grounded in univocal metaphysical truth.[8] In transposing the relation between the divine intellect and the human sensibility to the interior of the philosophical subject, Kantian metaphysics was no less hostile to the relativistic and pluralistic religious constitution than its confessional predecessors.[9] Not only did Kant insist that the legitimacy of the religious constitution depended on it being founded in the consensus of 'rational beings' – rather than in peace treaties between rival religious blocs – but he also declared that the constitutionally protected confessional religions were themselves destined to be displaced by a 'pure religion of reason' suited to mankind's rational maturity.[10]

Despite its historicization of Kantian metaphysics, Hegelian philosophy was extra-constitutional in the same manner. Hegel thus argued that the Janus-faced constitutional separation of church and state was a fracturing of the spirit that would be overcome through the dialectical development of a 'moral state'.[11] He further prophesied that the plurality of 'positive' constitutional religions would be replaced by a speculative, philosophical religion that reconciled the human and the divine in the course of the spirit's transition to full freedom and self-consciousness.[12] In this way, Hegel transposed the metaphysics of the divided self into a philosophical hermeneutics. This permitted Germany's historical religious constitution to be interpreted as symbol of a retarded stage in the spirit's progress towards historical self-consciousness. Hegel's philosophical history thus operated outside the disciplines of constitutional and ecclesiastical history that had allowed the Rankean historian to offer empirical accounts of church and constitution on the evidence of their documentary records. Instead, operating on the basis of an absolutely true metaphysical anthropology and cosmology, the Hegelian philosophical historian viewed church and state only as external symbols of an inner conflict between an abstract consciousness and its estranged concrete forms. From this dialectical method emerged a comportment or persona focused on achieving a specific kind of inner spiritual reconciliation, and the prophetic insight into the 'meaning' of history that resulted from this.

Thus, the conflict between Rankeans and Hegelians that broke out at the University of Berlin in the 1820s was not between the empiricist and idealist sides of the 'subject of history' – that is just a tale told by Hegelians – but was between two radically opposed intellectual conducts and ways of intellectual life. One of these had been formed through the integration of the erudite disciplines of constitutional and ecclesiastical history into the source-critical, 'impartial' methods of the Rankean empirical historian. The other had arisen from the integration of a specialized dialectical exercise in spiritual self-problematization and self-transformation into the hermeneutic-prophetic comportment of the Hegelian philosophical historian.

Cultural and political conflict at the University of Berlin

The latent conflict between constitutional religious pluralism and extra-constitutional Protestant rationalism had surfaced in several controversies at the end of the eighteenth century, most notably in those associated with the Prussian Religious Edict of 1788 and the associated attempt by the Prussian government to censor Kant's *Religion within the Bounds of Bare Reason*.[13] It did so again in the battle between empirical-contextual and philosophical-hermeneutic historians that erupted at the Prussian University of Berlin during the 1820s and 1830s. When Ranke arrived at the university in 1825 he was immediately drawn into a conflict between two mutually hostile factions: the 'historians' under the leadership of the Protestant theologian Friedrich Daniel Schleiermacher, assisted by the legal historian Friedrich von Savigny, and the 'philosophers', led by Hegel himself, who was at the zenith of his fame and influence.[14] In addition to Savigny and Schleiermacher, Ranke's immediate network consisted of the source-critical historians Barthold Niebuhr, Karl Gottlob Zumpt and Karl Lachmann, the philologist Johann Albrecht Eichhorn and the historian of philosophy Heinrich Ritter: a network embodying the configuration of pietistic, philological and historicist disciplines that informed Ranke's historiographic ethos and practice. Hegel's faction included the philosophical historians Heinrich Leo and Bruno Bauer, the Hegelian theologian Philipp Marheineke, the philosophical jurist Eduard Gans and a farther-flung array of Protestant rationalist theologians, including Karl Daub and Hermann Hinrichs at Heidelberg.

The Schleiermacher network was not formed on the basis of a shared method, theory or ideology but on cultural-political affinities between Schleiermacher's defence of confessional Protestantism against its transformation into moral philosophy, Savigny's defence of the historical constitutional order against its philosophical rationalization and Ranke's defence of empirical historiography against philosophical-historical hermeneutics. These affinities were rooted in the German constitutional-religious settlement discussed above; that is, in the relativistic ('secular') constitutional order that aimed to preserve the confessional religions, and the purely historical basis of which was captured in Rankean empirical historiography. More immediately, the Schleiermacher-Savigny-Ranke alliance had been forged by the need to defend this order against the extra-constitutional onslaught of Protestant rationalism in its Hegelian metaphysical form. For the Hegelians indeed sought to supplant the confessional ('positive') religions with a speculative, philosophical religion grounded in the spirit's achievement of self-determining self-consciousness, which would also serve as the basis of law and politics.[15] For their part, the links between the Hegelian philosophies of law, religion and history were forged by a single metaphysical doctrine, namely that all of these institutions were forms of *objective Geist*, or estranged expressions of the world spirit in its passage towards self-consciousness. This meant that constitutional arrangements designed to preserve them in their current form could only be regarded as illegitimate attempts to block the dialectical development of the human spirit. As one of the philosophical 'confessions' maintained by the relativistic religious constitution, Hegelian philosophy was thus engaged in an extra-constitutional struggle to undermine it, on the basis of the absolute truth of its own confessional metaphysics.

The fact that the two Berlin factions embodied fundamentally opposed cultural-political stances towards the German constitutional settlement meant that they did not engage on a shared ground of public reason, and explains the vehemence of their conflict. The two groups engaged in intellectual combat throughout the 1820s, in prefaces, journal articles, books and public lectures. But this combat was focused and intensified by a series of related developments towards the end of the decade.[16] Central here was Schleiermacher's successful campaign to block Hegel's election to the Berlin Academy of Sciences, which only ended with Hegel's death in 1831.[17] Once he realized that it was afoot, this campaign engendered a decisive response from Hegel. In 1827 he founded his own academy – Die Societät für wissenschaftliche Kritik – from which the Schleiermacher faction was excluded, and an associated journal, *Die Jahrbücher für wissenschaftliche Kritik*. The journal systematically rejected all articles critical of the Hegelian school, while publishing powerful critiques of the enemy, including Eduard Gans's review of works by Savigny, and Heinrich Leo's attacks on Ranke, to be discussed below.

While the underlying source of these conflicts lay in two fundamentally opposed intellectual comportments towards the religious-constitutional order, the manner in which they unfolded at Berlin University in the 1820s and 1830s was determined by two more immediate historical developments. First, Napoleon's dissolution of the German Empire and suspension of its constitution in 1806 had unleashed a flood of competing programmes for transforming the German constitution and 'state' – into, *inter alia*, a constitutional monarchy, a representative or popular democracy, a state dominated by Prussia (or Prussia and Austria) or a federation of existing states.[18] In the lead-up to the 1848 National Assembly, with the constitutional order in abeyance, it became possible for a variety of political parties and sects to claim that the constitution itself should be grounded in true rational or moral norms, thereby opening the way for left- and right-Hegelian philosophers to assume leadership roles in political factions opposed to public-law constitutionalism.[19] They could do this by purporting to show how 'history' itself had delegitimized a religious constitution that had retarded the spirit's coming to consciousness in a representative government and a post-confessional speculative-philosophical religion.

Second, in using the constitutional interregnum to pursue its longstanding objective of uniting the Calvinist and Lutheran religions – primarily as a means of bringing Prussia's powerful Lutheran estates to its Calvinist heel – the Prussian government made the multi-confessional religious constitution into a focal point for cultural and religious contestation in the years before the National Assembly of 1848.[20] The close connection between the Prussian government and the universities responsible for training its clergy and jurists meant that the Berlin academic factions could seek to align themselves with political factions in and around the government. Some Hegelian academics thus sought political patronage for their plans either to install an Hegelianized Protestantism as the new theology for a unified church, or to provide a rational basis for democracy. For their part, the Pietists defended their version of confessional Lutheranism, while some historians offered to provide an historical justification for the rise to dominance of the Prussian state.[21] And even where the political programmes of the academics proved abortive – disintegrating in the face of ruthless political factionalism and uncontrollable power-plays – these circumstances meant that the protagonists in academic disputes over philosophy, theology and history could view their teachings and writings as consequential in a wider religious and political order that was held to be in crisis.[22]

The character of the Hegelian way of operating in these fraught cultural and political circumstances can be seen in an essay that Hegel wrote in 1822, as a preface to a work of Protestant rationalism published by his former student Hermann Friedrich Hinrichs.[23] In a striking manoeuvre, Hegel constructed a vantage point for understanding the unstable constitutional religious order, in terms not of the political and religious forces that had destabilized it, but of a dialectical exercise to be performed by the philosopher on himself. This was the exercise of reconciling 'faith' and 'reason', theology and philosophy, viewed as the condition for the spirit's overcoming of its estranged, 'positive', religious expressions and achieving self-consciousness in a speculative, philosophical religion. Hegel could then characterize his cultural and political enemies in terms of their failure to achieve the dialectical reconciliation of faith and reason, declaring that this failure was the product of two faulty conceptions of faith, held respectively by the Schleiermacher faction and the defenders of the confessional religions.[24] In identifying faith with a purely subjective feeling, Hegel argued, Schleiermacher failed to engage with the objective metaphysical truths and spiritual realities of the Christian religion, leaving it stranded in the domain of ungrounded subjectivity.[25] For their part, by encasing the understanding in 'abstract' confessional formulas, the constitutionally recognized 'positive' religions had failed to engage with the concrete freedom of the spirit as it passes through the successive self-estrangements and sublations of the history of religion. What was required, Hegel proclaimed, was an approach that could allow the subjective or 'abstract' religious striving of the spirit to engage with a 'concrete' content or metaphysical truth that is '*an und für sich*' – in and for itself. The subsequent negation or sublation of this truth would then drive the spirit to a higher level at which faith and reason are reconciled in a speculative philosophical religion.[26]

Hegel then turned the same dialectical weaponry against the historians, declaring that in adopting a purely empirical approach to the history of religion they too had failed to reconcile faith and reason. Ignoring the scholarly methods used in empirical ecclesiastical history, Hegel targeted the manner in which this historiography combined a fideist or mystical conception of God's unknowability with a view of religions as purely human institutions. For Hegel, not only did this combination symbolize the failure to reconcile faith and knowledge, but in turning religion into a purely historical phenomenon it had led the historians to adopt an irreligious attitude towards it.[27] According to Hegel, in occupying themselves with the external facts of ecclesiastical history, the historians had failed to grasp the inner truth of religion. This truth took place as the self-manifestation of the spirit to philosophical consciousness in the present, for which an intellectual 'rebirth' was required. In other words, Hegel's dialectical method was an inner exercise that imbued him with the capacity to view the constitutional churches as transitory institutional forms of spirit's self-manifestation in history. He could claim to see through and beyond the complex historical culture in which the constitutional bracketing of religion and metaphysics had supported a fideist religious outlook, which had in turn facilitated the development of empirical constitutional and ecclesiastical historiographies.

In deploying this same inner-dialectical exercise, Hegel's followers acquired the intellectual weapons and emotional animus to prosecute their attack on Ranke and the empirical historians. In the process they developed a philosophical critique of 'historical empiricism' that even today has lost none of its force or condescension. In an early issue of the *Jahrbücher für wissenschaftliche Kritik*, in a review-essay ostensibly dealing with the universal historian Friedrich Schlosser, Heinrich Leo actually targeted Ranke, identified by his claim that history had to be based in 'naked facts'.[28] Deploying an array of Kantian and Hegelian weaponry, Leo launched a partisan attack on empirical historiography that had a long future ahead of it. In it he declared that since all historical knowledge – chronology, periodization, contextualization – involves acts of selection, it could not be based in given facts. Those who thought that it could were only adopting arbitrary or subjective principles of selection and, for this reason, their factual narrations amounted to a jumble of details disconnected from rational ordering. Similarly, in arguing that historical facts could be grounded in the documentary records left by participants, eye-witnesses and archivists, the 'defender of naked facts' failed to realize that any event could be described and reported in a myriad of ways by a myriad of witnesses. This meant that here too the facts depended on unacknowledged, transcendental acts of selection and narration.[29]

Only by viewing history as the manifestation of the spirit's process of self-determination and self-clarification, Leo argued, could the problem of interpreting historical events be solved. The truth of history thus lay not in the description of facts but in uncovering the hidden process in which, by reconciling its subjective and objective, normative and factual sides, the spirit of humanity comes to consciousness of itself as the truth underlying historical appearances. Leo could thus proclaim that '[h]istory is a spiritual totality and is the spirit of humanity itself – the process of the spirit is the process of history and this *process* is the *truth* and the *only* truth'.[30] In failing to achieve this standpoint, the works of the empirical historians disintegrated into a jumble of facts and 'curiosities' subtended by purely subjective principles of selection, lacking all insight into the hidden spiritual meaning of history.[31] These were precisely the dialectical terms in which Leo attacked two of Ranke's histories in a review published in 1828. Here Leo used Ranke's account of the emergence of the Spanish monarchy to illustrate his mocking claim that Ranke's history descended into a welter of minute details and curiosities lacking any meaningful structure.[32]

Ranke's response to the Hegelian attack can seem puzzling to modern eyes. It is true that he occasionally responded to hostile reviews, replying to Leo, for example, that his history of Spain indeed did have a unifying theme – namely, the emergence of the Spanish monarchy and state from a period of political and religious chaos during the sixteenth and seventeenth centuries.³³ But of course such a theme would not have counted as meaningful in the context of Leo's conception of history as the spirit's achievement of self-consciousness. The crucial observation to make here, however, is that if we take 'theory' in its Hayden White sense – as reflection on the transcendental conditions of historical experience and representation – then Ranke never offered a theoretical defence of his historiography. This was in part because Ranke's historical writing was not grounded in transcendental metaphors but in a battery of scholarly methods and techniques – for dating and validating source documents, contextualizing them in terms of the circumstances and purposes of their use, investigating their various receptions and uses – that he had taken over from ecclesiastical and constitutional history. But it was also because Leo's demand that Ranke provide a transcendental theorization of his practice did not spring from a shared human reason, but from an exercise in spiritual self-clarification that was internal to dialectical philosophy.

Ranke thus never developed a theoretical critique of Hegelian philosophical history and his critical reflections on it remain scattered throughout his vast corpus. Here their role was to warn readers against bringing the Hegelian viewpoint to Ranke's histories, with the reflections thus functioning as a kind of negative guide to reading the particular works in which they are embedded. All Ranke scholars owe a debt to Georg and Wilma Iggers for collecting and anthologizing these dispersed methodological reflections.³⁴ Nonetheless, in using these reflections to explicate Ranke's account of the difference between 'history' and 'philosophy', it is important to remember that he did not have a theory of this difference analogous to the kind provided by Hegel.

From Ranke's methodological reflections it is possible to draw out three key themes through which he signalled the difference between his empirical historiography and Hegel's philosophical kind. First, Ranke argued that the philosopher and the historian had fundamentally different and irreconcilable understandings of the relation between reason and history. If the former viewed history as a manifestation of reason or spirit, then the latter viewed philosophical reason as a manifestation of history. Ranke thus declared that the philosopher, like the theologian before him, views the entirety of history from the vantage point of a particular concept of humanity, and thence 'recognizes the truth of history only insofar as it is subject to his concept'.³⁵ The historical outlook is the inverse of this. It treats philosophical concepts and truths simply as facts or appearances, independently of their validity, as things done by philosophers, hence to be viewed as a plurality of competing truth-claims. In a radically historicizing claim that sounds as precociously modern as Leo's critique of his empiricism, Ranke thus observed that:

> History seeks to view the results of philosophy not as absolute, but only as appearances in time. It supposes that philosophy most properly lies in the history of philosophy; that is, in those theories that emerge from time to time, and, however much they contradict each other, are deemed to contain the absolute truth as recognizable by the human race... In this way history denies philosophy all absolute validity and comprehends it among the other appearances.[36]

In clarifying the manner in which empirical historiography viewed the rival truths of Kantian, Fichtean and Hegelian philosophies – that is, as a plurality of historical truth regimes, independently of their validity – Ranke displayed the roots of his empirical approach in German ecclesiastical and constitutional historiographies. For it was these historiographies that had perfected the humanist-philological methods for interpreting theological documents and doctrines as records of purely human activities, suspending their transcendent truth and meaning, and thence allowing philosophical writing and doctrine to be treated in the same way.

Second, Ranke argued that philosophical history and empirical history had divergent conceptions of historical truth and completely different methods for determining it. Tying its emergence directly to the philosophies of Fichte and Hegel, Ranke declared that philosophers understood the truth of history to be the spirit's development towards freedom and self-consciousness, which Ranke regarded as a philosophical task imposed on history from without.[37] In his view this spiritual, hermeneutic approach to historical truth turned history into the projection of a preconceived idea, immunizing it from challenge by relegating empirical investigations and evidence in favour of an inner exercise in dialectical self-clarification.[38] In notoriously declaring to the contrary that the historian should conceive truth in terms of describing the past 'wie es eigentlich gewesen' (as it actually was), Ranke has frequently been convicted of holding to an 'empiricist' or 'positivist' outlook arising from his failure to grasp facts as reifications of transcendental concepts. It should now be clear, however, that this view of him is nothing more than an application of the Hegelian template to Ranke's historiography. In fact, when Ranke spoke of describing the past as it actually was, his understanding of this goal was determined by the mastery of source-critical methods that permit the documentary records of events to be tested for their authenticity and interpreted in terms of their contextual uses and purposes, with a view to opening up existing histories to new investigations and evidence.[39] In a precocious investigation into the history of a sixteenth-century 'Spanish conspiracy' against the republic of Venice, for example, Ranke made use of the Venetian archives to show that this history was in fact a legend serving the interests of the Venetian state, and that some of the most celebrated accounts of it were based on a forged document.[40] In other words, the divergent Hegelian and Rankean understandings of historical truth did not signify a disagreement within a shared epistemic universe, but different regimes of truth: the one turned inwards through a hermeneutics of spiritual self-clarification, the other turned outwards through the philological and contextual interrogation of documentary evidence.

Third, in a set of remarks in the Introduction to his book on the epochs of modern history, Ranke characterized and criticized the notion of historical progress advanced by the 'Hegelian school'. In doing so, he exemplified two fundamentally different stances towards God's presence in history. Ranke described the Hegelian model of history as being grounded in the notion of humanity's possession of a vestigial spiritual nature shared with God. The Hegelians thus understood progress in terms of the dialectical development of this nature through epochal stages, leading up to God's coming to consciousness in man's final spiritual self-realization.[41] Displaying the double-sided empirical and fideist character of the German constitutional and ecclesiastical historiographies, Ranke rejected this model of historical progress on both empirical and ethical-theological grounds. Empirically, he argued, while there might be evidence of progress in particular spheres of life – military, agricultural, artistic – there was no historical evidence of mankind's overall moral or spiritual progress. In ethical terms he argued that the Hegelian conception of historical progress damaged the individual dignity of human beings by turning them into avatars of a self-generating world spirit, while theologically this conception insulted God by treating him pantheistically: '[p]ursued to its logical conclusion this view can lead only to pantheism. Mankind is then God in the process of becoming, who gives birth to himself through a spiritual process that lies in his nature.'[42] In distinguishing his own conception of the movement of history, Ranke denied that epochs form stepping-stones leading upwards towards the spiritual self-realization of humanity, insisting on the contrary that, like each human generation, so too:

> every epoch is immediate to God, and its worth is not all based on what derives from it but rests in its own existence, in its own self. In this way the contemplation of history, that is to say of individual life in history, acquires its own particular attraction, since now every epoch must be seen as something valid in itself and appears highly worthy of consideration.[43]

Ad personam

The most striking feature of modern intellectual histories of the conflict between the Hegelians and Rankeans is their remorselessly dialectical character. Rather than investigating them as rival intellectual cultures, differently rooted in German religious, political and cultural history, these histories have purported to understand the Hegelians and Rankeans by viewing their conflict in terms of the failure to reconcile a series of philosophical oppositions: between rationalism and empiricism, idealism and positivism, norms and facts, the transcendent and immanent, and so on. Typical of these accounts are those that view the conflict between the two intellectual cultures as a dialectical opposition between a positivist empiricism and a rationalist idealism that would be overcome in twentieth-century philosophical history.[44] No less representative, however, are those that treat the conflict as a minor difference between opposed tendencies internal to so-called 'German historicism';[45] or as rooted in an epistemological disagreement over the knowability of universal ideas in historical particulars.[46] The same dialectical template is also evident in a recent treatment of the conflict as indicative of the failure of Ranke's 'reflective history' to overcome the opposition between subjectivist fictions and undigested facts, which could only be achieved through Hegel's account of the unfolding of spirit or reason in concrete historical events and institutions.[47] Finally, note can be taken of a sophisticated account that situates Ranke's conflict with Leo and Hegel in the context of Ranke's failed attempt to integrate 'both the immanent and transcendent grounds of historical coherence in a vision of the empirically discernible progressive moralization of human existence through voluntary submission to transcendent spiritual authority...'[48]

It should be clear in light of the preceding discussion that this dialectical history of the conflict does little more than repeat the exercise in philosophical self-clarification that Hegel and Leo initially used as an intellectual and ethical weapon against the Rankeans. This approach views Ranke's empirical historiography as failing to retrieve its rational, ideal or transcendental grounds, and thence stalling the progressive moralization of human existence. It thus remains wholly internal to dialectical philosophical history understood as an exercise in spiritual self-clarification and anti-empirical academic combat. Modern dialectical histories of the conflict between empirical and philosophical historiographies thus replicate the basic philosophical exercise of Hegelian philosophical history. As a result, they also inherit the model of history as collective (philosophical) subjects coming to self-consciousness, together with the spiritual identity of the anti-empirical philosophical historian shaped by this exercise. In other words, not only is the modern dialectical historiography of the conflict between Rankean and Hegelian forms of history writing an extended exemplification of and partisan *apologia* for Hegelian philosophical history, but it is also an exercise for shaping the identity of the philosophical historian in the image of the coming to consciousness of a collective subject of history.

Given this contemporary intellectual context, the central role of the concept of the intellectual persona is to suspend the image of the philosophical subject's dialectical achievement of self-consciousness as a model for historical writing, and thence to make possible a quite different understanding of the conflict between the Hegelians and Rankeans. Two features of the persona concept are key to its performance of this task. First, rather than being a double-sided, empirical, transcendental figuration of the person oriented to philosophical self-clarification, the concept of persona provides an empirical approach to intellectual conducts and capacities that is oriented to an investigation of their ethical and technical conditions. It performs this role in part by approaching 'thought' in terms of particular 'arts' – of contemplation, calculation, observation, experiment, self-clarification – and in part by investigating the manner and degree to which these arts are anchored in the 'ascetic' cultivation of a particular kind of 'self' or personality.[49] Second, as a result, the concept of persona allows forms of intellectual personhood to be investigated in terms of diverse ethical and epistemic techniques for the shaping of intellectual conducts and comportments. This means that such comportments are viewed independently of their normative validity, and thence without regard to any notion of a normative hierarchy of personhood passing through dialectical stages of development towards self-consciousness and self-determination. Persona thus makes it possible to suspend dialectical accounts of the conflict between the Hegelians and Rankeans and to re-describe this in terms of the emergence of radically conflicting academic cultures for shaping the intellectual conduct and ethical identity of the 'historian'.

The key to understanding the persona of the dialectical philosophical historian lies in grasping that Hegelianism's double-sided philosophical anthropology – of man as a being divided between his ideas and senses, reason and faith, abstract thought and concrete embodiment – is not a theory capable of being true or false. Rather, it should be understood as a device for acting on the self in order to carry out a specific 'ethical work' on it.[50] The Hegelians used this anthropology to establish a new relation to themselves – as inwardly divided ethical subjects – and hence as compelled to pursue a certain kind of inner ethical reconciliation. In so doing they simultaneously transformed their way of looking at historical events and institutions, viewing these too as driven by the inner divisions through which spirit was unfolded in time. Hegel's divided subject of history was thus a device through which the philosophical historian could relate to himself as stationed at a particular moment in the unfolding of spirit in time, thereby simultaneously viewing history as a process that reconciled a divided collective subject or world spirit. The anthropology of the divided subject can thus be understood as a device in a conversion process through which academic intellectuals could come to conduct themselves in a new and profoundly elevated manner, as personally responsible for reconciling the ideal and the actual. The marks of this self-induced conversion experience are evident in Hegel's comment that:

> [t]o recognize reason as the rose in the cross of the present and thereby to enjoy the present, this is the rational insight which reconciles us to the actual, the reconciliation which philosophy affords to those in whom there has once arisen an inner voice bidding them to comprehend, not only to dwell in what is substantive while still retaining subjective freedom, but also to possess subjective freedom while still standing not in anything particular and accidental but in what exists absolutely.[51]

As a device for establishing a new relation to the self and attending to its 'inner voice', Hegelian philosophical anthropology thus formed part of a way of acting on and transforming the self, effecting a 'conversion of looking' that issued in the Hegelian view of history.

Structured by this act of inner division, Hegelian dialectical historical writing operates as a kind of spiritual exercise by which the philosophical historian shapes a special kind of ethical and cognitive persona. This is effected principally through the narration and inner reconciliation of historical oppositions. For example, by modelling his history of Christianity on the division between feeling and reason, the Hegelian ecclesiastical historian Richard Rothe viewed the separation of church and state as giving rise to a dialectical opposition or paradox. This arose between a subjectively sentimental religion that lacked the rationality to realize itself in society, and an objectively rational state that lacked the morality required for man's ethical realization.[52] By structuring his narrative in terms of this dialectical opposition, Rothe set the scene for its textual overcoming. This takes place when the sentimental religion and rational state exchange properties in the narrative crisis and resolution of 'sublation', thereby effecting in the form of a literary catharsis something that had not and would not take place in history: the *Aufhebung* and reunification of the church in the Christian state:

> Thus, in the highest pinnacle of its unfolding, in accordance with its two given sides – as religious and as human, as theological and as philosophical – the consciousness of our time drives powerfully towards the knowledge that not the church but the state alone is the form in which the religious, or more accurately, the Christian life in its consummation finds its true realization.[53]

Dialectical historical writing can thus be regarded as a text-based spiritual exercise, here permitting Rothe to groom his own 'self' as the consciousness formed in and of this cathartic exchange, thereby occupying the persona of the philosophical historian.

Finally, the philosophical-hermeneutic method – by which existing histories of religions, states and peoples were transformed into symbols of the dialectical unfolding of spirit in time – was a method through which the philosophical historian acted on himself in cultivating the persona of the academic prophet. This method provided the philosophical historian with the intellectual means and emotional drive to suspend his previous acceptance of empirical history, treating the latter as blocking his path to spiritual self-consciousness. He thus prepared himself for the 'conversion of looking' that would permit him to see the hidden, spiritual significance of historical events. It was this hermeneutic 'work of the self on the self' that imbued the persona of the philosophical historian with its prophetic dimension, for it allowed this figure to discern in any apparently historical event the hidden meaning of its stage in the dialectical unfolding of spirit in time, thereby judging its shortcomings and foreseeing the reconciled form of the future. In his lectures on the history of Jewish theocracy, Heinrich Leo could thus use the dialectic between the abstract and concrete to suspend existing ecclesiastical-historical accounts of Jewish monotheism and theocracy. He could then reinterpret these phenomena as symbols of the manner in which Jewish (commercially driven) abstraction had prevented this people from engaging with the concrete freedom of the religious spirit. This engagement could not occur until Protestant Christianity had championed the latter, reconciling law and faith in a free worship and thereby pointing towards the future supersession of confessional religion revealed to Leo.[54] Philosophical hermeneutics was thus a method for shaping a prophetic persona for the philosophical historian. It permitted him to transform historical facts into symbols that were in turn capable of being deciphered only by the higher self formed by the hermeneutic method.

The intellectual stance and scientific outlook of the Rankean empirical historians was also anchored in and configured by the cultivation of a particular intellectual persona or comportment, but of a very different kind to that groomed by the philosophical historians. This is because the twin cultural sources of Rankean historiography both approached the historical by removing it from knowledge of the transcendent: God, spirit or reason. This resulted in a radically historicized outlook in which history consisted of recorded acts and events or 'facts'. In suspending transcendental religious and philosophical norms in order to conclude its founding treaties, German constitutional law gave rise to a historiography that restricted itself to examining the documentary records of the treaties. This was a historiography that regarded juridical-political norms not as supervening on historical facts from an ideal sphere, but as arising from the contingent circumstances and instruments of the treaty negotiations.[55] For its part, ecclesiastical historiography approached church history via an institutional history of the activities of councils, curia, papacy and religious reformers, while biblical criticism deployed philological methods that allow biblical, theological and philosophical texts to be approached via the historical activities and circumstances of their writing. Ecclesiastical historiography and biblical criticism thus took the form of work on the documentary records of religious institutions and teachings understood as purely human activities. From here arose an outlook that viewed the history of the church as driven by similar ambitions, interests and rivalries to those found in the political sphere, and that regarded theological texts and doctrines not as manifestations of transcendent truths to the human mind, but as records of the intellectual activities and attitudes of particular religious factions.[56]

Crucially, however, this radical historicization of the church and theology was not driven by a rationalist or secularist philosophy. In fact, it was typically accompanied and supported by a fideist or pietist practice of religion in which the God who could not be known through the theological teachings of the churches nonetheless remained immediately present through faith and grace. Paradoxically, this 'mystical' stance towards spiritual truth allowed the churches to be viewed independently of their truth or falsity, thus historically or 'impartially'.[57] Rather than signifying the failure to reconcile faith and reason, this dualistic combination of fideist and empirical outlooks should be understood in terms of the acts that the Rankean historian performs on himself in the cultivation of a special scholarly persona. In declaring God to be an object of pure faith, lying outside historical knowledge and theological-philosophical reason, the Rankean historian enacts a remarkable dual configuration of the religious and scientific fields. For this permits him to relate to himself as a faithful Christian, while simultaneously constituting political and religious history as domains of purely human action or happenstance, 'facts', in keeping with the empirical methods of constitutional historiography and ecclesiastical history and biblical criticism.

This self-relation and self-cultivation was also executed in a particular form of historical writing. But this was a form that narrated the events of German constitutional and religious history in terms of the play of purely worldly ambitions, interests and forces, while simultaneously pointing to the presence of a God whose transcendence of human reason transforms history into a domain of empirical acts and circumstances. In this setting, accidents and coincidences come to play an important double role as cruces in Rankean historical narrative. They serve as the 'finger of God', pointing to his presence in history as something unfathomable, but thence indicating that history has to be viewed as determined entirely by human will and action: '[t]he moments that condition the progress of world history are, I would like to say, a divine secret: the value of man is grounded in his self-determination and activity'.[58] Rather than indicating a failure to integrate the subjective and objective, transcendent and immanent sides of an historical dialectic, the pietistic and empirical dimensions of Ranke's historical writing were thus anchored in the cultivation of a particular intellectual persona. This was a persona whose relation to himself as a believer in a God lying beyond human understanding facilitated a view of history as a domain of purely human acts and happenstance.

Finally, the source-critical methods through which he works on archival documents are also a way in which the Rankean historian works on his 'self' or scholarly persona, but in a different way to and to ends different from those methods that characterized Hegel's philosophical hermeneutics. Through the act of fideist scepticism by which he removes knowledge of God from the documentary records of human activities, the Rankean historian turns his mind not inwards towards a divided self, but outwards towards the documents deposited by the institutions of constitutional and ecclesiastical history, now viewed as records of purely human activities. This permitted Ranke to adopt an 'impartial' stance towards these documents, treating them as neither true nor false expressions of transcendental meaning, but as signs of events the evidentiary status of which have to be determined through source-critical techniques. Rankean impartiality thus emerged not as a defect in philosophical knowledge, but as the cultivated 'virtue' or disciplined comportment of a particular kind of intellectual persona.[59] Far from seeing it as an expression of transparent rationality, Ranke viewed this impartiality as grounded in a particular historical culture and mode of self-distanciation. In the preface to his history of the papacy, Ranke could thus acknowledge that the indifference towards the papacy resulting from a Protestant, source-critical investigation of its documentary records, differed from the veneration (or hatred) that might characterize the work of an Italian, Roman or Catholic, while nonetheless remaining indicative of a certain form of impartiality:

> In these respects [of veneration or hatred], a Protestant, a North German, cannot be expected to compete with [the Italian, Roman or Catholic]. He regards the papal power with feelings of indifference; and must, from the first, renounce such expression as arises from partiality or hostility... Popery can now inspire us with no other interest than what results from the development of its history and its former interest.[60]

Conclusion

The preceding discussion has shown that two opposed models for historical writing and the persona of the historian arose in the Protestant universities of early-nineteenth-century Germany. The conflict that gave rise to this development was not a dialectical one between the two sides of a single subject of history. Rather, it was a cultural and political one rooted in a constitutional religious settlement where rationalist contestation would issue in two radically and permanently opposed ways of cultivating the persona of the historian: those of the empirical, source-critical historian, and the dialectical-philosophical hermeneut.

Notes

1 Ernst Simon, *Ranke und Hegel* (Munich: Oldenbourg, 1928).
2 For a rare impartial comparison of the two methods, see ibid., pp 156–83.
3 See above all, Martin Heckel, 'Religionsfreiheit: Ein säkulare Verfassungsgarantie', in Heckel, *Gesammelte Schriften: Staat, Kirche, Recht, Geschichte*, ed. Klaus Schlaich, vol. 4 (Tübingen: J. C. B. Mohr, 1997), pp 647–849.
4 For classic examples, see Johann Jacob Moser, *Von der Teutschen Religions-Verfassung* (Frankfurt & Leipzig, 1774), and Johann Stephan Pütter, *An Historical Development of the Present Political Constitution of the Germanic Empire*, vol. 1, trans. J. Dornford (London: Payne, Davis and White, 1790).
5 For a key example, see Gottfried Arnold, *Unparteyische Kirchen- und Ketzer-Historie, von Anfang des Neuen Testaments bis auff das Jahr Christi 1688* (Frankfurt am Main: Thomas Fritsch, 1699).
6 The unsurpassed study of these developments remains Walter Sparn, *Wiederkehr der Metaphysik: Die ontologische Frage in der lutherischen Theologie des frühen 17. Jahrhunderts* (Stuttgart: Calwer Verlag, 1976).
7 See Christoph Scheibler, *Opus metaphysicum, duobus libris universum hujus scientiae systema comprehendens* (Giessen: Chemlini, 1617), bk. 1, pp 177–220, 341–62.
8 See, for example, Balthasar Meisner, *Dissertatio de legibus in quatuor libellos distributa* (Wittenberg: Raaben, 1616), pp 249–84.
9 For more, see Ian Hunter, 'Public law and the limits of philosophy: German idealism and the religious constitution', *Critical Inquiry*, 44 (2018), 528–53.
10 Immanuel Kant, 'On the common saying: that may be correct in theory, but it is of no use in practice', in Mary J. Gregor (ed.), *Immanuel Kant: Practical Philosophy* (Cambridge: Cambridge University Press, 1996), pp 273–310; Immanuel Kant, *Religion within the Bounds of Bare Reason*, trans. Werner S. Pluhar (Indianapolis, IN: Hackett, 2009), pp 120–37.
11 Georg Wilhelm Friedrich Hegel, 'The German constitution (1798–1802)', in Laurence Dickey and H. B. Nisbet (eds), *Political Writings* (Cambridge: Cambridge University Press, 1999), pp 6–101.
12 Georg Wilhelm Friedrich Hegel, *Lectures on the Philosophy of Religion: One-Volume Edition, the Lectures of 1827*, trans. R. F. Brown, P. C. Hodgson and J. M. Stewart (Los Angeles: University of California Press, 1988), pp 452–70.
13 Ian Hunter, 'Kant's *Religion* and Prussian religious policy', *Modern Intellectual History*, 2 (2005), 1–27.

14 For a detailed account of the composition of the factions, see Simon, *Ranke und Hegel*, pp 16–54.
15 See for example, Philipp Marheineke, *Einleitung in die öffentlichen Vorlesungen über die Bedeutung der hegelschen Philosophie in der christlichen Theologie* (Berlin: Enslin, 1842).
16 See Simon, *Ranke und Hegel*, pp 79–87.
17 For a helpful discussion, see Richard Crouter, 'Hegel and Schleiermacher at Berlin: a many-sided debate', *Journal of the American Academy of Religion*, 48 (1980), 19–43.
18 Michael Stolleis, *Public Law in Germany: 1800–1914* (New York: Berghahn Books, 2001), pp 90–160.
19 Gareth Stedman Jones, 'Religion and the origins of socialism', in Ira Katznelson and Gareth Stedman Jones (eds), *Religion and the Political Imagination* (Cambridge: Cambridge University Press, 2010), pp 171–89; Gareth Stedman Jones, 'The young Hegelians, Marx and Engels', in Gareth Stedman Jones and Gregory Claeys (eds), *The Cambridge History of Nineteenth-Century Political Thought* (Cambridge: Cambridge University Press, 2011), pp 556–600.
20 Christopher Clark, 'Confessional policy and the limits of state action: Frederick William III and the Prussian Union 1817–40', *The Historical Journal*, 39 (1996), 985–1004.
21 Simon, *Ranke und Hegel*, pp 106–20; John Edward Toews, *Hegelianism: The Path Toward Dialectical Humanism, 1805–1841* (Cambridge: Cambridge University Press, 1980), pp 203–54; Niklas Lenhard-Schramm, *Konstrukteure der Nation: Geschichtsprofessoren als politische Akteure in Vormärz und Revolution 1848/49* (Münster: Waxmann, 2014), pp 83–122.
22 Stefan Rebenich, 'Theodor Mommsen, die deutschen Professoren und die Revolution von 1848', in A. Demandt, A. Goltz and H. Schlange-Schöningen (eds), *Theodor Mommsen: Wissenschaft und Politik im 19. Jahrhundert* (Berlin: De Gruyter, 2005), pp 13–35.
23 Georg Wilhelm Friedrich Hegel, 'Foreword', in Hermann Friedrich Wilhelm Hinrichs, *Die Religion im inneren Verhältnisse zur Wissenschaft* (Heidelberg: Groos, 1822), pp i–xxviii. English translation in Peter C. Hodgson (ed.), *G. W. F. Hegel: Theologian of the Spirit* (Minneapolis, MN: Fortress Press, 1997), pp 156–71.
24 Hegel, 'Foreword', pp i–viii.
25 Ibid., pp xv–xx.
26 Ibid., pp ix–x.
27 Ibid., pp xxii–xxv.
28 Heinrich Leo, 'Universalhistorische Uebersicht der Geschichte der alten Welt und ihrer Kultur, von Friedrich Christoph Schlosser', *Jahrbücher für wissenschaftliche Kritik*, 43–4 (1827), 345–52; 45–6 (1827), 354–68; and 47–8 (1827), 370–83.
29 Ibid. (43–4), 349–50.
30 Ibid. (45–6), 355 (original emphases).
31 Ibid., 357.
32 Heinrich Leo (aka H. L. Manin), 'Geschichte' (review of Ranke's *Geschichten der romanischen und germanischen Völker*, 1824, and *Zur Kritik neuerer Geschichtschreiber*, 1824), *Ergänzungsblätter zur Jenaischen Allgemeinen Literatur Zeitung* (1828), no. 17, 130–6 and no. 18, 137–40.
33 Leopold von Ranke, 'Replik', *Allgemeine Literatur-Zeitung*, 131 (1828), 193–9. Reprinted under the title 'Erwiderung auf Heinrich Leo's Angriff (Frühling 1828)', in *Sämmtliche Werke*, vols 53, 54 (Leipzig: Duncker & Humblot, 1875), pp 659–66.
34 Leopold von Ranke, *The Theory and Practice of History*, ed. Georg G. Iggers, trans. Wilma A. Iggers (Abingdon: Routledge, 2011).
35 Leopold von Ranke, 'Idee der Universalhistorie', *Historische Zeitschrift*, 178 (1954 [ms. from the 1830s]), 293. English translation: Leopold von Ranke, 'On the character of historical science (a manuscript of the 1830s)', in Iggers, *Theory and Practice of History*, pp 8–16 (I have modified the translation by Wilma A. Iggers in several instances).
36 Ranke, 'Idee der Universalhistorie', 295.

37 Leopold von Ranke, 'The pitfalls of a philosophy of history (introduction to a lecture on universal history: a manuscript of the 1840s)', in Iggers, *Theory and Practice of History*, pp 17–19.
38 Ranke, 'Idee der Universalhistorie', 292–5.
39 Leopold von Ranke, *Geschichten der romanischen und germanischen Völker: von 1494 bis 1535*, vol. 1 (Leipzig: Reimer, 1824), pp v–vi.
40 Leopold von Ranke, *Ueber die Verschwörung gegen Venedig, im Jahre 1618: Mit Urkunden aus dem Venezianischen Archive* (Berlin: Duncker & Humblot, 1831), pp 2–11, 12–22.
41 Leopold von Ranke, 'On progress in history (from the first lecture to King Maximillian II of Bavaria, "On the epochs of modern history" – 1854)', in Iggers, *Theory and Practice of History*, pp 20–4.
42 Ibid., p. 22.
43 Ibid., p. 21.
44 Kurt Mautz, 'Leo und Ranke', *Deutsche Vierteljahrsschrift für Literaturwissenschaft und Geistesgeschichte*, 27 (1953), 207–35.
45 Ulrich Muhlack, *Geschichtswissenschaft im Humanismus und in der Aufklärung: Die Vorgeschichte des Historismus* (Munich: C. H. Beck, 1991), pp 412–35.
46 Frederick C. Beiser, 'Hegel and Ranke: a re-examination', in S. Houlgate and M. Baur (eds), *A Companion to Hegel* (Oxford: Blackwell, 2011), pp 332–50, at pp 338–40.
47 Peter C. Hodgson, *Shapes of Freedom: Hegel's Philosophy of World History in Theological Perspective* (Oxford: Oxford University Press, 2012), pp 18–20.
48 John E. Toews, *Becoming Historical: Cultural Reformation and Public Memory in Early Nineteenth-Century Berlin* (Cambridge: Cambridge University Press, 2004), p. 410.
49 Ian Hunter, 'The history of philosophy and the persona of the philosopher', *Modern Intellectual History*, 4 (2007), 571–600.
50 The phrase is borrowed from Michel Foucault, and throughout this section I have drawn on his approach to ethics in terms of 'practices of the self', as outlined in Foucault, *The Use of Pleasure*, trans. R. Hurley (Harmondsworth: Penguin Books, 1985), pp 3–32 and *The Hermeneutics of the Subject: Lectures at the Collège de France 1981–1982*, ed. Frédéric Gros, trans. Graham Burchell (New York: Picador, 2006), pp 1–24, 205–70.
51 Georg Wilhelm Friedrich Hegel, *Hegel's Philosophy of Right*, trans. T. M. Knox (Oxford: Oxford University Press, 1952), p. 12.
52 Richard Rothe, *Die Anfänge der Christlichen Kirche und ihrer Verfassung* (Wittenberg: Zimmermann, 1837), pp 126–34.
53 Ibid., pp 134–5.
54 Heinrich Leo, *Vorlesungen über die Geschichte des Jüdischen Staates* (Berlin: Duncker & Humblot, 1828), pp 54–62.
55 For a succinct rendition of this outlook, see Moser, *Teutschen Religions-Verfassung*, pp 6–22.
56 See, for example, Leopold von Ranke, *The History of the Popes during the Last Four Centuries*, vol. 1 (London: Bell, 1913 [orig. pub. 1834]).
57 Most famously in Arnold's *Unparteyische Kirchen- und Ketzer-Historie*. On the pietistic basis of Arnold's empirical history of the church and his conception of impartiality, see Sicco Lehmann-Brauns, *Weisheit in der Weltgeschichte: Philosophiegeschichte zwischen Barok und Aufklärung* (Tübingen: Niemeyer, 2004), pp 282–97.
58 Leopold von Ranke, *Deutsche Geschichte im Zeitalter der Reformation*, vol. 5, 5th edn (Leipzig: Duncker & Humblot, 1873 [orig. pub. 1843]), p. 46.
59 On historical personae as configurations of scholarly virtues, see Herman Paul, 'The virtues of a good historian in early Imperial Germany: Georg Waitz's contested example', *Modern Intellectual History*, 15 (2018), 681–709.
60 Leopold von Ranke, *Die römischen Päpste, ihr Kirche und ihr Staat im sechzehnten und siebzehnten Jahrhundert*, vol. 1 (Berlin: Duncker & Humblot, 1834), p. xv. In English: Ranke, *History of Popes during Last Four Centuries*, vol. 1, pp xii–xiii.

CHAPTER 2

Ranke vs Schlosser: pairs of personae in nineteenth-century German historiography

Herman Paul

Introduction

In 1877, the Berlin dramatist, novelist and literary critic Paul Lindau convened an imaginary parliament to discuss the question whether Friedrich Christoph Schlosser had been so great a historian as to deserve a commemorative address on the occasion of his hundredth birthday. The members of parliament whom Lindau invoked in the pages of *Der Salon*, a German cultural monthly, included both real and imaginary characters. Among the former were such well-known historians as Heinrich von Sybel, the director of the Prussian archives, and Heinrich von Treitschke, who occupied a chair at the University of Berlin as well as a seat in the Reichstag. Other real-life characters included Joseph Hillebrand, a Giessen-based philosopher, historian and novelist who had made no secret of his sympathy for Schlosser,[1] and Wilhelm Oncken, one of the thriving forces behind a Schlosser monument soon to be unveiled in the Frisian city of Jever.[2] Together with some eloquent parliamentarians born out of Lindau's own imagination, the four men engaged in spirited debate over Schlosser's merits as a historian, with applause and cheers from other delegates, a dignified president trying to keep order when emotions ran high and interruptions of a sort that led Treitschke to remark that it was advantageous not to understand everything that was said (a playful reference to his near-deafness).[3]

Although Lindau was known for his light-hearted, satirical prose,[4] one of the striking features of 'The Literary Parliament' is how historically accurate were the views that he ascribed to Hillebrand, Oncken, Sybel and Treitschke. Almost everything Lindau made them say about Schlosser was derived from their published work. This is most apparent in the case of Sybel, whose *Kleine historische Schriften* (1863) were quoted complete with quotation marks and page references.[5] But even where quotation marks were absent, Lindau did not give his imagination free rein. Hillebrand's statements were quoted literally from *Die deutsche Nationalliteratur seit dem Anfange des achtzehnten Jahrhunderts* (vol. 3, 1846), while a couple of other interventions in the debate seem to have been based on a 1857 brochure containing a collage of reviews of Schlosser's *Weltgeschichte für das deutsche Volk* (19 vols, 1844–57).[6] So, although 'The Literary Parliament' was a work of fiction, it was so only to a point: it mirrored part of a decades-long debate among German historians over Schlosser's professional merits.[7]

Much the same is true for Lindau's observation that historians discussed those merits in terms of virtues and vices. When Lindau invoked the 'representative H. v. Treitschke' as arguing that Schlosser had lacked 'one of the first virtues of the historian', he used a formula – the 'first' or 'highest' virtue – that historians had been using since at least the eighteenth century. The phrase referred not simply to dispositions or character traits that historians regarded as indispensable for historical scholarship, but more specifically to hierarchies of virtues: which of the virtues traditionally associated with historical studies deserved most weight? Lindau's literary parliament thus not only depicted German historians as discussing their professional vocation in terms of virtues, but more specifically also portrayed them as engaged in debate over the relative importance of those virtues.

The nineteenth-century debate over Schlosser's virtues and vices provides an interesting glimpse into why historians disagreed about their 'first' or 'highest' virtue and, more specifically, on how they conducted debate on so abstract a theme. I will argue that they did so under reference to embodied models of virtue that I call 'scholarly personae'. Although these personae were named after real-life historians such as Schlosser, they were usually highly stylized models, defined in contrast to each other and created in response to points of contestation in historians' understanding of their professional vocation. Scholarly personae, in short, represented different catalogues of virtues, or different answers to the question what made a good historian.

The highest virtue

When in 1842 the 65-year-old Schlosser, long-time professor of history in Heidelberg, announced his plan for a multi-volume world history, the *Allgemeine Zeitung* welcomed this idea effusively. It argued that no living German historian was better suited for this task than Schlosser, given his 'love of truth', 'objectivity', 'thoroughness' and 'sharp sight'

(*Scharfblick*) – virtues that distinguished the Heidelberg historian from authors whose 'pretended objectivity' was only a cover for 'diplomatic slyness' (*Schlauheit*).[8] When two years later Schlosser's opening volume arrived from the press, thanks mostly to the efforts of Schlosser's assistant Georg Ludwig Kriegk,[9] reviewers phrased their praise in terms of virtues, too. Drawing on gendered national stereotypes, they applauded Schlosser's 'German diligence', 'German thoroughness' and 'masculine enthusiasm for the higher moral law', which the *Frankfurter Journal* reckoned among 'the inherited virtues [*Erbtugenden*] of German character'. Some noted that Schlosser did not belong to 'the so-called objective school of history', given that he was intent on identifying moral rights and wrongs in history, thereby blaming especially the mighty and powerful for moral corruption. In these moral judgements, though, Schlosser was said to display 'the strictest conscientiousness' as well as 'the most beautiful feelings for justice'. Paired to 'uncompromising zeal for truth and truth alone', his 'impartiality' of judgement was hailed as a cardinal virtue for historians.[10]

This vocabulary of virtue was not particularly surprising, given that it dominated nineteenth-century German moral discourse more generally.[11] Also, Schlosser's reviewers stood in a long tradition of defining scholarly integrity in terms of virtues and vices. In early-modern Europe, 'love of truth', 'impartiality' and 'conscientiousness' already counted as scholarly virtues, with vices such as 'dogmatism' and 'speculation' serving as their negative counterparts.[12] As Stevin Shapin has demonstrated for seventeenth-century England, virtues in the sense of cultivated character traits were important because they served as markers of reliability: virtuous character was an index of scholarly trustworthiness.[13] Against this background, Kasper Risbjerg Eskildsen argues that nineteenth-century historians, just like their early-modern predecessors, were interested in virtues because they perceived them as guarantees of trustworthiness.[14]

This, however, is not the whole story. Apart from the fact that trustworthiness could be defined in various ways, Schlosser's example shows that creating reliable knowledge about the past was not unanimously regarded as the most important part of the historian's vocation. Schlosser, said the *Illustrirte Zeitung*, was more interested in fostering public morality than in 'empirical establishment of facts'.[15] Writing history with an eye to 'the circumstances of the time' and 'the needs of the present', another admirer declared, is what distinguishes 'the real historian' from those merely producing academic knowledge.[16] Although, of course, few denied the importance of acquiring reliable knowledge, disagreement existed on its relative significance *vis-à-vis* other historiographical aims. How important was factual accuracy in comparison to societal impact, style of writing in comparison to erudite learning, or political edification in comparison to methodological purity? Was it true, as Ludwig Häusser argued in 1841, that it amounts to a virtue not to keep digging in the 'rubbish' of historical records, but to allow the 'breath of the creative spirit' to blow through the dust?[17]

These were relevant questions at a time when Leopold von Ranke, F. C. A. Hasse and others had begun to convene academic historical seminars (*historische Übungen*) and when a specialized *Zeitschrift für Geschichtswissenschaft* (1844) appeared on the market, followed by the *Historische Zeitschrift* (1859).[18] Schlosser's *Weltgeschichte*, targeted at 'the German people', appeared at a time when German historians found themselves disagreeing over who were their prime audience: educated, middle-class readers or fellow historians in an emerging professional guild?[19] Although twentieth-century literature on 'professionalization' has highlighted the growing importance of professional peers as primary readers of historical literature, the emergence of more specialized audiences was neither linear nor uncontested. The dream of German unification, for instance, inspired quite a few historians to blur distinctions between historical writing and political journalism.[20] Opinions were sharply divided, however, on the extent to which the 'political professor' – a scholar putting his learning into the service of a nationalist cause – was an appropriate role model for historians.[21] Political and intellectual developments in mid-nineteenth-century Germany thus contributed to disagreement over the relative importance of the aims that historical studies could serve.

It was in relation to such prioritizing of aims that classic formulas regarding the 'first' or 'highest' virtue of the historian, such as those used by Treitschke and quoted by Lindau, gained in importance,[22] together with related terms like the historian's 'first duty', 'first task' or 'highest commandment'.[23] For the relative weight attached to virtues such as 'impartiality of judgement', 'zeal for truth' and 'feeling for justice' was corollary to the relative importance of the aims that historical study was supposed to serve. Thus, when historians argued that 'criticism' was 'the most indispensable quality of the historian' or, by contrast, presented 'a feeling for the scholarly needs of present-day man' as 'the first and greatest quality of the historian', such prioritizing of virtues amounted to taking stances on the historian's task.[24] Treitschke's verdict that Schlosser had lacked 'one of the first virtues of the historian', namely 'real historical objectivity', thus reveals at least as much about Treitschke's understanding of the historian's vocation as it does about Schlosser.[25]

Unsurprisingly, in Schlosser's case, such evaluations often focused on the appropriateness of moral judgement in history, given that the Heidelberg historian had not hidden his moral indignation at historical characters whom he perceived as engaged in corruption and injustice.[26] Because of this honest moral judging, argued the literary historian Heinrich Kurz in 1859, Schlosser 'still occupies one of the most prominent places among our history writers', despite others being more proficient in source criticism or more gifted with literary brilliance.[27] Considerably more critical, however, was Heinrich von Sybel's verdict that Schlosser had done a disservice to historical scholarship by subordinating the 'autonomy of historical writing' to 'other considerations' (*andere Rücksichten*), including especially moral reflection and judgement.[28] Other Ranke scholars joined Sybel in portraying Schlosser as engaged in judging the past with an eye to the present, more than in objective searching for 'historical truth'.[29]

After Schlosser's death in 1861, the debate continued with undiminished intensity. Schlosser's Heidelberg pupil Georg Gottfried Gervinus, of whom Lindau claimed that in Gervinus 'you see all Schlosser's failures and strengths even clearer than in himself',[30] poured oil on troubled waters by publishing a book-length obituary of his teacher that has rightly been described as a 'manifesto of the Schlosser school'.[31] Its tone of *apologia* elicited harsh criticism from Johann Wilhelm Löbell, one of Sybel's predecessors in Bonn, who argued that Schlosser's presumed virtues were better conceived of as vices.[32] Similarly, the young Carl von Noorden, a former student of Löbell and Sybel, castigated Schlosser for superimposing his own moral standards on the past, thereby showing an underdeveloped appreciation for the 'variety of human aspirations and spiritual persuasions'.[33] These attacks elicited further responses from the philosopher Wilhelm Dilthey, among others,[34] and resulted in a debate that exercised historians and non-historians alike, judging by private correspondence and printed statements on the 'battle' over Schlosser's virtues and vices.[35]

Contrastive models

Conspicuously, this dispute over the extent to which Schlosser embodied 'the ideal of a real historian' was soon indistinguishable from reflection on historiographical ideals as such.[36] The controversy over Schlosser's moralizing historiography, in other words, increasingly was also a debate on the desirability of historians acting as moral judges. Consequently, as von Noorden observed in 1862, Schlosser became gradually presented as a symbol of a morally driven sort of history writing. While Schlosser had initially simply been the name of an individual born in Jever in 1776, the mid-nineteenth-century debate over his virtues and vices turned the proper name into a more generic title, denoting a type of historian who issued explicit moral judgement on the past. This caused the debate over Schlosser to revolve around what von Noorden perceptively called his *idealisirten individuellen Eigenthümlichkeit* – the 'idealized individual distinctiveness' or schematized features that were perceived as distinguishing Schlosser's mode of history from others.[37]

Most prominent among those others was Ranke. Whenever mid-nineteenth-century historians evaluated the strengths and weaknesses of Schlosser's *Gelehrtentypus*, they compared Schlosser to Ranke. One of Lindau's characters, too, made such a comparison in declaring that 'Schlosser is Schiller, Ranke Goethe. Schlosser is a pronounced Kantian, Ranke a veiled Hegelian. Schlosser is formless in his writing, Ranke artistic in its form. The one is a male spirit, the other a female one.'[38] This echoed a *topos* that had emerged in the second quarter of the century, when Ranke was not yet primarily associated with objectivity, but with an artist's eye for colour, texture and detail as well as a talent for seeing the whole in the part, or the broad course of history reflected in individual moments of life.[39] Although Wilhelm Dilthey somewhat exaggerated when he remembered German historians in the 1830s and 1840s as being preoccupied with playing Ranke and Schlosser off against each other,[40] it is true that the two were frequently compared, not only on their styles of writing and philosophical orientations,[41] but also and especially on their attitudes towards moral judgement of the past. While Schlosser was turned into a representative of 'moralist' history, Ranke's refusal to let moral judgement prevail over silent wonder at the diversity of human existence became known as 'æstheticism'.[42]

This was not the only schematic contrast drawn between Schlosser and Ranke. Although both men held, or had held, university positions, Schlosser's admirers, such as the Heidelberg school teacher Georg Weber, turned their hero into a popular historian who positively distinguished himself from the academic historian that was Ranke. Unhindered by 'professorial guildism' and the 'vain haughtiness' of professional scholars, Schlosser had 'given voice and expression to the consciousness of the people', no matter how much mockery his work had provoked 'in the higher circles' of German society, wrote Weber in characteristic anti-elitist prose.[43] Moreover, as an 'advocate of the people', dressed in a prophet's cloak, Schlosser had called to account the mighty and powerful with a moral audacity that no state-paid academic was likely to display: 'Schlosser's world history is therefore a court of justice, to which those who are usually protected from judicial judgement are made to account...'[44]

As these examples illustrate, the names of Schlosser and Ranke did not refer merely to individuals; they corresponded to different models of how to be a historian, characterized by different catalogues of virtue.

Scholarly personae

When I designate such models of virtue as 'scholarly personae', I am using a term that historians of science have coined to draw attention to repertoires available for defining 'scholarly selfhood', or modes of being a scholar.[45] Yet as Gadi Algazi recently observed, historians have appropriated this concept in different ways for different purposes.[46] Some of them equate personae with templates for what societies understand or expect a scholar to be. Although such templates vary across time and space, they often do so only slowly and to limited extents: the early-modern trope of the absent-minded professor is still a recognizable stereotype. Such personae, moreover, are not limited to specific fields of enquiry: the absent-minded scholar can be a philologist, a chemist, or a mathematician.[47]

Other historians, by contrast, treat scholarly personae as 'masks' that can be put on and taken off as the situation requires. For them, personae are self-images that scholars cultivate in their attempts to claim authority or to demand recognition from others. Although such self-fashioning draws on culturally sanctioned scripts, the emphasis in this second approach lies on the politics of voice, dress and gesture.[48] So, whereas in Braudelian terms the first approach is located in the slowly changing realm of 'structural history', the second is a key example of *histoire événementielle* in so far as personae can differ from person to person and change from day to day.[49]

If the choice were just between these two approaches, interpreting the contrastive models of virtue embodied by Schlosser and Ranke in terms of scholarly personae would yield little insight. There is a third approach, however, located at an intermediate level between the structural and the *événementiel*, which fits the case study much better. Characteristic of this intermediate approach is that it defines scholarly personae as models of professional selfhood to which scholars in the past referred, positively or negatively, in articulating their views of that it meant to be a biologist, a chemist or an art historian. That is to say, first, that personae are treated as actors' categories – what were the models that scholars in the past found important enough to invoke in discussing their vocational identities? – and, second, that they usually, though not always, come in the plural. For just as the model of the 'pure scientist' only made sense in contrast to the 'applied scientist', so the nineteenth-century *Sachphilologe* was unimaginable without its implied other, the *Sprachphilologe*.[50] Scholarly personae, in this third approach, are therefore modes of being a scholar – discipline-specific in some cases, discipline-transcending in others – that were available to scholars in the past and served as points of orientation especially in contexts of disagreement about the purposes that scholarly enquiry should serve.[51]

Although nineteenth-century German historians rarely used the term 'persona',[52] the models they associated with Schlosser and Ranke were scholarly personae in Algazi's third sense of the word. They denoted different modes of being a historian, corresponding to distinct catalogues of virtues. In referring to the Schlosser and Ranke personae, I am not proposing an innovative tool for historiographical analysis, therefore; I am giving a name to a phenomenon that German historians discussed at the time, with some intensity, among themselves.

Areas of contestation

What difference, then, does a study of such personae make for our understanding of nineteenth-century German historiography? First, it allows us to explain why Schlosser continued to serve as a point of orientation, positively or negatively, for German historians even after his 'school' had disappeared. On the occasion of his centenary in 1876, commemorative speakers and writers almost unanimously agreed that Schlosser's days were over.[53] Even at Heidelberg, where Schlosser had taught for many years, Bernhard Erdmannsdörffer almost apologized for celebrating Schlosser's birthday: '[d]espite close personal memories, a broad gulf [*eine weite Kluft*] separates him and us'.[54] Nonetheless, Erdmannsdörffer saw in 'Schlosser's manner' something worth retrieving, without endorsing all of it.[55] While acknowledging that Schlosser's historical writing did not meet the standards of modern 'historical method and technique', he admired 'the depth and delicacy of his feeling' – a quality poorly nurtured among historians whose primary interest seemed to lie in methodological rigour.[56]

Even more positive was the Königsberg historian Franz Rühl, who in 1880 claimed Schlosser as a forerunner of universal history (*Universalgeschichte*). While relativizing the Schlosser–Ranke dichotomy, Rühl used Schlosser to promote an eighteenth-century cosmopolitan attitude conducive to transnational modes of history writing that nineteenth-century nationalists, to Rühl's regret, had failed to appreciate.[57] So, Rühl, too, invoked Schlosser as a contrastive model of virtue, even though the features of this persona had changed: the former moralist had now become a cosmopolitan rationalist.

What this example illustrates is that personae were not discussed in the abstract, but invoked in relation to fault lines or areas of contestation. The relevance of the Schlosser or Ranke persona was positively correlated to the contested character of the commitments they were perceived as embodying. This explains why Sybel could argue in 1886 that the old dichotomy between Ranke and Schlosser no longer made sense.[58] After the Franco-Prussian War and the *Kulturkampf*, among other things, issues of moral judgement had dropped down the historians' priority list. Other personae, such as the patriotic historian paradigmatically embodied by Treitschke, had made their appearance. Still, as Rühl's example shows, old names could reappear as labels for new personae, bearing on contemporary issues.

Much the same happened to Ranke. Once the Berlin *Altmeister* had ceased to be an antipode to Schlosser, he was reappropriated, most notably by Erdmannsdörffers's former student Max Lenz, as a larger-than-life example of 'objectivity'.[59] This new Rankean persona was intended as an alternative to Treitschke's, as Lenz explained to his Berlin students in 1901 by sharply contrasting Treitschke's political pathos with Ranke's sober objectivity.[60] At the same time, Catholic historians of traditional leaning habitually regarded Ranke as personifying such typically Protestant evils as scholarly naturalism, which excluded miracles from the realm of the possible.[61] For them, Ranke was an antipode to Johannes Janssen, the conservative Catholic apologist whose name in turn served as a byword for dogmatism in Lenz's Protestant circles.[62] Interestingly, younger Catholic scholars such as Georg Hüffer and Wilhelm Diekamp refused to choose between Ranke and Janssen and resolved this dilemma by invoking a third persona, embodied by the seventeenth-century Maurists, whom they perceived as harmoniously combining virtues of accuracy and criticism with faith and loyalty to the church.[63]

Navigating personae

This is not to say that every historian defined his own pairs of personae. To the contrary, all the contrasts mentioned so far – Schlosser vs Ranke, Ranke vs Treitschke, Ranke vs Janssen – were widely shared dichotomies. They served as coordinates on imaginary maps of the historical discipline, schematically representing different understandings of what counted as the historian's 'first' or 'highest' virtue. Yet while these maps were broadly shared, different historians made different use of them. If Schlosser and Ranke represented opposite ends of a spectrum, historians could position themselves at different points along this spectrum. They did not need to identify with a single persona, but could try to mediate or negotiate between several of them. Not all historians, in other words, were like Gervinus, who closely followed Schlosser's example, or Hubert Ermisch, who stayed loyal to the model of his teacher Georg Waitz.[64]

By drawing attention to historians who did not fit single categories, research focused on scholarly personae therefore allows, in the second place, for a higher degree of inclusion than histories of schools. Erdmannsdörffer is a case in point. As a former student of Johann Gustav Droysen and a close friend of Treitschke, whom he succeeded in 1874 as professor in Heidelberg, Erdmannsdörffer seemed predisposed towards membership of the 'Prussian Historical School'. It is no coincidence, however, that his name is absent from Robert Southard's study of this school.[65] As illustrated by his carefully restrained writing style, Erdmannsdörffer felt too much attracted to Rankean objectivity to fit Treitschke's mould.[66] Also, while his letters to Droysen reveal a lively interest in politics, he was never politically active.[67] His research, too, moved beyond the political by venturing into 'cultural history', as Karl Lamprecht would soon call it.[68] On top of that, Erdmannsdörffer did not have the rhetorical powers of his predecessors in Heidelberg, which forced him to develop an alternative to a tradition of spectacular lecturing associated with Häusser and Treitschke.[69] Erdmannsdörffer, in other words, wove his way between some of the dominant models of his time – engaging for many years in meticulous source-editing while longing for work of greater scope, and applauding Treitschke's nationalist historiography while himself striking more reserved tones.[70]

In such navigating, Erdmannsdörffer was not alone. In the closing decades of the nineteenth century, German historical studies were populated with figures like Friedrich von Bezold, who felt torn between his teachers Sybel and Waitz,[71] Ludwig Weiland, who tried to correct the limitations of Waitz-style source criticism with literary imagination as exemplified by Friedrich Christoph Dahlmann,[72] and Alfred Naudé, who resembled Erdmannsdörffer in trying to carve out a middle position between Treitschkean patriotism and Rankean objectivity.[73] What these examples show is that the historiographical landscape was not neatly divided into parcels or schools. There was space for dialogue and ambiguity. While some historians stuck to a single persona, not seldom out of faithfulness to a highly regarded teacher, others manoeuvred their own way, positioning themselves with nuance at some distance from the schematic positions that served as scholarly personae.

Political contexts

Naturally, the amount of freedom that scholars enjoyed in plotting their own professional path greatly differed. While Erdmannsdörffer only found himself confronted with Heidelberg expectations that he could not meet, other historians, especially in non-professorial positions, were significantly more restricted in their room to manoeuvre, if only because of political and religious sensibilities in the German Empire shortly after the *Kulturkampf*. Illustrative is the case of Waitz's former student Hermann Grauert, who shared with many Catholic historians of his generation a desire to overcome the dichotomy between Ranke and Janssen mentioned above. This became apparent in 1886, when Grauert wrote in the journal of the Catholic Görres Society a lengthy obituary of Waitz that was significantly more appreciative of Rankean objectivity than customary in Catholic circles.[74] The piece provoked a small revolt within the Görres Society and almost cost Grauert his editorship of the journal. Moving too close to Ranke, 'the most dangerous enemy of the Catholic church',[75] amounted to a career threat. This offers a clue to why Grauert subsequently kept silent about his preferred personae and, more generally, why many Catholic historians around 1900 thought it safer to engage in empirical research than to indulge in historiographical reflection.[76]

So, although scholarly personae, understood as coordinates on imaginary maps of the field, encourage research into map-making activities that help historians understand and articulate what it means to be a scholar, such research cannot ignore the social, political and religious realities in which such map-making took place. In so far as personae specified whether it was appropriate for historians to be patriotically committed to the nation or loyal to the Vatican, they were charged with political or religious meaning. Subsequently, praise and criticism of such personae amounted to taking a stand on contested issues. This in turn implies that the emergence, popularity and impact of these models cannot be understood without careful consideration of political and religious sensitivities in early Imperial Germany. A final, not exclusive, but important advantage, then, of studying personae is that it contributes to a deeply contextual understanding of what it meant to be a historian in an age when demarcations between history, politics and religion were as contested as those between history, literature and journalism.

Conclusion

Paul Lindau's parliamentary debate, with which I began this chapter, ended with a majority of the house voting in support of a commemorative address in Schlosser's honour. Ironically, however, the voters' motives were mixed: '[a] quarter of the majority... votes for it out of enthusiasm, a quarter out of generosity, so as not to spoil the committee's joy, a quarter in order to read their names among the contributors to a monument, a quarter because Schlosser's *Weltgeschichte* was one of their father's books, which they themselves have never read, though'.⁷⁷ In reality, erecting a *Denkmal* in Jever appeared even more difficult. Prominent historians such as Waitz refused to join the committee,⁷⁸ probably because Waitz's favourite virtues – 'criticism', 'penetration' and 'precision' – did not match Schlosser's.⁷⁹ Also, financial contributions fell painfully short. Only after two years' delay could a cheap and simple monument be unveiled.⁸⁰

In framing the German debate over Schlosser's monument in parliamentary terms, Lindau aptly conveyed the extent to which late-nineteenth-century German historical studies was a divided house. Not unlike the Reichstag, historical scholarship was divided into parties that found themselves disagreeing on fundamental issues.⁸¹ Although secondary literature conventionally refers to 'the' historical discipline in the singular, studying this discipline through the prism of scholarly personae reveals that its members not seldom identified with a specific persona, a 'highest virtue' or a particular model of professionalism more than with a discipline at large, on the nature of which they disagreed in the first place. Scholarly personae therefore help correct overly unified accounts of German historical scholarship by drawing attention to a disunity among historians that expressed itself in controversies like the long-running debate over Schlosser's historiographical merits.⁸²

Notes

1 Joseph Hillebrand, *Die deutsche Nationalliteratur seit dem Anfange des achtzehnten Jahrhunderts, besonders seit Lessing, bis auf die Gegenwart, historisch und ästhetisch-kritisch dargestellt*, vol. 3 (Hamburg: Friedrich und Andreas Perthes, 1846), p. 433.
2 'Schlosser-Denkmal', *Zeitung für das höhere Unterrichtswesen Deutschlands*, 4 (1875), 271; 'Das Schlosser-Denkmal in Jever', *Illustrirte Zeitung*, 71 (1878), 461–2.
3 [Paul Lindau], 'Das literarische Parlament', *Der Salon für Literatur, Kunst und Gesellschaft* (1877), 226–30.
4 Roland Berbig, 'Paul Lindau: Eine Literatenkarriere', in Peter Wruck (ed.), *Literarisches Leben in Berlin, 1871–1933* (Berlin: Akademie-Verlag, 1987), pp 88–125; Anneliese Eismann-Liche, 'Paul Lindau: Publizist und Romancier der Gründerjahre' (PhD thesis, University of Munster, 1981).
5 [Lindau], 'Literarische Parlament', 228, under reference to Heinrich von Sybel, *Kleine historische Schriften* (Munich: J. G. Cotta, 1863), pp 349, 350, 352.
6 *Friedrich Christoph Schlosser und dessen Weltgeschichte für das deutsche Volk: Eine Sammlung literarischer Urtheile* (Frankfurt am Main: Verlag der Expedition von Schlosser's Weltgeschichte, 1857).
7 Ellen-Charlotte Sellier-Bauer offers a brief overview of this *Historikerstreit* in *Friedrich Christoph Schlosser: Ein deutsches Gelehrtenleben im neunzehnten Jahrhundert* (Göttingen: V&R unipress, 2004), pp 24–33.
8 'Schlosser und seine neue Weltgeschichte', *Beilage zur Allgemeinen Zeitung* (30 May 1842).
9 F. C. Schlosser, 'Einleitende Vorrede des Verfassers der Weltgeschichte', in *F. C. Schlosser's Weltgeschichte für das deutsche Volk*, ed. G. L. Kriegk, vol. 1 (Frankfurt am Main:

Franz Varrentrapp, 1844), pp iii–xxiv. On Kriegk's role, see also Dagmar Stegmüller, 'Popularisierungsstrategien in Friedrich Christoph Schlossers "Weltgeschichte für das deutsche Volk"', in Carsten Kretschmann (ed.), *Wissenspopularisierung: Konzepte der Wissensverbreitung im Wandel* (Berlin: Akademie Verlag, 2003), pp 197–210, at pp 199–201.

10 *Düsseldorfer Journal* (20 January 1857); *Frankfurter Journal* (17 January 1857); *Illustrirte Zeitung* (27 December 1857), all as quoted in *Schlosser und dessen Weltgeschichte*, pp 12–14.
11 Manfred Hettling and Stefan-Ludwig Hoffmann (eds), *Der bürgerliche Wertehimmel: Innenansichten des 19. Jahrhunderts* (Göttingen: Vandenhoeck & Ruprecht, 2000).
12 Matthew L. Jones, *The Good Life in the Scientific Revolution: Descartes, Pascal, Leibniz, and the Cultivation of Virtue* (Chicago: University of Chicago Press, 2006); Sorana Corneanu, *Regimens of the Mind: Boyle, Locke, and the Early Modern Cultura Animi Tradition* (Chicago: University of Chicago Press, 2011); Sari Kivistö, *The Vices of Learning: Morality and Knowledge at Early Modern Universities* (Leiden: Brill, 2014); Kathryn Murphy and Anita Traninger (eds), *The Emergence of Impartiality* (Leiden: Brill, 2014).
13 Steven Shapin, *A Social History of Truth: Civility and Science in Seventeenth-Century England* (Chicago: University of Chicago Press, 1994).
14 Kasper Risbjerg Eskildsen, 'Inventing the archive: testimony and virtue in modern historiography', *History of the Human Sciences*, 26:4 (2013), 8–26, at 20.
15 *Illustrirte Zeitung* (27 December 1857), as quoted in *Schlosser und dessen Weltgeschichte*, p. 14.
16 G. G. Gervinus, *Friedrich Christoph Schlosser: Ein Nekrolog* (Leipzig: Wilhelm Engelmann, 1861), pp 58, 65.
17 Ludwig Häusser, 'Die historische Literatur und das deutsche Publikum' (1841), in Häusser, *Gesammelte Schriften*, vol. 1 (Berlin: Weidmann, 1869), pp 3–17, at pp 6, 5.
18 On *historische Übungen* as offered by Ranke and many of his students, see Hans-Jürgen Pandel, 'Von der Teegesellschaft zum Forschungsinstitut: Die historischen Seminare vom Beginn des 19. Jahrhunderts bis zum Ende des Kaiserreichs', in Horst Walter Blanke (ed.), *Transformationen des Historismus: Wissenschaftsorganisation und Bildungspolitik vor dem Ersten Weltkrieg* (Waltrop: Hartmut Spenner, 1994), pp 1–31 and Kasper Risbjerg Eskildsen, 'Private Übungen und verkörpertes Wissen: Zur Unterrichtspraxis der Geschichtswissenschaft im neunzehnten Jahrhundert', in Martin Kintzinger and Sita Steckel (eds), *Akademische Wissenskulturen: Praktiken des Lehrens und Forschens vom Mittelalter bis zur Moderne* (Basel: Schwabe, 2015), pp 143–61. On history journals in nineteenth-century Germany, see especially Theodor Schieder, 'Die deutsche Geschichtswissenschaft im Spiegel der Historischen Zeitschrift', *Historische Zeitschrift*, 189 (1959), 1–104.
19 Dieter Langewiesche, 'Die Geschichtsschreibung und ihr Publikum: Zum Verhältnis von Geschichtswissenschaft und Geschichtsmarkt', in Dieter Hein, Klaus Hildebrand and Andreas Schulz (eds), *Historie und Leben: Der Historiker als Wissenschaftler und Zeitgenosse: Festschrift für Lothar Gall zum 70. Geburtstag* (Munich: Oldenbourg, 2006), pp 311–26.
20 Niklas Lenhard-Schramm, *Konstrukteure der Nation: Geschichtsprofessoren als politische Akteure in Vormärz und Revolution 1848/49* (Münster: Waxmann, 2014); Robert Southard, *Droysen and the Prussian School of History* (Lexington, KY: University Press of Kentucky, 1995).
21 Ulrich Muhlack, 'Der "politische Professor" im Deutschland des 19. Jahrhunderts', in Ronald Burkholz, Christel Gärtner and Ferdinand Zehentreiter (eds), *Materialität des Geistes: Zur Sache Kultur: Im Diskurs mit Ulrich Oevermann* (Weilerswist: Velbrück, 2001), pp 185–204.
22 Heinrich von Treitschke, 'F. C. Dahlmann', in Treitschke, *Historische und politische Aufsätze vornehmlich zur neuesten deutschen Geschichte*, 2nd edn (Leipzig: S. Hirzel,

1865), pp 359–445, at p. 378; Karl Hillebrand, 'G. G. Gervinus', *Preußische Jahrbücher*, 32 (1873), 379–428, at 403; Ludwig Weiland, 'Zum Andenken an Reinhold Pauli: Vortrag gehalten auf der Versammlung zu Kiel', *Hansische Geschichtsblätter*, 12 (1883), 1–9, at 9.

23 Julian Schmidt, *Geschichte der deutschen Literatur im neunzehnten Jahrhundert*, vol. 3, 3rd edn (Leipzig: Friedrich Ludwig Herbig, 1856), p. 405; review of G. G. Gervinus, *Geschichte der neunzehnten Jahrhunderts seit den Wiener Verträgen*, vol. 1, *Die Grenzboten*, 14 (1855), 441–53, at 443; [Carl von Noorden], 'Zur Beurtheilung Friedrich Christoph Schlosser's', *Historische Zeitschrift*, 8 (1862), 117–40, at 132; Walther Schultze, 'Gerhard von Brogne und die Klosterreform in Niederlothringen und Flandern', *Forschungen zur deutschen Geschichte*, 25 (1885), 221–71, at 223; E. Reimann, *Abhandlungen zur Geschichte Friedrich des Grossen* (Gotha: Friedrich Andreas Perthes, 1892), p. 80 n. 3.

24 [G. G.] Gervinus, self-review of *Geschichte der deutschen Dichtung*, vol. 1, *Heidelberger Jahrbücher der Literatur*, 28 (1835), 900–15, at 911; Karl Weinhold, 'Festrede', in *Schiller-Denkmal: Festausgabe*, vol. 2 (Berlin: Riegel, 1860), pp 66–74, at p. 69; Richard Treitschke, 'Adolph Schmidt's Geschichte der Denk- und Glaubensfreiheit im ersten Jahrhundert der Kaiserherrschaft und des Christenthums', *Die Grenzboten*, 7 (1848), 117–23, 157–63, at 117.

25 [Lindau], 'Literarische Parlament', 229, quoting Treitschke, 'F. C. Dahlmann', p. 413.

26 Dagmar Stegmüller, 'Friedrich Christopher Schlosser und die Berliner Schule', in Ulrich Muhlack with Christian Mehr and Dagmar Stegmüller (eds), *Historisierung und gesellschaftlicher Wandel in Deutschland im 19. Jahrhundert* (Berlin: Akademie Verlag, 2003), pp 49–60, especially pp 58–9; Michael Gottlob, *Geschichtsschreibung zwischen Aufklärung und Historismus: Johannes von Müller und Friedrich Christoph Schlosser* (Frankfurt am Main: Peter Lang, 1989), pp 211–40; Georg Gülter, 'Die Geschichtsauffassung Friedrich Christoph Schlossers' (PhD thesis Ruprecht Karls University Heidelberg, 1966), pp 86–107.

27 Heinrich Kurz, *Geschichte der deutschen Literatur mit ausgewählte Stücken aus den Werken der vorzüglichsten Schriftsteller*, vol. 3 (Leipzig: B. G. Teubner, 1859), p. 687. Similarly: Heinrich Wuttke, 'Schlosser, der Geschichtsschreiber', *Die Grenzboten*, 3 (1844), 193–210.

28 [Heinrich] v[on] Sybel, review of F. C. Schlosser, *Geschichte des achtzehnten Jahrhunderts*, *Neue Jenaische Allgemeine Literatur-Zeitung*, 3 (1844), 53–63, 81–92, at 92. See also Heinrich von Sybel, 'Ueber den Stand der neueren deutschen Geschichtschreibung' (1856), in Sybel, *Kleine historische Schriften*, p. 352.

29 Georg Waitz, 'Deutsche Historiker der Gegenwart: Briefe an den Herausgeber (I)', *Allgemeine Zeitschrift für Geschichte*, 5 (1846), 520–35, at 522–3; cf. Stegmüller, 'Friedrich Christoph Schlosser', pp 49–52.

30 [Lindau], 'Literarische Parlament', 228.

31 G. P. Gooch, 'The growth of historical science', in A. W. Ward, G. W. Prothero and Stanley Leathes (eds), *The Cambridge Modern History*, vol. 12 (Cambridge: [Cambridge] University Press, 1910), pp 816–50, at p. 826.

32 [Johann Wilhelm Löbell], *Briefe über den Nekrolog Friedrich Christoph Schlossers von G. G. Gervinus: Ein Beitrag zur Charakteristik Schlossers vom litterarischen Standpunkt* (Chemnitz: Otto May, 1862), pp 23, 40.

33 [Von Noorden], 'Zur Beurtheilung', 136.

34 [Wilhelm Dilthey], 'Friedrich Christoph Schlosser', *Preußische Jahrbücher*, 9 (1862), 373–433; Georg Weber, 'Friedrich Christoph Schlosser', *Unsere Zeit*, 6 (1862), 314–26.

35 For example, Wilhelm Dilthey to Rudolf Haym, 31 October 1861, in Dilthey, *Briefwechsel*, ed. Gudrun Kühne-Bertam and Hans-Ulrich Lessing, vol. 1 (Göttingen: Vandenhoeck & Ruprecht, 2011), p. 201; Karl Dilthey to Wilhelm Dilthey, 29 May 1862, ibid., p. 247, and Karl Dilthey to Wilhelm Dilthey, November 1862, ibid., pp 260–2 (reporting on heated bar-room discussions in Bonn).

36 [Von Noorden], 'Zur Beurtheilung', 132.

37 Ibid., 126. One is reminded here of Johan Huizinga's distinction between 'Luther as a specimen of the biological species' and 'Luther as a historical phenomenon': J. Huizinga, 'De taak der cultuurgeschiedenis', in Huizinga, *Cultuurhistorische verkenningen* (Haarlem: H. D. Tjeenk Willink & Zoon, 1929), pp 1–85, at p. 26.
38 [Lindau], 'Literarische Parlament', 227.
39 Günter Johannes Henz, *Leopold von Ranke in Geschichtsdenken und Forschung*, vol. 1 (Berlin: Duncker & Humblot, 2014), pp 128, 129, 140, 145, 146. For a historiographical reappraisal of Ranke's visual æsthetics, see J. D. Braw, 'Vision as revision: Ranke and the beginning of modern history', *History and Theory*, 46 (2007), 45–60 and Daniel Fulda, *Wissenschaft aus Kunst: Die Entstehung der modernen deutschen Geschichtsschreibung 1760–1860* (Berlin, New York: Walter de Gruyter, 1996), pp 404–10.
40 Wilhelm Dilthey, 'Erinnerungen an deutsche Geschichtschreiber' (*c.* 1862), in Dilthey, *Vom Aufgang des geschichtlichen Bewusstseins: Jugendaufsätze und Erinnerungen*, ed. Erich Weniger (Leipzig, Berlin: B. G. Teubner, 1936), pp 215–31, at p. 215.
41 [Karl Hagen], 'Über den gegenwärtigen Stand der deutschen Geschichtschreibung (Beschluß)', *Der Adler*, 3 (1837), 9–11, at 10–11; 'Die Reformation in französischer und deutscher Auffassung', *Blätter für literarische Unterhaltung* (1840), 645–6, 649–50, 653–5, 817–19, 829–31, at 818; review of Leopold Ranke, *Deutsche Geschichte im Zeitalter der Reformation*, vols 4 and 5, *Leipziger Repertorium der deutschen und ausländischen Literatur*, 1:3 (1843), 565–72, at 565–6.
42 Julian Schmidt, *Geschichte der deutschen Nationalliteratur im neunzehnten Jahrhundert*, vol. 1 (Leipzig: Friedrich Ludwig Herbig, 1853), pp 318–32; A. Lübben, 'Zur Charakteristik dreier deutscher Geschichtschreiber', *Deutsche Monats-Hefte*, 6 (1855), 229–31; Kurz, *Geschichte*, vol. 3, p. 697.
43 Weber, 'Friedrich Christoph Schlosser', 325, 324.
44 Ibid., 326.
45 See the agenda-setting theme issue of *Science in Context*, 16:1–2 (2003), edited by Lorraine Daston and H. Otto Sibum.
46 Gadi Algazi, '*Exemplum* and *Wundertier*: three concepts of the scholarly persona', *Low Countries Historical Review*, 131:4 (2016), 8–32, at 9–16.
47 Lorraine Daston and H. Otto Sibum, 'Introduction: scientific personae and their histories', *Science in Context*, 16 (2003), 1–8. On absent-mindedness as an early-modern *topos*, see Gadi Algazi, 'Geistesabwesentheit: Gelehrte zu Hause um 1500', *Historische Anthropologie*, 13 (2005), 325–42 and 'Gelehrte Zerstreutheit und gelernte Vergesslichkeit: Bemerkungen zu ihrer Rolle in der Herausbildung des Gelehrtenhabitus', in Peter von Moos (ed.), *Der Fehltritt: Vergehen und Versehen in der Vormoderne* (Cologne: Böhlau, 2001), pp 235–50.
48 Mineke Bosch, 'Scholarly personae and twentieth-century historians: explorations of a concept', *Low Countries Historical Review*, 131:4 (2016), 33–54. See also Richard Kirwan, 'Introduction: scholarly self-fashioning and the cultural history of universities', in Kirwan (ed.), *Scholarly Self-Fashioning and Community in the Early Modern University* (Farnham: Ashgate, 2013), pp 1–20.
49 Fernand Braudel, 'Histoire et sciences sociales: la longue durée', *Annales*, 13 (1958), 725–53.
50 Paul Lucier, 'The origins of pure and applied science in gilded age America', *Isis*, 103 (2012), 527–36; R. Steven Turner, 'Historicism, *Kritik* and the Prussian professorate, 1790 to 1840', in Mayotte Bollack and Heinz Wismann (eds), *Philologie und Hermeneutik im 19. Jahrhundert*, vol. 2 (Göttingen: Vandenhoeck & Ruprecht, 1983), pp 450–89, at p. 466.
51 I elaborate on this third model in Herman Paul, 'The virtues and vices of Albert Naudé: toward a history of scholarly personae', *History of Humanities*, 1 (2016), 327–38 and 'Sources of the self: scholarly personae as repertoires of scholarly selfhood', *Low Countries Historical Review*, 131:4 (2016), 135–54.
52 See, however, Paul Yorck von Wartenburg to Wilhelm Dilthey, 6 July 1886, in Dilthey,

Briefwechsel, ed. Gudrun Kühne-Bertam and Hans-Ulrich Lessing, vol. 2 (Göttingen: Vandenhoeck & Ruprecht, 2015), p. 145.
53 Georg Weber, *Friedrich Christoph Schlosser der Historiker: Erinnerungsblätter aus seinem Leben und Wirken: Eine Festschrift zu seiner hundertjährigen Geburtstagsfeier am 17. November 1876* (Leipzig: Wilhelm Engelmann, 1876), p. vi.
54 B. Erdmannsdörffer, *Friedrich Christoph Schlosser (geb. 17. Nov. 1776, gest. 23 Sept. 1861): Gedächtnissrede zur Feier von Schlossers hundertjährigem Geburtstag am 17. November 1876 in der Aula der Universität Heidelberg gehalten* (Heidelberg: J. Hörning, 1876), p. 4.
55 Ibid.
56 Ibid., pp 21, 13.
57 Franz Rühl, 'Friedrich Christoph Schlosser', *Nord und Süd*, 13 (1880), 350–71. Note that this article appeared just before Ranke published the first volume (1881) of his *Weltgeschichte*. For Rühl's subsequent evaluation of the latter in comparison to Schlosser's, see Franz Rühl, 'Ueber den Begriff der Weltgeschichte', *Deutsche Revue*, 30:4 (1905), 110–22.
58 Heinrich v[on] Sybel, 'Gedächtnisrede auf Leopold v[on] Ranke, gehalten in der kgl. preußischen Akademie der Wissenschaften zu Berlin am 1. Juli 1886', *Historische Zeitschrift*, 56 (1886), 463–81, at 478. A similarly distanced stance was adopted by Franz X. von Wegele, *Geschichte der deutschen Historiographie seit dem Auftreten des Humanismus* (Munich: R. Oldenbourg, 1885), p. 1062.
59 Hans Heinz Krill, *Die Rankerenaissance: Max Lenz und Erich Marcks: Ein Beitrag zum historisch-politischen Denken in Deutschland, 1880–1935* (Berlin: Walter de Gruyter, 1962).
60 Berlin-Brandenburg Academy of Sciences and Humanities, Max Lenz papers, inv. no. 8, 'Geschichte der deutschen Geschichtschreibung' (1901), transcript by Martin Hass, 144–5.
61 Thomas Brechenmacher, *Großdeutsche Geschichtsschreibung im neunzehnten Jahrhundert: Die erste Generation (1830–48)* (Berlin: Duncker & Humblot, 1996), pp 460–75; Ulrich Muhlack, 'Die wissenschaftsgeschichtliche Bedeutung des Indexverfahrens gegen Rankes Papstgeschichte', in Hubert Wolf, Dominik Burkard and Ulrich Muhlack, *Rankes 'Päpste' auf dem Index: Dogma und Historie im Widerstreit* (Paderborn: Ferdinand Schöningh, 2003), pp 169–201, at pp 189–201.
62 Max Lehmann, *Friedrich der Grosse und der Ursprung des Siebenjährigen Krieges* (Leipzig: S. Hirzel, 1894), p. 139; Hans Delbrück, 'Ueber den Ursprung des Siebenjährigen Krieges (Nachtrag)', *Preußische Jahrbücher*, 86 (1896), 416–27, at 417–18.
63 Bernd Mütter, 'Georg Hüffer (1851–1922): Ein katholischer Historiker zwischen Kirche und Staat, Ultramontanismus und Historismus', *Westfälische Forschungen*, 61 (2011), 307–43, at 328.
64 Gangolf Hübringer, *Georg Gottfried Gervinus: Historisches Urteil und politische Kritik* (Göttingen: Vandenhoeck & Ruprecht, 1984); Michael Ansel, *G. G. Gervinus' "Geschichte der poetischen National-Literatur der Deutschen": Nationbildung auf literaturgeschichtlicher Grundlage* (Frankfurt am Main: Peter Lang, 1990); Jana Lehmann, *Hubert Ermisch 1850–1932: Ein Beitrag zur Geschichte der sächsischen Landesgeschichtsforschung* (Cologne: Böhlau, 2001).
65 Southard, *Droysen and the Prussian School*.
66 J. Wille, 'Bernhard Erdmannsdörffer', in Fr. von Weech and A. Krieger (eds), *Badische Biographien*, vol. 5 (Heidelberg: Carl Winter, 1906), pp 151–60, at p. 156.
67 Willy Andreas, 'Briefe Erdmannsdörffers an Johann Gustav Droysen', *Zeitschrift für die Geschichte des Oberrheins*, 81 (1929), 557–87.
68 G. v[on] Below, 'Bernhard Erdmannsdörffer', *Historische Vierteljahrschrift*, 4 (1901), 275–8, at 276.
69 Eberhard Gothein, 'Bernhard Erdmannsdörffer †: Ein Gedenkwort', *Preußische Jahrbücher*, 104 (1901), 15–22, at 20–1.
70 Bernhard Erdmannsdörffer to Heinrich von Treitschke, 18 June 1869 and 18

November 1877, Berlin State Library, Heinrich von Treitschke papers, inv. no. K5:164; B. Erdmannsdörffer, 'Treitschkes Deutsche Geschichte', *Die Grenzboten*, 42 (1883), 232–50.

71 Bonn University Archive, inv. no. Bh Bez., 'Lebenserinnerungen' (undated) by Friedrich von Bezold, 47.

72 Ludwig Weiland, *Friedrich Christoph Dahlmann: Rede zur Feier seines hundertjährigen Geburtstages am 13. Mai 1885 im Namen der Georg-Augusts-Universität gehalten* (Göttingen: Wilh. Fr. Kaestner, 1885) and *Georg Waitz (geb. 9. October 1813, gest. 24. Mai 1886): Rede gehalten in der öffentlichen Sitzung der K. Gesellschaft der Wissenschaften am 4. Dezember 1886* (Göttingen: Dieterichsche Verlags-Buchhandlung, 1886).

73 Paul, 'Virtues and vices', 334.

74 Herm[ann] Grauert, 'Georg Waitz', *Historisches Jahrbuch*, 8 (1887), 48–100. I discuss this case at greater length in Herman Paul, 'The virtues of a good historian in early Imperial Germany: Georg Waitz's contested example', *Modern Intellectual History*, 15 (2018), 681–709.

75 Gustav Schnürer to Heinrich Schrörs, 1 February 1888, as quoted in Gregor Klapczynski, *Katholischer Historismus? Zum historischen Denken in der deutschsprachigen Kirchengeschichte um 1900: Heinrich Schrörs, Albert Ehrhard, Joseph Schnitzer* (Stuttgart: W. Kohlhammer, 2013), pp 22–3 n. 58.

76 Bernd Mütter, *Die Geschichtswissenschaft in Münster zwischen Aufklärung und Historismus unter besonderer Berücksichtigung der historischen Disziplin an der Münsterschen Hochschule* (Munster: Aschendorff, 1980), p. 262.

77 [Lindau], 'Literarische Parlament', 230.

78 German Federal Archives Berlin, Georg Waitz papers, inv. no. 14, City of Jever to Georg Waitz, 13 January 1875; inv. no. 64, daily notes, January 1875.

79 G. Waitz, *Die historischen Übungen zu Göttingen: Glückwunschschreiben an Leopold von Ranke zum Tage der Feier seines fünfzigjährigen Doctorjubiläums, 20. Februar 1867* (Göttingen: W. Fr. Kästner, 1867), p. 4.

80 'Schlosser-Denkmal in Jever', 462.

81 Whereas 'parties' used to have a bad reputation as expressions of discord that were supposed to disappear in Germany's move towards national unity, by the 1870s increasing support had emerged for Treitschke's view that parties were indispensable agents of political struggle to the extent that they defended 'the interests of societal classes' (Heinrich von Treitschke, 'Parteien und Fractionen', *Preußische Jahrbücher*, 27 [1871], 175–208, 347–67, at 190). Although Lindau did not remotely share Treitschke's increasingly conservative political agenda, his portrayal of parties as interest groups closely resembled this Treitschkean view.

82 Drafts of this chapter were presented in London (February 2016), Leiden (January 2017) and Lund (April 2017). Thanks to Taru Haapala, Kari Palonen, Maria Karlsson and Johan Östling for their kind invitations, to the audiences at all three occasions for their perceptive feedback and to Andreas Biefang and Henk te Velde for useful suggestions. Funding was generously provided by the Netherlands Organization for Scientific Research (NWO).

CHAPTER 3

Fixing genius: the Romantic man of letters in the university era

Travis E. Ross

Introduction

In the spring of 1885, the popular English historian James Anthony Froude visited San Francisco and, in the media frenzy to report his every move, a literary weekly titled *The Wasp* scored quite a scoop. It alone reported the mortifying scene that took place at the luxurious Palace Hotel when Froude met the city's own famous and prolific historian Hubert Howe Bancroft. The two historians had a great deal in common. Both had prodigious catalogs. Both enjoyed popular, if sometimes embattled reputations as serious historians whose works held wide appeal within the nascent genre of history. That wide appeal was both difficult to muster and problematic to maintain since history as a genre was dividing externally from general literature and internally to target smaller groups of readers with rather different interests and epistemologies.[1] For all the pair appeared to have in common, though, *The Wasp* narrated in excruciating detail how neither Bancroft nor Froude could recognize the other as a historian.

'History writing is hard work, ain't it,' Bancroft blurted upon completing the short trek up Market Street from the offices of A. L. Bancroft & Company. 'I have found it so,' Froude replied, 'my literary work has been so incessant that I was forced to make a trip to the colonies for my health.' The businessman got right to the point: 'What do you pay your help on the other side of the water?' Froude did not understand. 'Why, your help,' Bancroft attempted to clarify, 'the fellows who write your books, you know.' 'Write my books – you are jesting, Mr. Bancroft,' Froude shot back, 'I write them myself.' Unaware of precisely how much he was giving away, Bancroft pressed on, convinced Froude was 'putting on airs with him.' 'Come now, I hope you are not offended,' Bancroft said. 'We are friends and there is nobody here. You need not object to giving the business away to me. I'll never blab a word of it. Don't talk to me as if I was a perfect stranger instead of being in the history business myself.' 'Mr. Bancroft,' Froude said, 'it may be news to you, and why I cannot possibly imagine, but I write my histories myself. None but myself compose a line of them. The style is my own, the information collected by myself and the deductions drawn by myself. You are certainly jesting when you talk about help. Do you not write those histories which I have read with such pleasure?' 'Sir,' Bancroft said, haughtily, 'you are looking at a business man. Do you think I find time to write histories?... No, sir, I hire help. I employ competent and energetic young gentlemen – university graduates, sir – men from the finest colleges of Europe – to write my histories, and I pay 'em for it. If I say to my help give us a chapter on the Missions and look smart about it, they do it, and mighty quick, too, I can tell you.' With that, the busy bookman excused himself to get back to work, leaving his English counterpart 'endeavoring to restore his equanimity by frequent application to the ice pitcher.'[2]

The Wasp had a certain advantage that allowed it to score such a scoop: it made the whole scene up. The famous and acerbic *litterateur* Ambrose Bierce edited the satirical literary magazine at the time, but he also wrote most of it, including this imagined encounter between 'two great historians.'[3] Per usual for *The Wasp*, much of the setup was true. Froude really was visiting San Francisco that spring. Bancroft really did pay a team of researchers and writers to write *The Works of Hubert Howe Bancroft*. The company's Dartmouth-educated librarian Henry Oak had transformed Bancroft's prodigious, ever-growing collection of rare books and manuscripts into a proprietary research library related to Pacific North America. Under the supervision of Oak and a handful of others, researchers and ghost-writers worked to refine the library's raw materials into the definitive history of Pacific North America from Alaska to Panama, inland to the Rocky Mountains, including all of Mexico and Central America, from antiquity to their present.[4] People of all sorts around North America and Europe subscribed to the thirty-nine-volume series, receiving a new 800-page volume quarterly between 1882 and 1890.[5]

One might empathize with the fictional Froude's exasperation. Whatever else was up for debate about history writing in those tumultuous decades, surely Bancroft's mobilization of wage laborers to research and to write history in their boss's name fell strictly out of bounds for ethical and epistemological reasons. Bierce clearly thought so. Between 1881 and the middle of 1885, *The Wasp* engaged in a merciless campaign to expose Bancroft as a 'literary impostor.'[6] In spite of Bierce's efforts, Bancroft's company successfully elicited prodigious intellectual and financial support for its enterprise from common and elite people on both sides of the Atlantic. It did that, not by hiding its collaborative research methods, but by describing them endlessly, proudly declaring how its economies of scope and scale would enable it to do in a decade what an ordinary historian could not do in a lifetime.[7] Meanwhile, Bierce struggled to convince anyone to join him in outrage over Bancroft's methods.[8] As early as 1903, however, the public could hardly bear what had become mere rumours: Bancroft had not personally written the massive series. Despite his individual authorship being blatantly ludicrous, Bancroft's unrivalled status in the public mind as the singular 'Historian of the Pacific Coast' had made it less conceivable to large portions of the population that Bancroft's *Works* had been 'written by any person other than Hubert Howe Bancroft.'[9] Within a decade or two, the methods that had once promised to make an impossibly large history possible had themselves become impossible as an explanation for a work of such grandeur and historical significance.

While 'models of scholarly selfhood do not change from day to day,' this case offers a bewildering example in which the persona of the serious historian *appears* to have changed overnight.[10] Not coincidentally, the same decades saw the rapid professionalization of history writing within American academe and a handful of increasingly professionalized state and local historical societies. Something did change around Bancroft's enterprise, but I argue that it was not the scholarly persona of the historian, the shared set of assumptions that defined a good historian and the best practices of the craft. Just as importantly, I argue that academic professionalization did not create – nor even attempt to create – a new scholarly persona. Instead, early academics worked to create the infrastructure to train and to sustain scholars who fit the persona established by the archival turn.[11] Bancroft *et al.* did the same, briefly outpacing their academic counterparts in the 1870s and 1880s. Bancroft's company and the early academic profession engaged in a similar project, with each enterprise working to demonstrate that it could address the economic and cultural challenges of the increasingly onerous expectations of the discipline, amplifying the virtues and diminishing the vices associated with the persona of the archival historian.[12]

The very different infrastructures these intellectual entrepreneurs created pushed them to cultivate in-house personae that initially look quite different: Bancroft & Company worked to demonstrate how their collaborative system animated a collective genius that exceeded the sum of its parts, making possible a kind of archival omniscience; conversely, the early American academic historian J. Franklin Jameson argued that academe could domesticate genius in the competent, professional scholar. I argue that, despite the differences separating the approaches each enterprise advanced or the modes in which each promoted itself, Bancroft's company and early academics responded to a relatively uniform set of expectations and concerns related to the character and working habits of historians aspiring to do history after the archival turn. Jameson and Bancroft *et al.* shared something else, though. The champions for each of those innovative enterprises demonstrated a surprising concern for claiming the mantle of a rather old-fashioned sense of genius and for demonstrating how their system could fix that problematic character. Whether because the image resonated with them personally or because they thought it would resonate with their internally diverse audiences, Bancroft *et al.* and Jameson invoked the image of the ideal Romantic author.

This chapter presents both a problem and an opportunity for studying the scholarly persona of the historian because it contains so many things that might legitimately qualify as a scholarly persona. For instance, it could compare Bancroft's corporate brain trust to Jameson's quintessential academic professional as competing personae. Alternatively, it could focus on how each of those in-house personae relied heavily on the shared cultural template of the Romantic man of letters, the lone genius who had little interest in fame or fortune, a character that had quickly become the nineteenth century's ideal author.[13] Instead, this chapter follows the dominant usage of the persona within this volume, examining the character of the ideal historian that had emerged from the archival turn and that both of these enterprises worked to replicate systematically and to sustain professionally. Disentangling these potential personae and the work they accomplished for their respective proponents, though, offers an opportunity to examine the payoffs and limitations of the persona model in general, but especially of different ways of defining the relationship between a scholarly persona and the repertoires, cultural templates, and individual personalities with which it is hopelessly bound up.

Helpfully, Gadi Algazi has delineated a taxonomy of the three potential uses of the scholarly persona, each of which has a ready exemplar in this story. First, the scholarly persona can refer to the careful curation of individual images that aspiring scholars create and maintain.[14] Bancroft's corporate genius and Jameson's quintessential professional certainly qualify as personae according to that definition. Rather than examine them as personae in their own right, this chapter uses those bits of self-styling to explore the scholarly persona in Algazi's second sense: 'the set of regulative ideals made flesh (at least partly)' shared and contested within a discipline, the contested list of virtues and vices that its practitioners must display or mitigate, respectively.[15] To whatever degree defining the historian constituted boundary work within an emerging discipline, it also occurred as an appeal for broad cultural legitimacy within a longstanding debate within general literature about how genuine men of letters could and could not legitimately engage with the marketplace both as a means of financial support and to distribute their work. The character of the Romantic genius certainly warrants analysis as a discipline-agnostic scholarly persona in Algazi's third sense: the 'cultural template for a codified social role' that offers 'essential cultural resource for forging personae' that 'need not coincide with any ideal espoused within a given community.'[16] Here, however, I have treated that character as a repertoire chosen by these champions of competing enterprises to render legible to outsiders the internal concerns that had remade the scholarly persona of the historian within the discipline of history after the archival turn.

The hero of the archives

Beginning earlier in the nineteenth century in Germany, serious practitioners of history had increasingly reimagined the archive as the place to recover historical truth and, therefore, as the primary worksite for historians.[17] That new mode of historical research both promised and demanded a lot, from its practitioners as well as its readers. The archival turn promised more reliable history since its sources were closer to past events. However, those sources were another step removed from actual readers, and so whatever additional trust they warranted had to be borrowed against the character of the archival historian.[18] The very transformation intended to make history writing more scientific had, ironically, made its core research moment nearly unrepeatable, removing even the pretence that other specialists could verify purported facts or assertions that seemed dubious or surprising.[19] Archival research, therefore, made the character of the historian more important than ever, launching a debate among likeminded historians about the virtues and vices of the archival historian and the proper balance between them. Underlying Bancroft's corporate genius and Jameson's network of competent academic professionals was a shared figure: the hero of the archives who could be trusted to examine critically *all* of the historical evidence, to reconstruct the past with neither compromise nor error, ruthlessly dispatching misinformation in the existing literature and in the historical record.

Whether that character proceeded from or merely took advantage of it, the Romantic man of letters offered a powerful, cross-cultural touchstone for a character who could be trusted to perform that onerous task. That figure had taken shape earlier in the century in Thomas Carlyle's series of lectures 'On Heroes, Hero-Worship, and the Heroic in History' (1840).[20] Carlyle began by examining the Romantic history of the 'hero as Divinity' (Odin), 'as Prophet' (Muhammad), 'as Poet' (Dante), and 'as Priest' (Luther). In the penultimate lecture, he turned to modern heroism: 'The

Hero as Man of Letters.' In it, Carlyle offered an optimistic examination of the problems and potential created in the previous century by the expansion of knowledge through books. 'Never till about a hundred years ago,' Carlyle asserted, 'was there seen any figure of a Great Soul living apart in that anomalous manner; endeavouring to speak forth the inspiration that was in him by Printed Books, and find place and subsistence by what the world would please to give him for doing that.'[21] As opposed to 'spurious' men of letters, Carlyle argued that the 'genuine Man of Letters' was 'inspired,' an imperfect signifier for the complex of heroic qualities for which 'we have no good name,' but that included 'originality,' 'sincerity,' and 'genius.'[22] Fulfilling the historical roles previously divided between the prophet, poet, and priest, the 'true Literary Man' guided the world, whether or not it acknowledged him in his lifetime with either respect or bread.[23]

Carlyle primarily concerned himself with the promises and the problems posed by the burgeoning book market in the nineteenth century. Books, he believed, had made an education and the life of the mind available to even middling people, but it also demanded an inquiry into what stood to be gained and lost when literary work could become a job. Having found his own financial support and intellectual platform as a professional lecturer, Carlyle boldly declared in that capacity and with no sense of irony: 'It is no evil to be poor,' adding, 'there ought to be Literary Men poor, – to shew whether they are genuine or not!'[24] Carlyle's genuine men of letters were a mendicant order; like their religious counterparts, legitimate authors performed poverty to signify their devotion. These Romanticized authors were *in* the market by necessity, but as a matter of principle they were not supposed to be *of* it. Carlyle's lectures anticipated how aspiring authors in the nineteenth century would feel compelled to protect their literary integrity against an increasing number of temptations to more than preserve their bodies at the expense of their authorial souls.

Carlyle established a powerful, resilient image of the genuine man of letters: self-made through deep reading, that lone genius wrote exclusively for the life of the mind, preferring poverty – if necessary – over writing to appeal to the whims of the mass market. That ideal, ironically, gained further power as the burgeoning market provided a growing number of ways to make a living by the pen. Rather than seriously defining a starving writer in a squalid garret who refused to write for money, Carlyle offered a powerful list of vices and virtues that would help aspiring *litterateurs* take advantage of the marketplace without being corrupted by its deleterious effects. He offered the same list as a means by which critical readers could judge the originality and sincerity of distant authors who could only be encountered only through the book trade. Rather than actually demanding its practitioners remain destitute, the Romantic authorial ideal eventually made aloofness from the market a potential selling point within it. Authors like Edgar Allan Poe or Herman Melville could create a market to support their literary efforts while fashioning authorial personae that appeared plausibly disinterested in the financial and literary success of those works in the market.[25] In other words, if done correctly, pretending not to care about fame or money could gain both for an author.[26]

That character provided a resilient, powerful touchstone for striking the proper balance between intellectual integrity and economic sustainability in the marketplace. The struggle to legitimize these innovative enterprises necessarily engaged with history's only default home at that time: the genre of history. In part, the question of how historians should support and disseminate their work played out within the larger debate about how all kinds of serious authors should legitimately use the market for those purposes. The idealized Romantic author imposed a set of external expectations on aspiring heads of enterprise like Bancroft or Jameson since each man hoped to convince a broad public that his enterprise could legitimately combine intellectual and economic labors without compromise. Neither Bancroft nor Jameson drew passively from that repertoire; both attempted to demonstrate that their enterprises could improve upon the recognizably flawed figure of the genius.

In the company of genius

Between roughly 1870 and 1885, Bancroft's promotional materials worked to demonstrate that its system alone could realize in full the promises of archival history while mitigating its most obvious problems. The company assumed that its diverse audience expected to hear a story that that hit certain points. Readers would care about the comprehensiveness of the sources consulted and about how the company had managed analysis that was simultaneously exhaustive and critical. It assumed those readers would have questions about how the company managed to engage in a research process that demanded the expenditure of so much cultural, economic, and political capital while insulating its writers from influence in the process. In each case, the champions of Bancroft's model worked to demonstrate that the economies of scope and scale afforded to it by the publishing house in which it was built offered a systematic solution to the problems inherent to archival history.

The company accomplished that by demonstrating how its unique enterprise animated a collective genius that exceeded the sum of its human parts. Promotional pieces often opened with a thumbnail biography of

Bancroft. 'Mr. Bancroft' usually disappeared rather quickly, though, replaced by a rotating stock of characters who were essentially discrete, anonymized functions of the historian. Writing in a signed article in *The Californian and Overland Monthly* that failed to identify her relationship to the company, its only female writer, Frances Fuller Victor, explained the collaborative system. First, 'readers' went over the whole collection of books and manuscripts, after which 'the secretary' transformed their notes into narrative. That early work allowed writers further down the line to write with near-omniscience, Victor claimed. The 'librarian' could know 'with certainty' anything in the library, from a 'single sheet to a heavy quarto'; the 'writer' could draw on, but also judge between *all* of the relevant sources. 'It is safe to assert,' she boldly declared, 'that no historical writing was ever done under better conditions.'[27] These faceless practitioners served a purpose: they promoted the image of the company's singular, collective genius. Connecting individual names and faces to discrete bits of work would have diminished the nearly divine omniscience that Victor and others worked tirelessly to describe.

Oak penned an extended conceit in the voice of the company's unnamed collective author in which he compared his own assisted authorship of the California volumes to the work of a hypothetical historian trying to write the same history by traditional means. Though written about his own experiences, from his own point of view, and with an 'I' that referred directly to himself, Oak's account of the writing process within the library was intended to describe the work done by Victor, Thomas Savage, or any of the lead authors working within the company's system. Taking himself as a representative author in a system that had many, Oak explained how the author took advantage of the labor of research assistants to make manageable an otherwise impossible task. The use of an anonymized, singular author as a stand-in for any of the company's several lead authors made Oak's description of the operation particularly vulnerable to his boss's misappropriation in *Literary Industries*.

Oak's comparison began with the assumption that the company's unrivalled research library might have offered it an advantage over its competition, but that it also exacerbated the familiar problem of archival history, demanding explanation. Oak had the advantage of having collapsed the successive nature of archival research into a single site in which documents could be re-examined and compared as necessary. While Oak's 'imaginary author' had to plod 'industriously through each work as he finds it, making careful notes' of what seemed important at the time, Oak could put 'ten men, each as capable in this kind of labour as [the conventional historian] or I, at work to extract everything under its proper heading.'[28] That allowed the author of a volume or section to 'tunnel the mountain of court records and legal briefs, bridge the marsh of United States government documents, and, stationing myself at a safe distance in the rear, hurl my forces against the solid columns of two hundred files of California newspapers.'[29] Oak's assisted authorship of the California volumes illustrated how the company's workshop combined his and other heavily augmented intellects into a collective genius that had achieved near-archival omniscience. Rather than argue that the company did acceptable archival history, Oak argued tirelessly that its system – and it alone – made the otherwise idealistic discipline of archival history tenable. A historian working by ordinary means, Oak claimed, necessarily had to 'confine himself to limited topics, or do his work superficially.'[30] He boldly declared: 'I claim that mine is the only method by which all the evidence on a great subject, or on many smaller subjects, can be brought out.'[31] Still, Oak argued that the company's methods differed from the methods of ordinary historians only in degree, not in type. The system multiplied the results yielded by the best practices of archival research and writing.[32]

Bancroft eventually usurped Oak's conceit, making it the core of his chapter 'My Method of Writing History' in *Literary Industries*.[33] Simply by appropriating Oak's 'I,' Bancroft effectively supplanted the collective genius into which the individual labors of Oak and his peers had been absorbed with a singular, individual genius. Bancroft generously lent that character his own name and face. That purloined letter angered Oak more for what it did to diminish the system he had devised, managed, and carefully explicated than for what it did to obscure any individual's contribution to the histories. Bancroft had written many pages in the histories, but he had not written them using the collaborative system, as his appropriation of Oak's conceit implied. While Oak believed he and his peers had written with near-omniscience, Bancroft, 'a rapid and strong writer naturally,' preferred to write based on his personal experiences rather than from either notes or sources. He filled his pages with 'long words,' 'fine sentences,' classical allusions, and 'brilliant theories' rather than history written from archival sources.[34] So, while Bancroft alone could claim unassisted authorship of his sections, that meant he had almost no legitimate claim to be an archival historian.[35]

Far worse than Bancroft's misrepresentation of his own method of writing, Bancroft's appropriation of Oak's conceit as a general statement about the whole series rendered it untrue in Oak's judgment because it reduced the company's collective genius to a single, heavily assisted and individually brilliant author. Oak had no qualms with using a first-person-singular pronoun to describe the heavily assisted authorship of the California histories (vols XVIII–XXII) of which he was the primary author. He would not have identified himself as the author of *The History of the Northwest*

Coast, however, even though he had written in it '73 p. on the "Oregon Question".'[36] Meanwhile, Oak did not object to his counterparts asserting their assisted authorship of other full volumes where appropriate: Bancroft had hired Victor to finish under his name her existing two-volume history of Oregon (vols XXIX and XXX).[37] So, while Oak's imaginative exploration of how the author worked within the system truthfully recounted his claim to assisted authorship of the California volumes, it proceeded on the assumption that no individual author could have made that statement about the full series. When Bancroft inserted the story unchanged into his ostensible memoir and the final volume of the series, he told exactly that lie.[38]

Beyond comprehensiveness in research, the company emphasized how its system insulated its workers from any concern other than historical truth. Ironically, Bancroft & Company achieved its distance from pecuniary concerns by pointing to Bancroft's personal wealth and business acumen. Having 'poured forth his money freely,' promotional materials explained that Bancroft had given 'no thought' to 'the cost' or 'the returns' when 'embarking in the work, except the general one that it would absorb the greatest part of his fortune. He had been fully taught, by his experiences as a publisher, that literary work of this kind does not pay.'[39] While other authors had to display at least a willingness to endure poverty for the sake of their integrity, the wealthy publisher had a ready-made explanation for how he could stand to lose a bit of money and for why he surely expected to, echoing the popular assumption that literary quality and financial gain are difficult, if not impossible, to reconcile. When the company embedded those assurances within marketing materials meant to drive the global sales of subscriptions to the histories, of course, it performed perfectly the familiar role of the Romantic man of letters in the marketplace.

Like other archival historians, Bancroft & Company had addressed the question of how it maintained its independence from the influence of the people and institutions who controlled the sources.[40] It certainly helped the company's case that it had a proprietary library acquired at auction or by outright donations.[41] Still, sometimes the company had to negotiate with important institutional partners, as Thomas Savage did in order to get permission to copy records controlled by Archbishop Joseph S. Alemany of San Francisco. Alemany enthusiastically welcomed Savage, but he also, subtly, insisted on the right to review the resulting histories 'lest unintentionally something might be stated inaccurately, which no doubt you would rectify.'[42] Bancroft had Savage copy the sources, later proclaiming in *Literary Industries*: 'it is needless to say that neither to the archbishop, nor to any person, living or dead, did I ever grant permission to revise or change my writings.'[43]

Whether in Oak's collective genius or in Bancroft's fictionalized self, the company's brain trust amplified the best qualities of the archival historian while diminishing the vices likely to afflict that character. Between its proprietary library and the collaborative system that examined it, the company could believably claim to have done research that critically examined the full weight of all the evidence available on its topic. Its hierarchical structure, meanwhile, made it possible to write histories ruthless in their pursuit of truth by ostensibly insulating the researchers and the writers from concerns about the political, financial, or cultural consequences. In so far as these materials targeted other insiders within the discipline, they demonstrated how their system had provided institutional structures that archival history increasingly demanded. Just as importantly, though, the company targeted members of the general public who thought far less about the methods of source criticism and far more about how the methods one used to judge between genuine and spurious men of letters.

Synthetic genius

Meanwhile, a new class of professional scholar-teachers began to fill professorships in the United States's new or newly reformed research institutions after receiving PhDs first from German universities and, after the founding of Johns Hopkins University in 1876, from American doctoral programs. Like Bancroft's staff had done, these new academic professionals weighed – but also weighted in their own favour – the advantages and disadvantages of their new enterprise for addressing familiar problems. A member of the first cohort to receive the new PhD in history from Hopkins, J. Franklin Jameson took the occasion provided by his inaugural lecture as the incoming Chair of the Department of History at the University of Chicago in 1902 to examine the influence that universities had had on historical writing in the previous two decades. Like Bancroft, Jameson worked to demonstrate that practitioners within his enterprise were meticulous and thorough researchers, that they relied on exhaustive research, and that they enjoyed sufficient political, cultural, and economic insulation from outside influence to tell the truth without compromise.[44]

At first glance, the repertoire of professionalism on which Jameson drew made the academic historian look like the antithesis both of Bancroft's corporate genius and of the Romantic man of letters. While Bancroft's genius had always achieved both fidelity and felicity in writing in order to appeal to common readers, the academic historian ostentatiously disregarded those readers. An unrepentant writer of wooden prose, the professional historian simply knew too much, had researched too deeply and too scrupulously. Steeped in the methods and minutiae of his esoteric discipline, he could never be bothered to polish the prose to accommodate non-specialist readers.[45] Ideally, American academe was supposed to create the infrastructures for the intellectual and economic support of research and writing that would never be economically or culturally viable in the marketplace; meanwhile, those history professors would pay back the public and their employers by making research-informed teaching accessible to an increasing segment of American society.

While Bancroft's system focused on the system that made the work, Jameson focused on the system that made scholars. Jameson fashioned the trained academic on a familiar character, arguing that graduate training could amplify the virtues and diminish the vices associated with the quintessential genius of pre-professional academe: the Oxford don. Most importantly, Jameson's academic professional was trained rather than born.[46] Professional academe could create genius, he argued, by teaching 'technical perfection' just as one could teach technical proficiency in any art; one 'could not,' Jameson lamented, imbue 'genius or originality' in those who 'do not possess it.'[47] As would become a central theme of his lecture, Jameson transformed that bit of self-deprecation into an inherent advantage for the resulting synthetic, systematic genius produced through graduate training. By juxtaposing the careful, reserved competence taught in graduate schools with the infamous brilliance and egotism of the don, Jameson argued that academic training and employment could synthesize and maintain a staider version of the genius that had previously been erratic both in its appearance and in its intellectual production.[48]

Jameson explored the trade-offs of creating a less original, staider version of genius in doctoral seminars and supporting its steady labor with middle-class professorships at the new and newly reformed research universities in the United States. Jameson's self-deprecating repertoire for the professional historian will likely sound surprisingly familiar to modern academics. That familiarity and the ways in which it obscured a direct appropriation of the Romantic genius as the hidden template for academic professionals surely warrants further introspection by historians of the humanities in the future. He lamented the peculiar dialect of 'doctor's-dissertation English,' for instance, which regrettably combined 'good English' with 'the scholastic jargon of a specialty, and undergraduate slang.'[49] Jameson mastered the art of subtly complimenting academic historians by deriding their ostensible weaknesses as the necessary price one paid for producing and sustaining a more stable form of genius. Taking the 'unchartered freedom' of history written 'in the age of brilliant amateurs' and sending it to school 'to learn how to read and interpret documents, how to sift and to weight evidences, how to avoid the blunders of amateurs and the vagaries of rhetoricians' had necessarily made history dull and boring, *per* the requirements of the archival historian.[50]

Beyond their writing style, Jameson paid particular attention to how the new influences of the profession conditioned these academic historians' engagement in the life of the mind. Jameson worried briefly that the seclusion of the ivory tower might keep academics worryingly insulated from the troubles of the world about which they wrote, but he accepted that the 'still air' of universities could 'powerfully [restrain] from partisanship and overstatement.'[51] Like their bad writing, the quiet, isolated worlds in which they lived and worked diminished the overall connection between scholars and wider society to the ultimate benefit of their intellectual production. That certainly aligned with the expectations of the genuine literary man, who ostensibly had to accept that writing for the acclaim of one's peers often negated finding fame or fortune. It also proceeded on the assumption that exacting, exhaustive history had little place in public. Still, he assumed that original research directly benefited the scholar, therefore indirectly benefitting the institution and its students, with historical instruction filling the gap left by the retreat of serious scholars from common readers.[52]

Just like those other authors, though, Jameson thought professional historians would have to work to maintain that distance. Though their isolation aided in their resistance to the deleterious influences of the marketplace, sometimes temptation would still prove too much. 'He plans a *magnum opus*', Jameson lamented, but then '[a]non the tempter' might persuade even the most serious historian to 'undertake some little caitiff book of a publisher's devising, utterly unneeded, but eminently vendible.'[53] Like men of the cloth who retreated to 'learned monastic communities,' the latter found quiet reprieve from the marketplace in the pious fraternity created by scholarly journals. Rather than serving 'to evoke originality' or 'to kindle the fires of genius,' these scholarly organs sought 'to regularize, to criticise, to restrain vagaries, and to set a standard of workmanship and to compel men to conform to it.'[54] Jameson took his place at the head of a long line of history professors who would joke that university employment 'virtually' constituted 'vows of poverty and obedience.'[55] Still, he worried that the need 'to conform to bourgeois standards [might] effectually stifle' the spirit of true intellectual pursuit.[56]

Modern academe, Jameson argued, replicated in highly trained individuals a very specific, rote form of genius that could not match the don, but that could surpass that character in reliability and stability, the traits required of the archival researcher. The infrastructure of modern academe and its mediocre pay scale insulated the professional scholar from the worst influences of the mass book market. Within the ivory tower, they could live the life of the mind apart from the need for bread with only the pesky interruptions produced by the many spirits within university bureaucracies who did not share the same ideals.[57] The new professional associations and their *Quarterlies* and *Reviews* provided opportunities for them to write important essays on impossibly esoteric topics for other likeminded scholars without having to worry about mass appeal. Though exhaustive research and a high demand for accuracy had necessarily narrowed the topic and claims most historians could make, Jameson suggested a kind of collaboration might begin to fix that over time.[58] Jameson suggested that historians might 'store up well-sifted materials which later may be used by masters of synthesis, of a type not yet evolved.'[59]

Conclusion

Despite the very different repertoires on which they drew, Jameson's curated image of the competent professional worked to address a similar set of expectations and concerns to those Bancroft and Oak imagined. Just as Bancroft's workshop had made it possible to do the otherwise impossibly onerous work of archival history by animating a genius that exceeded the sum of its human parts, Jameson claimed that academic seminars could synthesize a whole profession of standardized, reliable, interlocking replacements for the brilliant but erratic don. Just as Bancroft's enterprise had insulated its laborers from the deleterious effects of the marketplace, of political control over sources, and of the desire to write for fame rather than truth, so, too, did Jameson's university offer an internal reward system that isolated its practitioners and their work from nearly everyone but their peers. By populating an entire profession with systematically trained historians, the new profession promised to strike a balance between depth and breadth by creating a supply of bricks of uniform size and quality that later historians could figure out how to combine into something that would approach the scope of the grand narratives that the archival turn had seemed to make impossible, at least for the moment.

In other words, both of these enterprises assumed that the archival turn demanded a scrupulous researcher who could believably claim to have critically examined *all* of the relevant sources on a question before reconstructing from them absolute historical truth, told without regard for the personal, professional, political, and economic consequences of that ruthless devotion to accuracy. Both enterprises tried to demonstrate that their system gave its practitioners the skills and the resources as well as the independence to do all of that with the assumption that, under ordinary circumstances, an individual historian could not yet hope to do any of it.

Like most contributions to this volume, this chapter has defined scholarly personae as a shared set of intradisciplinary expectations about what it takes to be a good archival historian. This story presents alternative ways of delineating between a scholarly persona, its cultural source material, specific disciplinary concerns, and the repertoires of its performance. Because this chapter focuses on competition for legitimacy between novel historical enterprises rather than between individuals, it has made explicit some of the implicit problems of vocabulary for persona studies. Featured herein are any number of cultural templates, touchstones, and repertoires that could be identified as a scholarly persona. Should Bancroft's fictional version of himself, or Oak's collective genius, or Jameson's professional qualify as personae? This chapter uses those curations of in-house personae to examine what their practitioners thought was the common denominator of expectations for the historian after the archival turn. As a means for performing the proper relationship between intellectual and economic work and as a means of portraying trustworthiness to a broad audience, however, the ideal Romantic author might have warranted examination as a scholarly persona of the humanist after the emergence of the mass book market. In that sense, archival historians might only have adapted that existing character to their own discipline-specific questions and concerns.

The problems are semantic, but they are not trivial. Determining what to identify as a scholarly persona and what to reduce to a template on which it is based or to the repertoire with which it is performed, for instance, can produce very different arguments. I know this from experience. These permutations divide over whether the chapter defines history as a discipline or as a genre. The chosen version traces the emergence of the persona of the historian from within the discipline created by the archival turn, that necessarily engaged with broader public expectations because that discipline still wrote for a mixed marketplace. The path not taken might have examined the emergence of a scholarly persona of the historian as a specific form of the idealized author. In that alternate version, this chapter would have examined how two aspiring enterprises worked to demonstrate to a broad public that they had domesticated genius, transforming the inherently erratic and ephemeral quality into something dependable and reproducible. By suggesting that academic professionalization made it possible to believe in genius, rendering what had always been an obviously unrealizable ideal into a job description, that version would have better explained how Bancroft's status as the unrivalled historian of the Pacific made it impossible for common readers to imagine he had not written the more than 30,000 pages of his histories on his own. It would further have suggested why academics have had a particularly difficult time accepting the rumours of the death of the author as an individual, inspired genius solely responsible for a text.[60]

Notes

1. On the print history of history in England, see Leslie Howsam, *Past into Print: The Publishing of History in Britain, 1850–1950* (London: British Library, 2009); on the emergence of serious history as a genre in that era, and especially of Froude's embattled place as a test case within that boundary work, see Ian Hesketh, 'Diagnosing Froude's disease: boundary work and the discipline of history in late-Victorian Britain', *History and Theory*, 47:3 (2008), 373–95; Ian Hesketh, 'Writing history in Macaulay's shadow: J. R. Seeley, E. A. Freeman, and the audience for scientific history in late Victorian Britain', *Journal of the Canadian Historical Association*, 22:2 (2011), 30.
2. 'Two great historians, the meeting of James Anthony Froude and Hubert H. Bancroft', *The Wasp* (25 April 1885).
3. Ibid. Until his feud with new management led to his dismissal in the spring of 1886, Bierce exercised nearly full control of the magazine. 'In addition to "Prattle,"' Kenneth M. Johnson asserts, Bierce 'wrote practically all the editorials and dominated all departments.' Kenneth M. Johnson (ed.), *The Sting of The Wasp: Political & Satirical Cartoons from the Truculent Early San Francisco Weekly, with an Introduction & Comments by Kenneth M. Johnson* (San Francisco: Book Club of California, 1967), p. 10.
4. The company succeeded. Bancroft's histories established the historiography for most state and local histories within that vast region. For the better part of a century, the widely available volumes remained a reliable first stop for researchers working on any topic in western North America. Earl Pomeroy, 'Old lamps for new: The cultural lag in Pacific Coast historiography', *Arizona and the West*, 2:2 (1960), 107–26; Charles S. Peterson, 'Hubert Howe Bancroft: First Western regionalist', in Richard W. Etulain (ed.) *Writing Western History: Essays on Major Western Historians* (Reno, NV: University of Nevada Press, 2002).
5. The series began by reissuing the five-volume series *The Native Races of the Pacific States*, which it had completed as a potentially self-contained set in 1874–75 to test (or to build) the market for the larger series in the 1880s. Harry Clark, *A Venture in History: The Production, Publication, and Sale of the Works of Hubert Howe Bancroft* (Berkeley, CA: University of California Press, 1973), p. 59.
6. The first reference to Bancroft as a 'literary impostor' appeared early in 1883: 'Our roasted historian', *The Wasp* (17 February 1883).
7. A. L. Bancroft & Company, *A Brief Account of the Literary Undertakings of Hubert Howe Bancroft* (London: Trübner & Company, 1883), p. 9.
8. Oak claimed Bancroft overemphasized his system for its positive effect on public opinion. Henry Lebbeus Oak, *'Literary Industries' in a New Light: A Statement on the Authorship of Bancroft's Native Races and History of the Pacific States, with Comments on Those Works and the System by Which They Were Written* (San Francisco: Bacon Printing Company, 1893), p. 35. For a list of the leading lights of Victorian science and literature who praised Bancroft's enterprise as of 1883, see Bancroft & Company, *Brief Account*. In January 1883, Charles H. Phelps wrote a letter to the *New York Evening Post* (objecting to Bancroft's enterprise) that shared a great deal in common with Bierce's criticisms. Phelps had edited *The Californian* before it became the *Overland Monthly* and knew at least one of Bancroft's staff writers. Bierce reprinted Phelps' letter with an introduction noting their shared outrage, going so far as to imply that his campaign against Bancroft in *The Wasp* had spurred Phelps toward his position. 'Our roasted historian'; Clark, *A Venture in History*, pp 289–90.

9 William Alfred Morris, 'The origin and authorship of the Bancroft Pacific States publications: A history of a history', *The Quarterly of the Oregon Historical Society*, 4:4 (1903), 290–1.
10 Herman Paul, 'What is a scholarly persona? Ten theses on virtues, skills, and desires', *History and Theory*, 53:3 (2014), 354.
11 Herman Paul has examined the emergence and contestation of this persona elsewhere, in greater detail than I will here: Herman Paul, 'The heroic study of records: The contested persona of the archival historian', *History of the Human Sciences*, 26:4 (2013), 67–83.
12 I follow the historian Rob Townsend in distinguishing between the historical discipline and its several professions. Robert B. Townsend, *History's Babel: Scholarship, Professionalization, and the Historical Enterprise in the United States, 1880–1940* (Chicago: University of Chicago Press, 2013), pp 3–4.
13 Christine Haynes, 'Reassessing "genius" in studies of authorship: The state of the discipline', *Book History*, 8:1 (2005), 287–320.
14 Gadi Algazi, '*Exemplum* and *Wundertier*: Three concepts of the scholarly persona', *Low Countries Historical Review*, 131:4 (2016), 9–10.
15 Ibid., 10–11.
16 Ibid., 8, 11–12.
17 Kasper Risbjerg Eskildsen, 'Inventing the archive: Testimony and virtue in modern historiography', *History of the Human Sciences*, 26:4 (2013), 18–19.
18 Ibid., 18–19; Paul, 'Heroic study of records', 72; Herman Paul, 'The virtues of a good historian in early Imperial Germany: Georg Waitz's contested example', *Modern Intellectual History*, 15 (2018), 681–709.
19 As historian Anthony Grafton cogently argued in his masterful history of the footnote, the 'strings of coded references to unpublished documents' that make up citations to archival sources often mean that only historians working on closely associated topics could hope to 'identify the catch in any given set of notes with ease and expertise.' Anthony Grafton, *The Footnote: A Curious History* (Cambridge, MA: Harvard University Press, 1997), p. 7.
20 Haynes, 'Reassessing "genius"', 287.
21 Thomas Carlyle, *On Heroes, Hero-Worship and the Heroic in History* (London: Chapman and Hall, 1842), pp 242–3.
22 Ibid., p. 244.
23 Ibid., p. 246.
24 Ibid., p. 261.
25 The negotiation of this new space as a potentially transformative but anxiety-provoking way to support the creation of a distinctly American literature, like the advent of that literature itself, lagged somewhat behind its European forebears. Geoffrey Turnovsky, *The Literary Market: Authorship and Modernity in the Old Regime* (Philadelphia, PA: University of Pennsylvania Press, 2011); Sheila Post-Lauria, *Correspondent Colorings: Melville in the Marketplace* (Amherst, MA: University of Massachusetts Press, 1996); Terence Whalen, *Edgar Allan Poe and the Masses: The Political Economy of Literature in Antebellum America* (Princeton, NJ: Princeton University Press, 1999); Michael S. Kearns, *Writing for the Street, Writing in the Garret: Melville, Dickinson, and Private Publication* (Columbus, OH: Ohio State University Press, 2010).
26 According to H. J. Jackson, the Romantic ideal of authorship 'turns out to be less uniform, less revolutionary, and less tied to one period' than one might expect, a fact that only makes the study of it more important as 'a cluster of ideas that are not only historically significant but also still operative in the modern world.' H. J. Jackson, *Those Who Write for Immortality: Romantic Reputations and the Dream of Lasting Fame* (New Haven, CT: Yale University Press, 2015), pp x, 232 n. 4, 110.
27 Frances Fuller Victor, 'The Bancroft Historical Library', *The Californian and Overland Monthly*, 6:36 (1882), 494.

28 Hubert Howe Bancroft, *Literary Industries* (San Francisco: The History Company, 1890), p. 596.
29 Ibid.
30 Oak, *'Literary Industries' in a New Light*, p. 48; Bancroft, *Literary Industries*, p. 598.
31 Oak, *'Literary Industries' in a New Light*, p. 48; Bancroft, *Literary Industries*, p. 598.
32 For whatever reason, Oak omitted this assertion from Bancroft's *Literary Industries* with an ellipsis in his reproduction of it. Oak, *'Literary Industries' in a New Light*, p. 48; Bancroft, *Literary Industries*, p. 598.
33 Oak, *'Literary Industries' in a New Light*, p. 29; Bancroft, *Literary Industries*, p. 592.
34 Oak, *'Literary Industries' in a New Light*, p. 57.
35 For instance, Bancroft wrote in three consecutive chapters a first-person narration of his journey to California in 1852 from New York (via two steamers with an intermediary transit across the isthmus of Panama) that stood in for a more systematic history of that popular method of getting to California. Confirming Oak's diagnosis, these chapters run just over one hundred pages and contain no citations other than a few internal cross-references. Hubert Howe Bancroft, *California Inter Pocula* (San Francisco: The History Company, 1888), pp 121–2, for instance. The chapters are: Chapter VI: 'The voyage to California – New York to Chagres'; Chapter VII: 'The voyage to California – isthmus of Panama'; and Chapter VIII: 'The voyage to California – Panama to San Francisco'.
36 Oak, *'Literary Industries' in a New Light*, p. 42.
37 Oak noted that Victor had exhibited 'her volumes' with 'her name on back and title' at the Chicago World's Fair and elsewhere. He considered her 'claim and action' to be 'entirely justifiable and proper' (ibid., p. 38). He eventually did exactly that, and a set of his volumes are cataloged as such at Dartmouth, Oak's *alma mater*. Henry Lebbeus Oak, *Works of Henry L. Oak.*, 11 vols (s.i.: s.n., 1875–93), online at http://libcat.dartmouth.edu/record=b1300440~S1.
38 Bancroft made it worse when he split the final volume off in a popular edition, with an introduction written by George Frederic Parsons to celebrate Bancroft's genius individually. George Frederic Parsons, *On the Completion of the Historical Section of the Works of Hubert Howe Bancroft* (San Francisco: History Company, 1891); Hubert Howe Bancroft, *Literary Industries: A Memoir* (New York City: Harper & Brothers, 1891).
39 Bancroft & Company, *Brief Account*, p. 11.
40 Eskildsen, 'Inventing the archive', 18–19.
41 Bancroft, *Literary Industries*, pp 199, 394.
42 Ibid., p. 472.
43 Ibid., pp 472–3. The company similarly negotiated the cooperation of the Church of Jesus Christ of Latter-day Saints, without which it could not have written the history of Utah. Bancroft spent much of 1884 in Salt Lake City and, though he failed to mention it in *Literary Industries*, he reviewed the manuscript with church leaders in September of that year. According to church leader Wilford Woodruff, since Bancroft 'was giving both sides of the question for and against' the church, he offered its leaders 'the privilege of correcting any mistakes on our side.' LDS Church History Library, MS 1352, Wilford Woodruff, 'Wilford Woodruff Journals and Papers' 1828–98, quoted in George Ellsworth, 'Hubert Howe Bancroft and the history of Utah', *Utah Historical Quarterly*, 22:2 (1954), 114.
44 For a more thorough analysis of professionalization as a performance, see Peter Novick, *That Noble Dream: The 'Objectivity Question' and the American Historical Profession* (Cambridge: Cambridge University Press, 1988), ch. 2. Maleness proved especially important to these professionals' self-representation as well as their denunciation of others as feminized amateurs. See, for example, Bonnie G. Smith, *The Gender of History: Men, Women, and Historical Practice* (Cambridge, MA: Harvard University Press, 1998) and Julie Des Jardins, *Women and the Historical Enterprise in America: Gender, Race,*

and the Politics of Memory, 1880–1945 (Chapel Hill, NC: University of North Carolina Press, 2003).
45 This way of performing erudition and expertise as drudgery has not gone anywhere. In his own amusing departure from that dour demeanor, Grafton satirizes this performance by comparing the tedium of a footnote to the 'high whine of the dentist's drill,' both of which serve to reassure: 'the pain inflicted... is not random but directed, part of the cost that the benefits of modern science and technology exact.' Grafton, *Footnote*, p. 5.
46 John Franklin Jameson, 'The influence of universities upon historical writing', *University Record (University of Chicago)*, 6:40 (1902), 298.
47 Ibid.
48 Ibid.
49 Ibid.
50 Ibid.
51 Ibid., 299.
52 J. Franklin (John Franklin) Jameson, John Bach McMaster, and Edward Channing, *The Present State of Historical Writing in America* (Worcester, MA: The Davis Press, 1910), p. 12.
53 Jameson, 'Influence of universities', 299–300.
54 Ibid., 299.
55 Ibid., 300.
56 Ibid.
57 Ibid., 299.
58 In support of their own system, Bancroft and Oak had identified this as a fundamental limitation of individual scholarship. Bancroft, *Literary Industries*, p. 598.
59 Jameson, 'Influence of universities', 300.
60 On the death of the author, see Roland Barthes, 'Death of the author', trans. Richard Howard, *Aspen*, 5:6 (1967). For the ways in which rumors of that author's death have been somewhat exaggerated, see Haynes, 'Reassessing "genius"', 314–16.

CHAPTER 4

Generational continuities and composite personae: French historiography from the 1870s to the 1950s

Camille Creyghton

Introduction

One of the most polemical texts the French historical innovator Lucien Febvre (1878–1956) ever produced is entitled: 'On a form of history that is not ours'.[1] It is an article reviewing a small guide to historical method by 'his old friend' the medievalist Louis Halphen that, according to Febvre, missed the whole point of what doing history should be by 'refusing to think the human fact... professing pure and simple submission to the facts, as if the facts were in no way of his fabrication, as if they weren't chosen by him'.[2] Although Halphen, born in 1880, was of the same generation as Febvre, the latter condemned the book and the author as belonging to a previous generation with ideas on how to write history that by then had been totally superseded by Febvre himself and his fellow new historians. This 'histoire historisante' (historicizing history), as he called it, would be characterized by the exclusive stress on the methodological quest for clear and undisputable historical facts, distilled out of archival documents that had stood the test of reliability, and by a lack of interpretative and synthesizing force. Its practitioners would, consequently, be pure erudites – in the pejorative sense of the term – without any gift for historical imagination and concealing this lack of talent behind their overt praise for the strictest kind of objectivity. Ironically, some forty years before, it had been Halphen himself who, in a letter in which he defended his ideas on historical research against the harsh critiques of another innovator Henri Berr, coined the epithet 'histoire historisante'.[3] Thanks to Berr, and later on Febvre, the proudly self-given title for a history that would meet the requirements of 'objective' science turned out as a nickname for all sins that a historian could commit while working too meticulously and recoiling from all subjective interference.

Febvre was quite successful with his condemnation of the kind of history that was written before him: he thereby contributed a great deal to the establishment of a standard narrative on French historiography from the nineteenth century onwards, in which historians are classified according to three successive generations, schools or paradigms with wholly different and mutually exclusive ways of doing research and writing history: the Romanticist generation of, roughly, the years 1830–70 with Jules Michelet as its most notable representative; the 'methodological' or positivist generation of the period 1870–1930, exemplified by the textbook of Charles-Victor Langlois and Charles Seignobos that nowadays is more mocked than read; and the generation of the *Annales* historians to which Febvre himself belonged.[4]

Yet, as this chapter will show, with respect to the scholarly personae valued by successive generations of historians many of the distinguishing traits become blurred and the differences appear to be not so much important as to be mutually exclusive. The positivists had much in common with the Romanticists and the *Annales* historians learnt more from the positivists than Febvre ever acknowledged. What was considered as 'not ours' in fact appeared not so irrelevant and old-fashioned at all. This chapter explores the opportunities that are opened up by introducing the concept of scholarly personae in the study of French historiography, especially concerning the period 1870–1950. It will demonstrate that this approach prompts an important reconsideration of the standard narrative, putting into perspective the sharp distinctions that structure it. However, it will also argue for a broader and more open interpretation of the persona concept than has been adopted to date, as this appears necessary for understanding some complexities or internal tensions *within* the discourses of different French historians about what it takes to be a historian, which in part stem from the fact that historians play different roles at the same time, each demanding different epistemic and moral virtues.

In what follows, I undertake case studies of two pairs of historians of different generations; both are pairs of masters and students, traditionally classified in two different 'paradigms'. The first case study concerns Gabriel Monod (1844–1912), founder of the first French journal exclusively devoted to professional history, the *Revue historique*, and one of his last graduate students, Lucien Febvre, who would co-found the most important rival journal *Annales* in 1929. The second pair consists of Charles Seignobos, whose name mainly lives on in the combination 'Langlois-Seignobos' serving as a shorthand for their supposedly old-fashioned textbook, and his student Marc Bloch, the other *Annales* founder. These two double case studies allow a comparison of the scholarly personae of two different generations of French historiography and the detection, apart from the well-known generational gaps in research interests and method, of the dispositions, cultivated character traits and ideals that were shared by the different generations and transmitted by the 'doctor fathers' – to borrow a German expression – to their sons. All four historians discussed were central figures in the French historical profession of their times, holding important university positions and signing crucial publications for the profession as a whole. They were not particularly representative of the profession, therefore, but their opinions and writings guided it. This last is the reason why they can nevertheless stand for more than their individual case and inform us about some fundamental traits of the French historian's scholarly personae in this period.

Erudition and imagination: Gabriel Monod and Lucien Febvre

Monod rightfully counts as one of the leading French historians of the last quarter of the nineteenth century, although he owes this reputation not so much to his own research on early medieval sources as to his teaching and his organization of the historical profession.[5] More than any other historian of the period, Monod devoted his energy to teaching and writing on how to practise history and to what ends. Apart from being the founder, and for a long time the sole director, of the *Revue historique*, he was also a professor at the prestigious Ecole normale supérieure and the Ecole pratique des Hautes Etudes, which was established in 1868 as an innovative institution for providing practical training in research. There, he introduced into France the seminar system for research training with which he had become acquainted as a student of Georg Waitz in Göttingen. In addition, from 1905 till 1910 he held a special chair in 'general history and historical methodology' at the Collège de France. However, he probably derives most of his influence from the 'Bulletin historique', the regular chronicle of the profession in the *Revue historique*, in which book reviews were published alongside discussions of education policy and obituaries of deceased colleagues. Monod was the main contributor to this 'Bulletin historique', sometimes assisted by others but in other periods more or less alone, from the start of the journal in 1876 until his death in 1912. The 'Bulletin historique' was not only a valuable source of information for the professional historian, it also set the standards of what good professional history should be.

Monod's ideas appear to have been remarkably consistent throughout his career, although he significantly shifted the emphasis of his arguments as the professionalization of historical research he had been advocating since 1876 materialized and its drawbacks became apparent. His opening text of the *Revue historique*, which can be considered a 'manifesto' for professional history writing, provided both an overview of the development of historical writing in France since the sixteenth century and a plea for pursuing this development by introducing scientific methods to historical research.[6] Part of the inspiration for this 'scientific' history could be found in the indigenous French tradition of erudition embodied in Mabillon and Du Cange, but for more recent inspiration one should look to the German universities, to Ranke, Niebuhr or Waitz. Although Monod recognized that some German historical work tended to suffer from over-specialization and a lack of a sense of synthesis, he considered it the model that French historians – until then too inclined to reach hasty generalizations – should follow. Whereas in France erudite research had always been separated from history writing, with style prevailing over exactitude and scientific rigour, henceforth, according to Monod, erudition should become part and parcel of historical practice. That meant, in the first place, a temporary postponement of historical synthesis until more erudite research had provided a firm basis for it. Second, it meant that serious training was needed on methods of source criticism and the necessary auxiliary sciences, in order to prepare young historians for the analytical work that in the end should permit the writing of 'scientific' historical syntheses.[7]

Monod remained loyal to these ideas on the order of historical work and the importance of erudition until the end of his career. Still in 1908, he published a significant text, written in connection with his teaching at the Collège de France, in which he repeated that historical synthesis should be built onto the 'positive and firm results' of analysis. However, while he admitted that 'historical critique and the auxiliary sciences that are connected with it provide a kind of satisfaction to those who occupy themselves with them' and that they 'operate by truly scientific procedures', he now insisted that this was not enough for true history writing.[8] In fact, it was only half the work: '[t]he historian has accomplished only half of his task if he has just united and classified the materials of which historical reality is made. In order to provide an understanding of this reality, he has to give it life... After studying the past as a scholar, the historian, in order to portray it, must make an effort of personal creation and must add art to science. In so doing, he recreates the past in himself. Science decomposes the elements of life. Only art recreates them.'[9]

For Monod, erudition, with all its usefulness, was in danger of becoming an end in itself – actually, he saw that danger materialized in the increasing number of detailed historical studies in which all attempts at saying something meaningful about a larger issue had been abandoned. At the beginning of the twentieth century, Monod therefore shifted the emphasis in his methodological texts towards a plea for synthesis, which he voiced with a wording that calls to mind the dictum of the Romantic historian Jules Michelet that history should be a 'resurrection of the past'.[10] Indeed, once he realized the shortcomings of historical erudition, Monod devoted much of his energy to the study and propagation of the work of this illustrious forebear, although he also constantly stated that, since Michelet had lacked the disinterestedness and scientific rigour needed for analysis, he could not be an example for modern scientific historians in any direct sense.[11] Instead, modern historians should look, according to Monod, to the developments in the new social sciences, notably social psychology, in order to gain better insight into human life, and hence into human life in the past.[12] But what could be learned from Michelet is that, for synthesis, something more and something other than erudition was needed, which did not pertain to the domain of science but to the domain of art. History thus became for Monod a 'double operation', in which a 'large part is left... to the subjective qualities of the strength of thought and of imagination'.[13] Hence, imagination, empathy with human beings of the past and artful creation were not to be banned from scientific history writing: not even were they just fanciful additions, but an essential part of good historical work, without which it was not complete.

Tragically enough, Monod knew very well that he himself was not able to live up to this ideal, that he did not meet his own criteria, since he was better at erudite source work than the writing of well-rounded books. He never even finished his doctorate. At the end of his life, Monod was a historian *manqué* in his own eyes, who realized that his main legacy would be his methodological texts and his students. But that did not prevent him from formulating this high ideal.

Monod's doctoral student Lucien Febvre was undoubtedly more successful in writing books: in 1911 he graduated with a dissertation on 'Philippe II et la Franche-Comté', after brilliant studies at the Ecole normale supérieure.[14] After World War I, in which he served, he became one of the young French academics to be catapulted into the (by then again French) University of Strasbourg. In 1933 he was appointed at the Collège de France to a chair of 'history of modern civilization', a position which he held until his retirement in 1949. As is well known, in 1929 he established a new journal, together with his younger Strasburgian colleague Marc Bloch, thus repeating what his thesis supervisor had done before. While the *Revue historique* had had the professionalization of the practice of history as its mission, Febvre's and Bloch's *Annales d'histoire économique et sociale* should be associated with the debate on what had become an increasingly pressing issue since the start of the twentieth century: the position of the (by that time well-established) historical discipline *vis-à-vis* the newly emerging social sciences.[15] Febvre's and Bloch's way of resolving the issue was one of synthesis of disciplines, but without relinquishing, as Durkheimian sociologists tended to do, the specificity of the historical discipline. Instead, by giving history a central position as the discipline that integrated sociology, geography and psychology in order to provide a comprehensive understanding of past society, they in fact confirmed the position as 'queen discipline' that it had acquired during the nineteenth century.[16]

Febvre has the reputation of being a radically innovating historian who completely rejected the heritage of the older generation of 'positivists' or *méthodiques*, a reputation that he himself, a somewhat irascible character who was best able to articulate his ideas while attacking those of others, cultivated assiduously. Yet upon closer inspection he appears to have adopted much of Monod, and not just the strategy of making his mark on the historical discipline by establishing a journal and filling its book review section. This concerns in the first place his deference to Michelet as the forebear of the discipline, and especially of the kind of comprehensive history he advocated, although Febvre, like Monod, never directly followed the example of this nineteenth-century Romanticist. Michelet stood for a history that portrayed both the 'material' (the economic and social) and 'spiritual' (the cultural and mental) aspects of past societies.[17] Furthermore, reference to Michelet was a device for Febvre to criticize the generation of positivist historians before him, which – according to Febvre, thus glossing over his own supervisor's ample meditation on Michelet – had retreated from the tasks Michelet had set the historian: to write history that reconstructed the entirety of past life.

In addition to the Michelet reference, Febvre also adopted from Monod a good part of his ideas on history as a scientific activity, which he updated, as Monod had started doing himself towards the end of his career, by integrating insights from the newer social sciences and reflections on the philosophy of science that had become urgent since the early twentieth-century revolutions in physics, chemistry and biology.[18] In an address in 1941 to first-year history students of the Ecole normale supérieure, published afterwards as a programmatic text in the *Annales*, he discussed these ideas at length. Because of the genre of the text, it can be said to expressly transmit a certain persona of the historian. Its title, 'To live history (Vivre l'histoire)', underscored this: '[t]hat which Michelet attempted to do, with his authority and the ardour of his words and the radiance of his genius, that's indeed, relatively speaking, what I want to attempt here with you... : to give you the sentiment that one could live one's life as a historian.'[19] This life as a historian, then, was the life of a scientist, since for Febvre history was, although not a science in the strict sense as physics could be, a 'scientifically conducted study', which meant that it had to start with 'two operations, the same that form the basis of all modern scientific work: to set problems and to formulate hypotheses'.[20] Instead of just embarking on the exploration of a mass of sources, including archives, and then writing down whatever facts could be established from them, historians had to start from questions, imposed by current issues in society, in order to answer them in a systematic way and thus reconstruct a part of past life.

Febvre's sometimes virulent criticism of 'erudite' historians notwithstanding, he never rejected erudition *per se*. On the contrary, good source work and critical sense were as important for him as for Monod or other historians from the previous generation: it was not only Febvre's own research that testified to this, but also his countless reviews of other historians' books. But erudition should not become a goal in itself. It should merely be part of a larger endeavour that had to start with a good question – or 'problem' or 'hypothesis', to use the more modern terms he preferred – and lead to a synthesis. And, endorsing Monod's ideas on the realization of such a synthesis, he stated that beside erudition something else, or more, should also come into play that can best be described as imagination:

> [t]he synthesis of the historian can only take place within him. It brings together the dead elements of the past that once was the living present and that stopped living; the problem being thus to reconstruct life as it was when these elements were not dead but living. It is therefore the synthesis of a chemist, but in the mind of the operator, in the thought of the historian. And the retort here is: should one say the heart or the mind or the soul of the historian? Let's say his personality.[21]

Febvre preferred a comparison with a chemist – who had not totally lost all association with the alchemist creating gold out of lead – to one with an artist, thus staying within the realm of science. Nevertheless, it is clear that for Febvre historical synthesis depended on the historian's personality and thus could never be realized through cumulating the results of previous erudite undertakings of different and interchangeable historians. Moreover, it should be noted that the 'chemist' Febvre had in mind here was Marcellin Berthelot, who had himself compared chemical synthesis with art.[22]

Hence, in Febvre's as in Monod's case, there is a fusion of repertoires derived from science, such as the epistemic virtues of objectivity or the values of proof and certainty, and other repertoires, derived from art and pointing in the direction of personal involvement and imagination. The persona of the historian they constructed was a synthesis in itself that could not be captured with the name of Michelet alone, and was strategically directed against other – too one-sidedly erudite – historians. Most importantly, however, there appears to have been considerable continuity between this leader of the *Annales* and the chief representative of the previous generation.

Academic disinterestedness and engagement: Charles Seignobos and Marc Bloch

Such continuity can also be traced in the case of another teacher, the Sorbonne Professor Charles Seignobos, who was the object of Febvre's most severe condemnations, and his student and *Annales* co-founder Marc Bloch.[23] The latter had followed Seignobos's lectures at the Sorbonne and, although distancing himself from many of Seignobos's principles in his *Apologie pour l'histoire*, in that same book he also acknowledged his debt to him and defended him against Febvre's attacks.[24] This, however, did not prevent Febvre from being rather successful in portraying Seignobos as the narrow-minded representative of the positivist fact-fetishists *par excellence*, thus hampering serious evaluation of his legacy. While both Seignobos and Bloch had their ideas on the merits of erudition and imagination in historical work too, they are discussed here particularly for their attempts at reconciling academic disinterestedness and engagement.

Although a decade younger than Monod and living well into the twentieth century, the apex of Seignobos's career chronologically coincided with Monod's lecturing at the Collège de France. His most influential publications on historical method, *Introduction à l'étude historique* co-authored with Charles-Victor Langlois and *La méthode historique appliquée aux sciences sociales*, date from 1898 and 1901, while he was appointed professor of historical method at the Sorbonne in 1907, where he had previously taught in substitute positions since 1898. As he was very reluctant about cooperation with the emerging social sciences, the programme of his major methodological works was primarily to make historical research a purely academic occupation without intended societal outreach, to the point that even Monod came to criticize their hypercriticism.[25] It is, however, important to keep in mind here that these works were written in reaction to the success of Durkheimian sociology, which tended to treat historical research as mere preliminary work in a far more ambitious programme. Although Seignobos's attempts to temper the expectations of what historical research could arrive at were genuine, they should also be read against their polemical background and not immediately be taken at face value.

Seignobos's conviction that historical research had to be disinterested and detached from the pressing but also transient demands of society did not imply that he suffered from academicism. On the contrary: not only was he a sociable man who preferred to spend his leisure time at the seaside with a number of other distinguished academics such as the Curies and the mathematician Emile Borel, he was also, like Monod, a very active Dreyfusard; a member of the central committee of the Dreyfusard Human Rights League; an advocate of the 'Leftist Bloc' of 1899.[26] His commitment to the propagation of human rights was well known and he spent much of his energy on writing journalistic pieces in which he used his historical insight to understand present-day situations and that he published not only in French, but also in German and English periodicals. In 1901 he started the international pacifistic weekly *L'Européen* with the Dutch jurist Willem van der Vlugt; this continued to appear until 1914. During World War I, he delivered a couple of lectures on the 'reorganisation of France' that should be undertaken when peace returned.[27] His biography was, therefore, anything but an indication of narrow-mindedness.

His broad interests were also reflected in the volume with a selection of his work that his students edited in his honour.[28] It consists of three equal parts: original historical work, pedagogical texts and journalism. While clearly distinguished, the three genres and the three different activities they were associated with – research, teaching and political engagement – were connected for Seignobos and all were part of his self-conception as a historian. Seignobos did not consider this as contradicting the disinterestedness he prescribed for historical research: rather, the role of a researcher was only one of the various roles historians had to play, alongside those of a teacher and of a citizen who incidentally, because of his training and mode of thought, was able to add a dimension to current debates that others could not provide.[29] Hence, while political engagement, for instance in the form of journalistic activities, could be part and parcel of the life of a historian, historical research proper should remain immune from current concerns.

This was also the case for teaching, which in Third Republic France in itself was seen as a civil service and an expression of republican engagement. For Seignobos, history teaching was an 'instrument of political education', important not only for 'a part of the pupils, but for the entire nation', because it enabled them 'to understand the world in which they will live, to become interested in it and prepared to take action in it'.[30] 'Because history is the true civil education, it is the mission of the professors of history to provide future citizens with political instruction,' Seignobos continued.[31] And hence, for him, teaching – and the writing of textbooks – was the highest vocation of the historian, to which he himself devoted the best of his energy. This explains why Seignobos, his alleged interest in social, institutional and economic history notwithstanding, did not succeed to any great extent in writing historical narratives that went beyond the sequence of well-established facts and provided a meaningful explanation.³² His *Histoire sincère de la nation française* was meant to be an accessible synthesis of French history with special attention to sentiments, beliefs, habits and ideas, but in fact chiefly dealt with political history.³³ As in a textbook, important notions were italicized for reasons of clarity and the narrative was interrupted by a subheading before every bit of new information, which precluded argumentative complexity. Like Monod, Seignobos partly failed in his ambitions, because his methods and research practices remained those of a teacher and in the end he did not manage to fully meet the requirements for historical research he himself had formulated.

Perhaps Marc Bloch fared better in this respect. The innovative nature of his research is beyond doubt, as is his engagement. Despite health problems, at the age of 53 he volunteered for the French army during World War II and, after demobilization, based himself and his family in his holiday home in the unoccupied part of the country and continued working in so far as that was possible under the increasing threats he had to face because of his Jewish background. In 1943, he became a member of the armed resistance in the vicinity of Lyons. After being arrested by the Gestapo, he was executed on 16 June 1944.

This engagement till death provides a major explanation for the exemplary role that intellectuals and historians, particularly in France, ascribe to Bloch even to the present day.³⁴ However, as is widely recognized, his historical research, too, contributes to his reputation. Bloch pioneered the use of new kinds of historical sources such as material relics and art, and the application of anthropological insights in the study of medieval society. Although he several times failed to be elected a professor at the Collège de France, which he took as a bitter disappointment, he forged a brilliant career that started with a lectureship in Strasbourg and ended at the Sorbonne. Finally, he was of course well known as the younger co-founder of the *Annales*. In addition to his research-based work, and while in hiding during the war, he wrote two short books, published posthumously.

First, *Etrange Défaite* (*Strange Defeat*), in which he examined both the immediate military causes and the deeply rooted cultural explanations for France's defeat in World War II and heavily criticized the French educational system. The book was in itself a kind of historical engagement: on its very first pages Bloch made clear that he wrote as a historian and applied the same 'habits of critique, observation and honesty' to France's current situation that he had learned to apply in studying the past.³⁵ Moreover a large part of the book is devoted to a critical discussion of the urgent need to reform history education in schools in order to make the programme more attractive, more conducive to patriotism and more productive in instilling in young pupils insight into historical developments and the changeability of society that would arm them for an uncertain future. Although the educational programme Bloch proposed was undoubtedly much more modern and much less centred on the study of political facts than Seignobos's, the plea was essentially the same.

History education, but this time the education of the professional historian, was the subject of his second war book: the unfinished *Apologie pour l'histoire, ou: Métier d'historien* (*An Apologia for History, or: The Historian's Craft*), which is one of the shortest and sharpest introductions to the practices and aims of historical research ever written. Bloch opened his *apologia* with the question what could be the use of writing history, which he subsequently answered by saying that history should first be a science aiming not only to know but also to understand the past and to provide explanations for its development. But finally, he added, 'it is undeniable that a science will always seem to us somehow incomplete if it cannot, sooner or later, in one way or another, aid us to live better'.[36] 'The good historian,' he said later on, 'is like the giant of the fairy tale. He knows that wherever he catches the scent of human flesh, there his quarry lies.'[37] His answer was openly directed against 'orthodox positivists', by which he had in mind Seignobos among others, and it was in fact closer to Febvre's or even Monod's ideas than it seemed to Seignobos's.[38]

However, in some respects, Bloch was quite close to Seignobos. The fact that Bloch ended up in the Sorbonne while Febvre succeeded in securing a position at the Collège de France was attributable to the contingencies of academic politicking, further marred by anti-Semitism. But it in the meantime reflected their different professional norms quite well. Whereas the co-editor of the *Annales* preferred the bold statements needed for public speech, Bloch was more a man of prudence who was cautious about too easily throwing out the babies with the bath water. In particular, he was more devoted than Febvre to a kind of disinterested academic rigour that he had inherited, as he confessed himself, from Seignobos and Numa Denis Fustel de Coulanges.[39] Indeed, the subtitle of his historical *apologia* – 'métier de l'historien' or 'the historian's craft' – was deliberate: history was for Bloch a craft, a kind of meticulous manual work, as it had been for Seignobos. He therefore shared with Seignobos his criticism of Durkheim's all too easy reduction of historical manual work to the status of mere preparation for true social science.[40]

More important even was his use of the metaphor of the *juge d'instruction*, the public prosecutor who researches a case and brings it before the court, for the historian in his pursuit of truth.[41] In 1935, he introduced it in a book review and in the subsequent, discordant exchange of correspondence with Febvre about that text, and he still employed it, albeit more hesitatingly, in *Apologie pour l'histoire*.[42] The metaphor is rooted in an early-modern tradition of comparing the practice of history with the judicial domain, although the fact that Bloch chose the *juge d'instruction*, who does not pass judgment himself, and not the judge proper was an important shift.[43] This metaphor provides the best illustration of Bloch's conception of the persona of the historian, expressing first the requirement for historians to do meticulous source work, trying to 'hear' and judge the value of all 'testimonies' in order to find out the truth about the past. But second and not unimportant is the fact that the ultimate aim of all this, just as that of the judicial system, was the well-being of society. Hence, both in Bloch's and in Seignobos's case, the requirement of academic disinterestedness for historical research went hand in hand with an overt engagement with society as regards the ultimate aims of that research. And without these aims, doing historical research would be utterly senseless.

In this respect too, Bloch truly remained closer to his former professor than to his *Annales* colleague Febvre, a fact of which they were both aware. Febvre unequivocally rejected the metaphor of the *juge d'instruction*, which, in his view, would reduce historical enquiry to the dimensions of a conflict between two persons. For expressing this opinion, he accused Bloch in a gross but fundamentally correct manner of 'integral Seignobosism'.[44] Meanwhile, as was the case with erudition and imagination, there was a degree of friction between disinterestedness and engagement, even if not clearly perceived by these historians. It surfaced in Seignobos's failure to write a meaningful history for the society of his day and thus really connect the two poles. But it never occurred to anyone to resolve it by giving up one of the poles.

Conclusion

The personae of the historian formulated by Monod, Febvre, Seignobos and Bloch are all complex wholes in which several roles, all with their own requirements, several opinions about what good historical practice is and several epistemic and moral virtues came together. For all of them, a good historian was not just someone who was good at archival research, or good at teaching, or good at writing, or politically engaged: ideally, historians should be and do all these at once in order to qualify as a good historian. Meanwhile Monod, Febvre, Seignobos and Bloch all had their own ideas and preferences about which of these roles and activities had priority and how exactly to bring them about.

Still, what strikes us most while studying them is the overlap in their epistemological and methodological opinions, their professional ethics and their role perception, in short: in the personae of the historian they conceived. Especially within the couples of teachers and students, the continuities from one generation to another exceeded the differences. The younger historians tended to use more modern words and phrases and brought their ideas into line with contemporary scientific and societal developments, but the shift was not fundamental since the underlying principles remained very similar. Instead of two radically different generations, we rather see a kind of Venn diagram of partly overlapping and partly individualized sets of virtues, role perceptions and epistemological or methodological opinions. Hence, the major gain of studying French historiography with a persona approach and looking into the practices and moral economy of these historians is that it enables us to understand the different, competing schools and generations without falling into the trap of their rhetoric and reproducing their self-images, and also without ignoring these altogether. It thus permits us to detect continuities and similarities these historians were unable or unwilling to see themselves.

However, in order to see beyond the self-images historians created, the personae concept should be taken in a sufficiently broad and flexible manner. For instance, personae are decidedly related in one way or another to examples, forebears or parent figures, but they do not entirely coincide with them. The reference to Michelet was essential to Monod's and Febvre's formulations of the persona of the historian, but they never took Michelet as a direct example, nor did the personae they conceived resemble in any way the Romanticist historian. Rather, the persona concept is particularly useful for figuring out the ways in which historians dealt with their forebears or examples, what they took over from them and what they rejected, and how they reinterpreted their examples for reconciling their lessons with the progress of scholarship.

Secondly, the concept gains in explanatory value if it leaves space for a gap between the desired scholarly self and the realized; between ideals and ambitions on one hand and reality on the other. In that way, it accounts for the fact that ideals by definition are not fully realizable, since reality always gets in the way with all its imperfections, demands and distractions, such as political developments that call for an urgent reaction. Until now, indeed, personae have sometimes been conceptualized as unstable, but most often this instability is conceived as something external, stemming from the fact that they are contested from outside or in competition with each other. When they introduced the concept of personae, Lorraine Daston and Otto Sibum used it to describe at a macro level how different historical societies conceive of the social position of the 'scientist' or 'scholar' and ascribe a special kind of cultural identity or personhood to it. Frictions, then, are conceived as dissonances between the prevailing scholarly persona in a society and the ways in which individual scientists or scholars organize their lives.[45] Herman Paul, by contrast, has shown that the concept can be productively applied at a micro level, to grasp competing conceptions within a discipline of what it takes to be a good practitioner of that discipline.[46] However, the flip-side of these attempts to distinguish different personae within disciplines has been a rather homogeneous characterization of the personae themselves, in which a particular persona is tied to one particular role scholars can take, which in turn is connected to an inspiring model or parent figure. For example, Paul showed how in Germany historians used the names of particular father figures as shorthand for competing types of historian, each connected to their own set of ideals and virtues.[47] Yet, the cases of these four French historians, especially of Monod and Seignobos, show that personae, considered at this micro level, can be complex amalgams of different and sometimes competing ideals and virtues. These historians not only had to choose between different available models for being a historian, but were also obliged to unite different, not fully compatible modes and roles within their being a historian, and in addition to learn to live with their shortcomings.

Lastly, and further pursuing this line of argument, the value all these historians attached to activities other than historical research proper calls for an approach that accounts for more than just the historian *qua* researcher and includes other roles historians assumed and considered part and parcel of their being a historian. Especially in the French case, where historians were in the first place considered teachers, where history was the 'queen discipline' of the republican education system and historians frequently took up public responsibilities, the personae concept is particularly useful, provided it allows us to account for the multiplicity of roles that historians perform all at once. Instead of being connected to different personae between which historians could choose, such as seems to have been the case in the debates about their profession among German historians described by Paul, different and sometimes competing professional roles went together in one and the same persona, since a good historian was expected to fulfil them all. The personae these French historians created were composite wholes of different kinds of role-specific behaviour, epistemic and moral virtues, and opinions on method, epistemics and objectives. Conceived in this way, the personae concept also leaves room for internal tensions in the lives and work of historians that stem from role conflicts and from the fact that the constellations of virtues assembled in a persona always have to be weighed against each other. It is a basic assumption in virtue ethics and virtue epistemology that virtues in principle cannot be realized all at once and that the ethical or epistemic 'good life' precisely consists in the ability to find a balance between them in concrete situations. The cases of these French historians and their ways of evaluating their own and each other's behaviour illustrate just that. Hence, the personae concept should provide space for this balancing and deliberating. Understood in this broad way, this chapter shows, the personae concept enables us to significantly enrich our understanding of the history of French historiography.

Notes

1 I wish to thank Gadi Algazi for his comments on an earlier version of this chapter.
2 Lucien Febvre, 'Sur une forme d'histoire qui n'est pas la nôtre. L'histoire historisante', *Annales: Histoire, sciences sociales*, 3 (1948), 21–4, at 24: 'Un historien qui refuse de penser le fait humain, un historien qui professe la soumission pure et simple à ces faits, comme si les faits n'étaient point de sa fabrication, comme s'ils n'avaient point été choisis par lui.' The text is reprinted in Lucien Febvre, *Vivre l'histoire*, ed. Brigitte Mazon and Bertrand Müller (Paris: Robert Laffont, 2009), pp 100–4.
3 Published in Louis Halphen and Henri Berr, 'Histoire traditionnelle et synthèse historique', *Revue de synthèse historique*, 23:68 (1911), 121–30.
4 For the standard narratives, see for example: André Burguière, *L'Ecole des Annales: Une histoire intellectuelle* (Paris, Odile Jacob, 2006); Peter Burke, *The French Historical Revolution: The Annales School 1929–89* (Cambridge: Polity Press, 1990); Charles-Olivier Carbonell, *Histoire et historiens: La Mutation idéologique des historiens français* (Toulouse: Privat, 1976); Christian Delacroix, François Dosse and Patrick Garcia, *Les courants historiques en France, XIXe–XXe siècle* (Paris: Gallimard, 2007); Isabel Noronha-DiVanna, *Writing History in the Third Republic* (Newcastle-upon-Tyne: Cambridge Scholars Publishing, 2010).
5 The best biography to date is still Rémy Rioux, 'Gabriel Monod: visions de l'histoire et pratique du métier d'historien, 1882–1912' (Master's thesis, Université Paris I, 1990).
6 Gabriel Monod, 'Du progrès des études historiques en France depuis le XVIe siècle', *Revue historique*, 1:1 (1876), 5–38. The text is called a 'manifesto' in Delacroix, Dosse and Garcia, *Courants historiques*, p. 117. The terms 'science' and 'scientific' were frequently used by French historians in the period. Although those who were familiar with the German context knew that the German word *Wissenschaft* has a broader meaning than the French *science*, they used the latter as a translation for it. The narrowing effect of this translation may possibly explain the strict scientism and the misunderstandings that followed from that in some French debates on the epistemology of history.
7 Monod, 'Progrès des études', 34–5.
8 Gabriel Monod, 'La méthode en histoire: synthèse', *Revue bleue*, 5th series, 9:16 (1908), 486–93, at 486: 'La critique historique et les sciences auxiliaires qui s'y rattachent offrent ceci de satisfaisant à ceux qui s'y livrent qu'elles peuvent opérer par des procédés vraiment scientifiques et arriver à des résultats positifs et certains.'
9 Ibid., 492: 'L'historien n'aura accompli que la moitié de sa tâche s'il a seulement réuni et classé les matériaux dont la réalité historique a été faite. Pour faire comprendre cette réalité, il faut qu'il lui donne la vie... L'historien, après avoir étudié le passé en savant, doit pour le faire comprendre et le décrire, faire un effort de création personnelle et ajouter l'art à la science. Il le recrée en quelque mesure en lui-même. La science décompose les éléments de la vie. L'art seul la recrée.'
10 Jules Michelet, 'Préface à l'*Histoire de France*', in *Oeuvres complètes*, ed. Paul Viallaneix, vol. 4 (Paris: Flammarion, 1974), pp 11–27, at p. 12. On Monod and Michelet, see my

thesis: 'La survivance de Michelet: historiographie et politique en France depuis 1870' (PhD dissertation, University of Amsterdam, 2016).
11 Gabriel Monod, 'Michelet, de 1843 à 1852: leçon d'ouverture du cours d'histoire générale et de méthode historique au Collège de France (10 décembre 1908)', *Revue de synthèse historique*, 17 (1908), 261–72.
12 Gabriel Monod, 'Bulletin historique', *Revue historique*, 72 (1901), 375.
13 Monod, 'La méthode en histoire: synthèse', 487: 'On conçoit quelles précautions exige cette double opération... et la large part qui y est laissée... aux qualités subjectives de force de pensée et d'imagination.'
14 Among the numerous biographical studies of Febvre, Bertrand Müller, *Lucien Febvre: Lecteur et critique* (Paris: Albin Michel, 2003) is most prominent.
15 Laurent Mucchielli, 'Aux origines de la Nouvelle histoire', in Mucchielli, *Mythes et histoire des sciences humaines* (Paris: La découverte, 2004), pp 93–128.
16 Burguière, *Ecole des Annales*, pp 10–13.
17 Michelet, 'Préface à l'*Histoire de France*', p. 13.
18 Enrico Castelli Gattinara, *Les Inquiétudes de la raison: Epistémologie et histoire en France dans l'entre-deux-guerres* (Paris: Editions de l'EHESS, 1998).
19 Lucien Febvre, 'Propos d'initiation: vivre l'histoire', *Mélanges d'histoire sociale* [war-time title of the *Annales*], 3 (1943), 5–18, at 8: '[C]e que tentait Michelet, avec son autorité et l'ardeur de sa parole et le rayonnement de son génie – c'est bien cependant, toutes proportions gardées, ce que je voudrais tenter avec vous... : vous donner le sentiment qu'on peut vivre sa vie en étant historien.' The text is reprinted in: Febvre, *Vivre l'histoire*, pp 21–35.
20 Ibid., p. 8: '"Scientifiquement conduite", la formule implique deux opérations, celles-là mêmes qui se trouvent à la base de tout travail scientifique moderne: poser des problèmes et formuler des hypothèses.'
21 Lucien Febvre, *Michelet et la Renaissance*, ed. Fernand Braudel and Paule Braudel (Paris: Flammarion, 1992), p. 110: 'La synthèse de l'historien... ne peut s'opérer qu'au dedans de lui. Elle met en présence les uns des autres des éléments morts, du passé qui fut du présent vivant et qui a cessé de vivre, le problème étant de reconstituer la vie telle qu'elle fut quand ces éléments n'étaient pas morts mais vivants. Il s'agit donc d'une synthèse du chimiste, mais dans la pensée de l'opérateur, dans la pensée de l'historien. Et la cornue ici, c'est, faut-il dire le coeur, ou l'esprit ou l'âme de l'historien? Disons sa personnalité.'
22 Ibid., p. 115.
23 Of Febvre's numerous attacks on Seignobos, the most notorious is 'Entre l'histoire à thèse et l'histoire manuel: deux esquisses récentes d'histoire de France: M. Benda, M. Seignobos', *Revue de synthèse*, 5:3 (1933), 205–36, reprinted in an attenuated form in Febvre, *Vivre l'histoire*, pp 71–88.
24 Marc Bloch, *Apologie pour l'histoire, ou: Métier d'historien* (Paris: Armand Colin, 1949), p. 109; Bloch to Febvre, 22 June 1938, in Marc Bloch and Lucien Febvre, *Correspondance*, ed. Bertrand Müller, vol. 3 (Paris: Fayard, 2003), p. 26.
25 Gabriel Monod, 'Bulletin historique', *Revue historique*, 23:2 (1898), 129–34; Gabriel Monod, 'Bulletin historique', *Revue historique*, 26:3 (1901), 880.
26 Christophe Charle, 'Charles Seignobos, historien pacifiste et européen: les aspects méconnus d'un professeur à la Sorbonne', *Revue de la BNF*, 32:2 (2009), 18–29.
27 Charles Seignobos, *La réorganisation de la France: Conférences faites a l'Ecole des hautes études sociales, novembre 1915 à janvier 1916* (Paris: Alcan, 1917).
28 Charles Seignobos, *Etudes de politique et d'histoire*, ed. Joseph Letaconnoux (Paris: Presses universitaires de France, 1934).
29 Christophe Charle, 'L'historien entre science et politique: Charles Seignobos', in Charle, *Paris fin de siècle: Culture et politique* (Paris: Seuil, 1998), pp 125–52, at p. 146.
30 Charles Seignobos, 'L'enseignement de l'histoire comme instrument d'éducation politique [1907]', in Seignobos, *Etudes de politique et d'histoire*, pp 109–32, at p. 110: 'non à une partie seulement des élèves, mais à toute la nation. Ce qui est utile à tous les élèves,

c'est de comprendre le monde où ils vont vivre, de s'y intéresser et d'être prêts à y agir.'
31 Ibid., p. 132: 'Puisque l'histoire est le véritable enseignement civique, c'est sur les professeurs d'histoire que retombe la mission de faire l'instruction politique des futurs citoyens.'
32 Here I follow the interpretation of Antoine Prost, 'Charles Seignobos revisité', *Vingtième siècle. Revue d'histoire*, 43 (1994), 100–18.
33 Charles Seignobos, *Histoire sincère de la nation française: Essai d'une histoire de l'évolution du peuple français* (Paris: Rieder, 1933).
34 For example: Vincent Duclert, *L'avenir de l'histoire* (Paris: Armand Colin, 2010).
35 Marc Bloch, *L'étrange défaite: Témoignage écrit en 1940* (Paris: Editions Franc-Tireur, 1946), p. 22: 'Ce sont ces mêmes habitudes de critique, d'observation et, j'espère, d'honnêteté.' There are several subsequent editions and it has been republished in Marc Bloch, *L'histoire, la guerre et la résistance* (Paris: Gallimard, 2006).
36 Marc Bloch, *The Historian's Craft*, trans. Peter Putnam (Manchester: Manchester University Press, 1954), p. 10. Original: Bloch, *Apologie pour l'histoire*, p. 9: 'Il n'est point niable, pourtant, qu'une science nous paraîtra toujours avoir quelque chose d'incomplet si elle ne doit pas, tôt ou tard, nous aider à mieux vivre.' The book is also republished in Bloch, *L'Histoire, la guerre et la résistance*.
37 Bloch, *The Historian's Craft*, p. 26. Original: Bloch, *Apologie pour l'histoire*, p. 4: 'Le bon historien, lui, ressemble à l'ogre de la légende. Là où il flaire la chair humaine, il sait que là est son gibier.'
38 Bloch, *The Historian's Craft*, p. 9.
39 Bloch to Febvre, 24 August 1934, in Bloch and Febvre, *Correspondance*, vol. 2, p. 148.
40 Bloch, *Apologie pour l'histoire*, p. xv.
41 Ulrich Raulff, *Ein Historiker im 20. Jahrhundert: Marc Bloch* (Frankfurt am Main: S. Fischer, 1995), pp 181–204.
42 Marc Bloch, 'Une introduction à la recherche historique', *Annales d'histoire économique et sociale*, 8:37 (1936), 51–2; Bloch to Febvre, 3 December 1935 and subsequent letters until 13 December, in Bloch and Febvre, *Correspondance*, vol. 2, pp 343–51; Bloch, *Apologie pour l'histoire*, pp 17 and 41.
43 Barbara Shapiro, *A Culture of Fact: England, 1550–1720* (Ithaca, NY: Cornell University Press, 2003), pp 34–62.
44 Febvre to Bloch, dated by Bertrand Müller 8 December 1935, but more probably to be dated between 9 and 13 December, in Bloch and Febvre, *Correspondance*, vol. 2, pp 347–8.
45 Lorraine Daston and H. Otto Sibum, 'Introduction: scientific personae and their histories', *Science in Context*, 16 (2003), 1–8.
46 Herman Paul, 'What is a scholarly persona? Ten theses on virtues, skills, and desires', *History and Theory*, 53 (2014), 348–71. For an insightful discussion of the different levels at which the concept can be applied: Gadi Algazi, '*Exemplum* and *Wundertier*: three concepts of the scholarly persona', *Low Countries Historical Review*, 131:4 (2016), 8–32.
47 Herman Paul, 'The virtues of a good historian in early Imperial Germany: Georg Waitz's contested example', *Modern Intellectual History*, 15 (2018), 681–709.

CHAPTER 5

Pasha and his historic harem: Edward A. Freeman, Edith Thompson and the gendered personae of late-Victorian historians

Elise Garritzen

Introduction

When in 1869 Edith Thompson (1848–1929) published her first review-essay in history, Edward Freeman (1823–92) concluded that she was now 'part of "we"'.[1] The 'we' were the historians who pledged in the name of detachment and inductive presentation of facts, and cultivated the virtues, skills and habits that comprised the idealized persona of a professional historian. Persona in this sense is, as Gadi Algazi defines it, a set of regulative ideals of what it takes to be a philosopher, scholar or, in this case, a historian. Persona embodies constellations of virtues and dispositions which are considered necessary for history writing at a specific historical moment. Personae serve various purposes that define the desired constellations.[2] For the self-proclaimed professional historians this goal was to erect a boundary between themselves and the amateurish history writing in Victorian Britain. Freeman was one of the best-known representatives of the emerging professional community. He was the author of the *History of the Norman Conquest of England* and the Regius Professor of Modern History at Oxford from 1884 onwards.[3] Notwithstanding his lofty words, as a woman Thompson was not eligible for full membership of this group, where men set the standards for a proper historian. Just as gender was an essential organizing concept in Victorian society, it was implicit in the personae historians promoted. Nevertheless, gender remains largely unaddressed in the context of historians' scholarly personae despite the growing interest the question of personae has generated recently.[4] This chapter addresses the gap by taking Freeman and Thompson as examples and exploring how gendered personae were constructed and maintained, how the gendered assumptions shaped research and how women adjusted to and possibly challenged the restrictions placed on them.

Approaching Victorian historiography in terms of public, professional men and domestic, amateur women would be too simplistic. The situation was messier than this, as Bremner and Conlin have emphasized.[5] 'Persona' as an analytical concept can help in mapping out the complex nature of Victorian history writing. Indeed, the distinctions between scientific and non-scientific narrative history were anything but sharp. Even the term 'historian' resists clear definition because history writing comprised actors ranging from antiquarians, biographers and genealogists to amateurs and professionals. History was written in different registers and published in various formats. For the contemporaries, the labels were evident and each category placed distinct demands on personae.[6] Furthermore, the gender line was less defined than the traditional historiographical narratives propose: men and women did not write history in entirely separate spheres.[7] Nor was the gendered persona only about women, but about men as well; it served diverse purposes from maintaining the gendered social order to defining the types of manliness historians emulated.[8] When John Doran ventured to write a history of eminent women, a topic oozing femininity, Freeman accused him of inaccuracy, carelessness and lack of self-restraint, all traits associated with female historians.[9] There were certain similarities in the personae men and women cultivated. Accuracy, precision, diligence and honesty were scholarly virtues that crossed the gender line. Nevertheless, it would be naive to suggest a gender equality among nineteenth-century historians: the professionals were steeped in the masculine culture that prevailed in the universities and scholarly networks. It is not a coincidence that Dean Church complemented Freeman for the *manly* style of his *Norman Conquest*.[10] The personae were rooted in sociocultural forces such as gender, class and ethnicity.[11]

Gender was biological fact for the Victorians and could not be learned, cultivated or regulated like skills, virtues and vices. Consequently, gender limited the selection of personae historians could adopt. Freeman did not entirely dismiss women as historians, but structured a hierarchical division of tasks. He expected men to conduct original research and produce new knowledge. Women had more modest, yet important, positions on the outskirts of the professional community. They assisted men in scholarly pursuits, just as Freeman's wife and daughters did when they composed indexes to his books, proofread his sheets or corrected and collated his citations.[12] Moreover, Freeman considered women perfect for summarizing the studies men had produced. As an editor to the series 'Historic Course for Schools' he appointed Thompson and two other women to contribute to it, prompting John Richard Green to grant him the title 'Pasha of History' surrounded by his 'historic harem'.[13] Yet he did not seem to have encouraged women to conduct original research. The submission to men's interpretations and the lack of independence set the frame for women's historical pursuits – and for their persona. This reproduced the idea of active and independent men and nurturing, accommodating and compliant women. Edith Thompson and her *History of England* ticked all the boxes, making her a perfect fit for Freeman's gendered division of tasks.

Edith Thompson has not attracted much attention in the conventional historiographical accounts, which tend to prioritize men's historical pursuits. We owe it largely to Amanda Capern and Leslie Howsam that her name has surfaced in historiographical research at all. What we know of Thompson is that she was a daughter of a London judge and received education at home. She came to know Freeman through his daughters.[14] The first letter from Freeman to Thompson is dated in 1868; in it he sent her the second volume of his *Norman Conquest* as a token of his gratitude for her help and the many 'pleasing' conversations they had had about history. This was the beginning both of a long friendship and of Thompson's career in history.[15] As so often was the case with Victorian women historians, her work was enabled by the support of an eminent man.[16] This did not lessen the meaning historical pursuits had for her: they provided her social networks and an intellectual purpose for life. In addition to the *History of England* (1874) which she wrote for the series Freeman edited, Thompson contributed to the *Saturday Review* and succeeded Freeman as one of the journal's main reviewers of history books. In this role, she became familiar with the latest currents of historical research. She also supplied altogether 15,000 entries to the *Oxford English Dictionary*, edited a collection of original documents about 'the Wars of York and Lancaster' (1892) and contributed to the biographical dictionary Leslie Stephen was composing.[17] She thus produced many types of historical text – except what could be called a scientific monograph.

It is significant that Freeman did not automatically expel Thompson or other women from his scholarly networks. Thompson occupied a position that was both attached to and separate from the professional establishment and her actions contributed to the reputation of this community. The question of reputation surfaced continuously in Freeman's correspondence, suggesting that a positive reputation was considered crucial for the credibility of an individual historian and the learned community. Consequently, it was paramount to conduct oneself in a manner that reproduced the virtues and values of a desired persona because public appearances were used for judging individual status and collective respectability. For this reason, Freeman guided Thompson whenever he noticed that she was taking steps that could harm either her, his own or the scholarly community's reputation. In 1870, he discovered that she had published an article in the *Graphic*, an illustrated magazine that he judged highly unsuitable for a dignified historian. He wrote to her that '[a]n illustrated paper…

is quite beneath you or any of *us*'. Assuming that Thompson would be embarrassed at having descended to the 'lower stratum' of publishing, he promised to keep the article a secret.[18] The reference to 'us' indicates the collective responsibility to uphold reputation and the curious position Thompson enjoyed on the outskirts of the professional community.

What made this management of reputation challenging was that reputation required cultural recognition beyond the scholarly community. While persona was something that historians constructed and performed, reputation was granted by the public. As Geoffrey Cubitt maintains, audiences participate in crafting public images by assessing texts, biographies and authors' public appearances to ascribe to them a reputation.[19] Gaining and maintaining a desired reputation can therefore be challenging because the presumed ideas that are woven into the texture of public imagination do not necessarily correspond with the self-image scholars cherish.[20] The caution Freeman invested in the curation of his public appearances suggests that he was nevertheless convinced that historians could influence their reputation. He emphasized how it was vital to pay attention to the impressions historians made on the 'public'. He also kept close track of what was written about him.[21] In order to establish epistemic authority and to gain scholarly reputation it was necessary to publicly articulate professionalism in publications, research practices and conduct. Freeman's fear of inappropriate reputation was one of the major factors that would influence the process of publishing Thompson's *History of England*.

Historians in many guises

It was taken more or less for granted that women could not become professional historians. The question, then, was whether women were eligible to write popular histories, as they had done earlier, because the nascent professional community began to claim a stake in popular publishing and to establish new standards for it. Their attempt to instal themselves as authorities both in scholarly and popular histories is one indication of this era as a transitional period in British historiography. As Stefan Collini has suggested, literary men were positioned between two cultures: they were no longer men of letters, yet they were not representatives of distinct disciplines either, as they were to be around 1900 when 'intellectual distinction was becoming increasingly a matter of "scholarship", and scholarship was becoming increasingly an academic activity'.[22] Because of this fluidity, the boundaries were permeable and a professional could shift from the role of an academic to that of a populariser.

According to Ian Hesketh, once a historian had proven his scholarly skills by publishing a scientific monograph, he was free to produce popular histories as long as he remained faithful to the methodological and epistemological notions of the discipline.[23] Freeman, who embraced this principle wholeheartedly, maintained in his *Old English History for Children* how his object was 'to show that clear, accurate, and scientific views of history... may be easily given to children'.[24] Even the primers should not have been marred by insufficient methodological and intellectual vigour. In practical terms, a properly produced popular history rested on detachment, utilized the latest research on the topic, pledged itself to minute accuracy and avoided picturesqueness. There was no going back to the old, sloppy ways of writing popular history, J. R. Green, the champion of popularizing, assured his readers.[25] Professionals, thus, did not reject popular histories as such, but as part of their boundary work they scorned the vulgar populariser who failed to meet their high standards.

The interest that the professionals showed in popularizing history derived, first, from the realization that multi-volume scientific studies attracted only a limited academic readership. To spread the results of their research – and their scholarly and cultural authority – they had to compress their scholarly works into a more digestible form.[26] Second, there were the financial realities. The scholarly volumes rarely brought profits whereas the steadily selling textbooks promised a more reliable income. The demand for popular histories grew during the second half of the century as increasing literacy and reducing production costs expanded the market for inexpensive popular histories.[27] As the number of university positions remained low, even the professionals often earned a living by publishing anything from book reviews to essays and histories. The economic stress was accentuated by the fact that financial independence and the ability to maintain a household were essential proofs of masculine respectability. Freeman's constant preoccupation with publishing contracts and sales figures is just one example of the economic strains historians faced. '[A]s a father of a family' he could not afford not to ask questions about profits, royalties and the terms that the publishers offered to him.[28] There were then many reasons why professionals were keen to participate in popularizing history and by setting methodological standards for such books they rendered popularizing a respectable pursuit for an educated middle-class man.

Erecting a normative boundary between proper and improper popular history had some implications for women because some began to question their ability to master the new requirements.[29] When James Bryce heard that Freeman had recruited female authors, he claimed that 'these little things [textbooks] must be done by big people – they are the most difficult things of all to do, and that till big people can find time to do them they had better wait'.[30] Women obviously did not count as 'big people' for Bryce. Even so, many admitted that some tasks were suitable for women as long as they adhered to the new standards. Freeman insisted that those feminine 'creatures' who uncritically repeated silly, unhistorical stories were not welcome to write history.[31] Freeman was not the only man who enlisted women to write primers and textbooks. Mandell Creighton employed women to contribute to the series 'Historical Biographies' that he edited.

The late-Victorian era was a transitional period for women as well, as they gradually moved away from the flourishing mid-Victorian tradition of authoring short biographies of eminent women, a tradition that Freeman had labelled in 1855 'the greatest possible hindrance to historical knowledge', ridiculing the flippancy and prejudices that reigned in these pretty little volumes. Although women's presence in the lecture halls in Oxford and Cambridge increased, they were still considered amateurs during this period.[32] Not everyone, though, settled for popularizing. As women tried to navigate between social, cultural and scholarly limitations in modernizing Britain, some ignored the restrictions and began to conduct independent historical research. In Freeman's circles, we can identify at least two such women. Alice Stopford Green (1847–1929) formulated a revisionist interpretation about the history of Ireland and assumed a political role, using history for ideological causes. Kate Norgate (1853–1929) made a praised contribution to the study of early English history. Because as independent women they did not behave according to the socially prescribed conventions, Freeman struggled to get along with them.[33] I come back to Norgate later on because she helps to further illustrate why Freeman considered Thompson to represent the perfect type of a woman historian.

Freeman, the masculine historian

The constellations of virtues were given gendered meanings. Freeman's biographer W. R. W. Stephens asserted in 1895 that 'intellectual gifts' and 'certain moral qualities' made Freeman a great historian. The moral qualities included 'the virtues of *Manliness*'. According to Stephens, the masculine virtues Freeman fostered were endurance, perseverance, restraint in 'vexations and pleasures' and, most importantly, an independence of mind and the 'moral courage' to defend one's own views.[34] To further evoke an image of a manly historian, Stephens demonstrated Freeman's ability to sustain mental and physical fatigue when visiting historical sites. Rob Boddice, however, has maintained that Freeman cherished the mid-Victorian domesticated and intellectual type of manliness, preferring the seclusion of his study to the bodily prowess of the late-Victorian masculine ideal.[35] Indeed, Freeman engaged in a fierce attack on field sports, despised those who risked their lives in mountaineering and exercised moderation when describing the obstacles he faced during his excursions.[36] Nevertheless, for Stephens, writing at a time when domestic masculinity had lost its vogue, it was vital to project an image of Freeman as a masculine adventurer who climbed mountains and rambled battlefields to explore historical sites. Freeman did not just sit in his domestic study: his excursions 'involved an amount of physical and mental labour, such as few men would be capable of undergoing'. In comparison with the standard depictions of masculinity, which overflowed with bodily trials, imperial adventures and sports, Stephens's description of a historian physically exhausted by long days of 'walking about and sketching, and taking notes of places or buildings' appear rather modest.[37]

The masculine ideology underpinned the virtue discourse. The virtues that Stephens considered manly – endurance, industry, independence, pluck and moral courage – corresponded with the virtues that were considered essential both for a masculine middle-class character and for the persona of a proper historian, and thus indispensable for intellectual pursuits.[38] When Thompson began to write the *History of England* Freeman reported how she had 'set to work manfully', judging her against the masculine standards that were perceived as 'normal'.[39] However, he did not quite believe that women could conduct research 'manfully'. He emphasized how nothing could be achieved without effort. A real historian worked not only when it was pleasant, but also when it was unpleasant. However, he considered industry and perseverance masculine qualities and cautioned Thompson not to overtax herself. Her feminine constitution was unfit for unyielding intellectual exertion and industry: he advised her to abstain from working in the evenings.[40] Freeman was also concerned about her rashness and guided her to cultivate a more disciplined self: 'I can't get rid of a notion that you are a bit desultory and do things by fits and starts', he once observed.[41] Lack of self-restraint was a vice and a feminine trait.

Independence, submissiveness and the making of Edith Thompson's *History of England*

The process of publishing Thompson's *History of England* confirms that submissiveness was considered an essential quality in a woman historian. The book was issued in Macmillan's series *Historic Course for Schools*. The aim was to replace the existing 'wretched compilations' by putting forth 'clear and correct views of history in simple language, and in the smallest compass and cheapest form possible'.[42] Freeman first recruited Thompson and then continued to fill the other vacancies, preferably with women.[43] He himself wrote the opening volume, *General Sketch of European History*, to delineate the interpretative outlines of the series. Green was amused by the plan and began to talk about Freeman's 'historic harem'.[44]

Indeed, the plan was extraordinary. Publishers preferred experienced editors and authors for their textbook series. First, a well-known author would lend authority to an educational book, increasing its marketability. Second, as Alexander Macmillan explained, part of his publishing 'mission' was didactic: it was 'a great boon to the public' to offer them 'perfect knowledge' and therefore he wished to enlist distinguished scholars instead of 'writers who are popular in the worst sense of the term'.[45] Since Freeman chose a different path, the reputation of the series was to rest on him alone. His name vouched for the quality of each volume and each volume contributed to his reputation. Accordingly, he demanded that authors subscribe to his historiographical views.

Since Freeman was so concerned about his reputation it is necessary to ask why he preferred inexperienced female authors. Ian Hesketh has speculated that Freeman recruited 'she-bodies' because their gender rendered them ideal for the task. Women were often employed as populisers of science for children because it was believed that their nurturing maternal nature helped them to address young readers.[46] In Freeman's case, this is not confirmed or disproved by the sources. A more likely explanation, however, is that he was seeking contributors whom he could control.[47] He needed compliant assistants, not independent authors who would threaten his reputation with unorthodox interpretations or narrative choices. In reality, however, the authors occasionally produced 'stuff' that he was 'thoroughly ashamed' of and that he feared might contaminate his reputable name.[48]

Freeman's reasoning became evident when he failed to find enough women for his project and had to rely on men to complete the series. As a second-best choice, he recruited young men who had not yet established themselves as authorities in history. Macmillan proposed some recognized names, but Freeman refused them by appealing to his responsibility for the content and quality of each volume. Consequently, the contributors had to be willing to 'knock under' him. This he could not ask from any established male historian because 'If he differs from me on any point, he has as good a right to his opinion as he has to mine'.[49] Freeman was confident that women – or fresh young men – would willingly submit to his views and he was pleased to see how well Thompson internalized his ideas. In the preface that he wrote for her book, he affirmed how the author took 'for granted the views and divisions laid down in my *General Sketch of European History*'.⁵⁰

It is obvious, then, that Freeman expected women to be submissive, but as independence was an important scholarly and promotional virtue in history books, Freeman emphasized in the same preface how Thompson's book was 'strictly the work of its author'. He explained that he had given it only enough supervision 'to secure its general accuracy'. The 'details of the narrative, both as to their choice and their treatment' were Thompson's responsibility because in those points he had not 'thought it right to go beyond suggestion'.⁵¹ This was a rather bold statement from someone who knew the book's publishing history. In fact, the content was shaped by Freeman and the text edited by Green.

As an editor, Freeman reminded Thompson how picking holes in her text was his duty.⁵² Her duty was to make the corrections without objections. Freeman was astonished when she disagreed with some of the requested revisions. She, for example, held fast to her positive depiction of Albert, Prince Consort. When Freeman demanded modifications, she refused to delete the attributes she had assigned to Albert. This brought her into conflict with Freeman whose offensive outburst impelled her to seek advice from Alexander Macmillan. She was convinced that there was nothing incorrect in that specific paragraph. Macmillan agreed with her and considered Freeman simply wicked. The publisher, adopting a paternal role, set to protect the 'dear good girl' whom he judged to be 'accurate as to facts' and 'innocent' in her opinions. He told Freeman that he had gone too far with his obsession about his historical views. To Thompson Macmillan replied that if the contested sentences '*accidentally*' slipped into the final proofs, he was 'willing to take the blame'.⁵³

This, however, did not happen. Eventually it was Thompson who had to give in. This was made clear to her by George Craik, one of Macmillan's editorial staff. Craik admitted that Thompson's original version was more appealing than the one Freeman suggested, yet it was wise to edit the section according to Freeman's instructions. From a publisher's point of view this was vital: Freeman's authority was 'of great consequence' and the publisher was 'glad of his assistance & the help of his name'.⁵⁴ Unknown authors, let alone an unknown woman, had a great disadvantage in the competitive book market. Freeman's name was calculated to assure success and therefore the priority was to keep Freeman content.

As a young woman Thompson had few means to resist Freeman or the publisher, but she never accepted the changes she had been forced to make to the contested paragraph. When she was given the opportunity to revise the book in 1900, when Freeman was no longer alive, she did not hesitate to rewrite the 'stiff' passage. She recalled how Freeman had had 'strong feelings' about it and had objected it as 'Albert-worship'.[55] This rather strong wording deviates from the respectful tone she usually adopted when talking about Freeman and betrays her resentment of his editorial authority in the matter. As she was no longer obliged to follow Freeman's orders, she removed the first edition's paragraph, which stated nothing but the facts about Victoria's enthronement, marriage and Albert's death. She expanded the section depicting Victoria and Albert in much more empathetic fashion than what Freeman had ordered her to write.[56]

While Freeman influenced the content of Thompson's book, Green adjusted the manuscript into a textbook format. It was too long for its purpose and Macmillan assigned Green to help Thompson to shorten it by at least 250 pages.[57] To Freeman's annoyance, Green found the manuscript 'a capital piece of work done by any clever woman, and as dull as an old almanac!'[58] Freeman's and Green's disagreement about style is well known.[59] Freeman privileged in textbooks the same exactness and pedantry that he expected of scientific histories. This kind of 'dry rattle of names and dates', Green claimed, 'set boys against history'. For the purposes of this article, these rival stylistic notions are less important than the fact that Green cast the entire blame for Thompson's 'unreadable' manuscript on Freeman and his overbearing editorial authority. Green even wondered whether Freeman had forbidden his 'harem' to mention 'the Beautiful and Interesting' – the stories and anecdotes which Green appreciated in popular histories – and claimed how 'a clever girl like this [Thompson] would do better if you left her a bit alone'.[60]

According to Macmillan, an editor was in charge for 'the general *plan & scale*'. Publishing history was indeed a collaborative venture, as Leslie Howsam has highlighted. It involved authors, editors, publishers and readers.[61] Nonetheless, Green correctly maintained that Freeman took his editorial responsibility too far, turning his 'harem' into mere secretaries who reproduced his historical notions. Freeman was so convinced of his own opinions and so concerned about his reputation that he demanded the authors repeat his historical thinking and narrative preferences. He preferred, therefore, obedient women, often represented as innocent young girls, whom he could patronize.

Thompson's *History of England* was complimented for its accuracy and taken into use in schools in Britain and North America. It went through a number of reprints and revisions. The teacher–student relationship of Thompson and Freeman altered when she became a published historian. Gradually she became Freeman's confidante. He no longer gave her instructions on how to be a historian. Instead, he appreciated her observations about historical scholarship and shared with other historians the ideas that their discussions had provoked.⁶² Yet he did not encourage her to conduct original research. He made only cursory suggestions in this direction, appealing to Thompson to contribute to the *English Historical Review* because 'she should certainly help *us*', the professional historians, to cement the scholarly character of the recently founded professional journal.⁶³ Thompson responded to this with ten book reviews, altogether, but she never submitted a research article to the *Review*. Freeman, too, let drop the subject of Thompson writing scholarly articles. It did not quite seem to occur to him that Thompson, who conversed with him in private about old-English manuscripts and historical details, could have appeared in public as an independent scholar.

Thompson, Freeman and the virtue of loyalty

Loyalty was a core scholarly virtue and had gendered connotations. In Thompson's case, loyalty took at least two distinct meanings. First, it was a form of feminine emotional care and companionship. Second, it was about faithfulness to specific historical ideas. In the first case, we need to shift attention from Thompson to Kate Norgate, to understand how loyalty was translated into care and how this made Thompson the type of a feminine historian that Freeman preferred. At the heart of the matter was that Norgate adopted the persona of an overtly serious historian, a manifestly masculine disposition. Her unconventional conduct confused and annoyed Freeman. Giving such importance to forms of conduct illustrates how personae also included qualities that were not directly linked to epistemology and research practices, yet were judged essential for consolidating a persona.

Kate Norgate, the daughter of a London bookseller, had been a protégée of Green.⁶⁴ After his death in 1883, she received some help from Freeman 'for the sake of his friend [Green]', as she formulated this in the preface to her first study, *England under the Angevin Kings* (1887).⁶⁵ The book was welcomed approvingly by the scholarly community. The *Edinburgh Review* complemented her 'exact and conscientious examination' of sources and 'the soundest sobriety of judgment'. Even more importantly, the reviewer congratulated her for avoiding the vices of her mentors: she had resisted the 'pictorial effects' of Green and refrained from 'loading her pages with matter which… is only too likely to clog or weary the reader', as Freeman tended to do.⁶⁶ An obituary in *The Times* in 1935 gave a less favourable image of her as a historian: she represented 'the pre-academic period' of women historians. She was reduced to someone whose 'generalizations do not always carry conviction' and whose merits rested mostly on her ability to 'tell a tale admirably'.[67] In the 1930s, Norgate appeared an antiquated historian, though one who could not be entirely ignored by a leading newspaper either.

For Freeman, Norgate was an 'intellectual daughter' of Green and he did not refer to the assistance he gave to her. He nevertheless applauded her book in the *English Historical Review*, declaring how '[t]he addition of a new member to the company of those who are reading and writing history in the right way is indeed a thing to be glad at'. Indeed, her book was 'empathetically scholarly' and she had earned a 'place among genuine historical scholars'. Nonetheless, he recognized a gendered weakness in the book. 'It is manifest,' he wrote, that there were 'some things' in history that 'an old man can deal with less shrinking than a young woman'. Occasionally, out of feminine discretion, Norgate had avoided the necessary 'plainness of speech', but this moderation was the only sign 'of anything that can be called feminine weakness' in the book.[68]

Supposed feminine inability to manage indecent sources was not, however, what most troubled Freeman. The problem was that Norgate was markedly serious and socially restrained. This was not becoming in a woman. To add weight to this observation, Freeman mentioned that other men similarly recognized her social awkwardness; in other words, her failure to act according to her gender. Norgate was 'just the opposite' of the chatty and social Thompson, whose company Freeman truly enjoyed. He returned to the topic several times and planned to introduce the two women so that Thompson could teach Norgate to talk.[69]

Compassion, care and sociability were virtues that domesticated middle-class women were expected to cultivate and Freeman anticipated them also from women historians. He had been disappointed when he had discovered Thompson gaining seriousness while she was writing the *History of England*. He had met her in London expecting animated company. Instead, he had been confronted with a list of questions about historical research. He was relieved that Thompson did not repeat this another time: the serious 'woman of business', the type that Norgate represented, was far from the ideal Freeman cherished. He longed for those meetings with Thompson which he described as '[b]almy, and soft, and soothing to the mind'. After the 'merry days' of her visits, his days were 'dull'.[70] Time and again he yearned to meet her and his pleas were underpinned by emotional apprehensions as he anticipated calming support, care and nurture as only his loyal Edith Thompson could provide. She was the one he could count on while the 'carl bodies' cast him aside as soon as they made it on their own.[71]

Loyalty as a form of care and sociability was underpinned with gendered expectations. The second type of loyalty, allegiance to Freeman's historical views, was less obviously gendered yet troubled Thompson repeatedly after his death in 1892. She continued to revere him as her 'honoured friend and teacher' and defended him when his scholarly integrity was questioned.[72] Nonetheless, she deviated from some of his interpretations and narrative demands, such as the paragraph about Victoria and Albert, when she edited her book two more times. Gaining independence in matters that concerned her book, however, was undermined by her limited ability to negotiate with the publisher.

Thompson acknowledged that it was historians' duty to maintain accuracy and the up-to-date quality of their publications. Even so, her allegiance to Freeman forced her to ask how extensively she could alter the text. This tested both her loyalty to him and her honesty towards her readers. The paratexts in the *History of England* identified Freeman as the editor and Thompson feared that readers might assume that the alterations had his approval.[73] Honesty and transparency towards readers were essential virtues and their violation could have hurt the sales and damaged a reputation. Thompson, grasping the importance of a sound reputation, was therefore extremely cautious about the sincerity of her paratextual promises.[74] She refused to call the 1901 edition '*new* or *revised*' because the revisions were not sufficient enough to 'justify those expressions'.[75] As a solution to her problem, she proposed to Macmillan paratextual modifications to give less prominence to Freeman's editorial role. Macmillan refused this because Freeman's name still had commercial appeal. The half-title page continued to introduce him as the editor and the reprinted preface from the original edition further enhanced his editorial presence.[76]

Thompson faced even a greater dilemma when she edited her book for the last time between 1916 and 1923. Macmillan charged her to write an additional chapter that brought the narrative up to the present day. Thompson, however, wanted also to revise the section in which she discussed the 'Aryan *race* theory' that Freeman had advocated zealously. World War I had prompted her to reassess the theory. 'Events have proved that, if we are Teutonic, our Teutonism is very different from that of the Germans', she concluded. She doubted again 'how far I am at liberty to modify the... views of my dear master', but she was nonetheless convinced about the urgency of the modifications. She pledged loyalty to Freeman's theory immediately, on the first page, and wanted therefore to rewrite the opening paragraph.[77] She needed the publisher's approval for that. In spite of her arguments about the outdatedness of the theory, Frederick Macmillan refused to grant her permission for the revisions. The intention was to sell off the remaining stock by adding an entirely new chapter to the existing unbound text.[78] Any other modifications would have required casting some of the type anew, increasing the production costs significantly. The publisher was unwilling to do this.

Thompson was frustrated that her book continued to praise 'the great *Aryan* family of mankind'.[79] As the author of a textbook history, as an ageing woman and as someone who had entered the publishing world in an era when the author–publisher relationship had rested on mutual friendship, she had few means to negotiate with her publishers in an age when publishing had become modern business. The skills and knowledge about publishing she had learned from Freeman were no longer applicable. Her sadness was intensified by the realization that her *History*, too, appeared uncomfortably antiquated in the Britain of the 1920s. With decided melancholy she remarked on the low sales and feared that her *History* 'may not be pacifist or socialist enough for the present authorities'.[80]

Scholarly personae, gender and Victorian historians

Historical research in Victorian Britain was defined by overlapping, parallel and even rivalling modes of studying the past. As this chapter has suggested, the boundaries between various practices and styles were fluid. Freeman articulated himself as a professional, yet mastered different styles and formats of history writing; women were not treated as professionals, yet Kate Norgate was complimented for her scholarly talent. Categories such as 'amateur' and 'professional' are therefore too generic to describe the richness of late-Victorian historiographical practices. The concept of personae is well suited for framing this plurality of approaches. As Herman Paul has illustrated in the case of German academic history, by focusing on personae as schematic models of virtues, skills and dispositions we can draw imaginary maps of different positions historians held and identify how these positions were related to each other.[81] Adopting such an approach can make a significant contribution to a more nuanced understanding of how history was written in Victorian Britain.

Furthermore, this chapter has illustrated how virtue discourse, research practices and scholarly conduct were given gendered meanings and how the gendered personae were open for multiple interpretations and redefinitions on a case-by-case basis. The personae were constantly renegotiated because the presence of women such as Thompson at the borders of the professional community challenged the limits gender imposed on personae, on their public display and on the reputation of the scholarly community. While gender informed and restricted the personae historians emulated, it was also a constitutive factor in Victorian society, defining middle-class identities. Because the dyad feminine/masculine structured historians' world views on many different levels, it is necessary to further probe the problems represented by the bond between gender and scholarly personae. There are promising examples of linking historians' scholarly personae to broader cultural factors, for instance in the context of political and religious sensibilities, but with few exceptions the gendered aspects of historians' personae have attracted less attention.[82] Yet in order to better understand scholarly personae, we also have to explore the historians' entangled scholarly, social and cultural positions.

Notes

I would like to thank Leslie Howsam, Markku Peltonen, Josephine Hoegaerts and the members of the research seminar in intellectual history at the University of Helsinki for their comments and suggestions. Funding was provided by the University of Helsinki and the Jenny and Antti Wihuri Foundation.

1 Hull History Centre, Hull (hereafter HHC), U DX/9/13, Freeman to Thompson, 12 September 1869.
2 Gadi Algazi, '*Exemplum* and *Wundertier*: three concepts of the scholarly persona', *Low Countries Historical Review*, 131:4 (2016), 10–11; Lorraine Daston and H. Otto Sibum, 'Introduction: scientific personae and their histories', *Science in Context*, 16 (2003), 3–7; Herman Paul, 'What is a scholarly persona? Ten theses on virtues, skills, and desires', *History and Theory*, 53 (2014), 353–4; Ian Hesketh, *The Science of History in Victorian Britain* (London: Pickering & Chatto, 2011), p. 95.
3 On Freeman, see G. A. Bremner and Jonathan Conlin (eds), *Making History: Edward Augustus Freeman and Victorian Cultural Politics* (Oxford: Oxford University Press, 2015).
4 See, however, Falko Schnicke, *Die männliche Disziplin: Zur Vergeschlectlichung der deutschen Geschichtswissenschaft 1780–1900* (Göttingen: Wallstein Verlag, 2015); Rozemarijn van de Wal, 'Constructing the persona of a professional historian: on Eileen Power's early career persona formation and her years in Paris, 1910–1911', *Persona Studies*, 4:1 (2018), 32–44.
5 G. A. Bremner and Jonathan Conlin, '1066 and all that: E. A. Freeman and the importance of being memorable', in Bremner and Conlin (eds), *Making History*, pp 11–12; Leslie Howsam, 'Academic discipline or literary genre? The establishment of boundaries in historical writing', *Victorian Literature and Culture*, 32 (2004), 528.
6 For example J. H. Round argued that a family biographer or a professed genealogist should be criticized by 'a separate standard'. W. Raymond Powell, *John Horace Round: Historian and Gentleman of Essex* (Chelmsford: Essex Record Office, 2001), p. 71; Philippa Levine, *The Amateur and the Professional: Antiquarians, Historians and Archæologists in Victorian England, 1838–1886* (Cambridge: Cambridge University Press, 1986).
7 The title of John Kenyon's *The History Men: The Historical Profession in England since the Renaissance* (London: Weidenfeld and Nicolson, 1993) is indicative. Women's invisibility in historiographical studies has been countered by stressing how they wrote history despite their gender. Bonnie G. Smith, *The Gender of History: Men, Women, and Historical Practice* (Cambridge, MA: Harvard University Press, 2000); Julie Des Jardins, *Women and the Historical Enterprise in America: Gender, Race, and the Politics of Memory, 1880–1945* (Chapel Hill, NC: University of North Carolina Press, 2003); Maxine Berg, *A Woman in History: Eileen Power, 1889–1940* (Cambridge: Cambridge

University Press, 1996); Nadia Clare Smith, *A 'Manly Study'? Irish Women Historians, 1868–1949* (Basingstoke: Palgrave Macmillan, 2006).

8   Erika Lorraine Milam and Robert A. Nye, 'An introduction to *Scientific Masculinities*', *Osiris*, 31:1 (2015), 2–5.

9   [Edward Freeman], 'The art of history-making', *Saturday Review* (17 November 1855), 52–3.

10 John Rylands Library, Manchester (hereafter JRL), FA1/7/70, Church to Freeman, 18 September 1869; Paul R. Deslandes, *Oxbridge Men: British Masculinity and the Undergraduate Experience, 1850–1920* (Bloomington, IN: Indiana University Press, 2005), pp 1–8.

11 Nationality was considered to condition interpretative abilities. J. R. Green claimed that Ranke's understanding of English 'things' was 'inadequate and miserable' because he had not experienced the political life in England from 'his own very boyhood'. Green to Freeman, 30 September 1878, in Leslie Stephen (ed.), *Letters of John Richard Green* (London: Macmillan, 1902), p. 476.

12 W. R. W. Stephens, *The Life and Letters of Edward A. Freeman DCL, LLD*, vol. 2 (London: Macmillan, 1895), pp 50–1.

13 Green to Freeman, June 1870, in Stephen, *Letters*, p. 254.

14 Amanda L. Capern, 'Thompson, Edith', *Oxford Dictionary of National Biography* (hereafter *ODNB*), online at https://doi.org/10.1093/ref:odnb/64832; Amanda Capern, 'Anatomy of a friendship: E. A. Freeman and Edith Thompson', *Paragon Review*, 6 (1997), 25–9; Howsam, 'Academic discipline', 534–42.

15 HHC, U DX/9/1, Freeman to Thompson, 19 May 1868. The 196 letters from Freeman to Thompson attest to their closeness. Thompson's letters to Freeman have not survived.

16 Ann Mitchell, '"The busy daughters of Clio": women writers of history from 1820 to 1880', *Women's History Review*, 7:1 (1998), 113–14.

17 Capern, 'Thompson'.

18 HHC, U DX/9/21, Freeman to Thompson, 4 September 1870. The italics in all the quotations are in the originals.

19 Geoffrey Cubitt, 'Introduction: heroic reputations and exemplary lives', in Cubitt and Allen Warren (eds), *Heroic Reputations and Exemplary Lives* (Manchester: Manchester University Press, 2000), p. 3; Daston and Sibun, 'Introduction', 5; John Rodden, *The Politics of Literary Reputation: The Making and Claiming of 'St George' Orwell* (Oxford: Oxford University Press, 1989), pp 4, 51.

20 Algazi, '*Exemplum*', 19–25.

21 JRL, FA1/8/1–30, Freeman to Green, 11 February 1872; JRL, FA1/8/61–108, Freeman to Green, 22 September 1878.

22 Stefan Collini, *Public Moralists: Political Thought and Intellectual Life in Britain 1850–1930* (Oxford: Oxford University Press, 1991), pp 16–23.

23 Hesketh, *Science of History*, pp 115–19.

24 Edward A. Freeman, *Old English History for Children* (London: Macmillan, 1869), p. v.

25 Green to Freeman, 1869, in Stephen, *Letters*, p. 237; Rosemary Jann, *The Art and Science of Victorian History* (Columbus: Ohio State University Press, 1985), pp 185–8. Green (1837–83) reshuffled the conventional interpretations of English history and narrative structures when he told the tale of social history of England in his best-selling *A Short History of the English People* (London: Macmillan, 1874). Anthony Brundage, *The People's Historian: John Richard Green and the Writing of History in Victorian England* (Westport, CT: Greenwood Press, 1994), pp 1–3.

26 Rosemary Jann, 'From amateur to professional: the case of the Oxbridge historians', *Journal of British Studies*, 22:2 (1983), 137–8.

27 Leslie Howsam, *Past into Print: The Publishing of History in Britain 1850–1950* (Toronto: University of Toronto Press, 2009), p. 26.

28 British Library, London (hereafter BL), Add. MSS 55049, Freeman to Macmillan, 20

February 1870; John Tosh, *A Man's Place: Masculinity and the Middle-Class Home in Victorian England* (New Haven, CT: Yale University Press, 1999), p. 3.
29 Frederick York Powell was known for his contempt for 'the plain female historians'. Oliver Elton, *Frederick York Powell: A Life and a Selection from his Letters and Occasional Writings*, vol. 1 (Oxford: Clarendon Press, 1906), p. 300.
30 Bryce's words were delivered to Freeman by Green, 27 June 1871; in Stephen, *Letters*, p. 305.
31 BL, Add. MSS 55053, Freeman to George Macmillan, undated [1889].
32 [Freeman], 'Art of history-making', 52; Rohan Amanda Maitzen, *Gender, Genre, and Victorian Historical Writing* (New York: Garland, 1998); Mitchell, 'Busy daughters', 107–9; Deslandes, *Oxbridge Men*, p. 185.
33 HHC, U DX/9/159, Freeman to Thompson, 6 April 1888; Elise Garritzen, 'Framing and re-framing meanings in history books: the original and posthumous paratexts in J. R. Green's *Short History of the English People*', *History of Humanities*, 3:1 (2018), 177–97; F. M. Powicke and P. Millican, 'Norgate, Kate', *ODNB*, online at https://doi.org/10.1093/ref.odnb/35248.
34 Stephens, *Life and Letters*, vol. 2, pp 462–4.
35 Rob Boddice, 'Manliness and the "morality of field sports": E. A. Freeman and Anthony Trollope, 1869–71', *The Historian*, 70:1 (2008), 25.
36 Stephens, *Life and Letters*, vol. 1, pp 293, 357–74; William M. Aird, '"Seeing things with our own eyes": E. A. Freeman's historical travels', in Bremner and Conlin (eds), *Making History*, p. 94; Edward A. Freeman, *Sketches from the Subject and Neighbouring Lands of Venice* (London: Macmillan, 1881), pp 24–6.
37 Stephens, *Life and Letters*, vol. 1, p. 293; Tosh, *A Man's Place*, pp 174–5.
38 Mike Huggins, *Vice and the Victorians* (London: Bloomsbury, 2016), pp 173–82; Collini, *Public Moralists*, pp 91–117, 186.
39 BL, Add. MSS 55049, Freeman to Macmillan, 4 December 1870.
40 HHC, U DX/9/6, Freeman to Thompson, 10 June 1869; HHC, U DX/9/26, Freeman to Thompson, 19 February 1871; Edward A. Freeman, 'On the study of history', *Fortnightly Review* (Spring 1881), 319.
41 HHC, U DX/9/13, Freeman to Thompson, 12 September 1869.
42 Stephens, *Life and Letters*, vol. 2, p. 31. About the entire series: Howsam, 'Academic discipline', 534–42.
43 Eventually only two other volumes were written by women: Margaret MacArthur produced *History of Scotland* and Charlotte Yonge produced *History of France*.
44 Green to Freeman, June 1870 in Stephen, *Letters*, p. 254.
45 Macmillan to Airy, 23 January 1861 in George A. Macmillan (ed.), *Letters of Alexander Macmillan* (printed for private circulation, 1908), p. 75; Howsam, *Past into Print*, pp 26–7.
46 Hesketh, *Science of History*, pp 125–6.
47 This is implied in Howsam, 'Academic discipline', 538.
48 BL, Add. MSS 55050, Freeman to Macmillan, 22 February 1874; BL, Add. MSS 55051, Freeman to Craik, 20 August 1877.
49 BL, Add. MSS 55050, Freeman to Macmillan, 19 January 1872 and 19 September 1873.
50 Edward A. Freeman, 'Preface', in Edith Thompson, *History of England* (London: Macmillan, 1874), pp v–vi.
51 Ibid.
52 HHC, U DX/9/35, Freeman to Thompson, 21 April 1872.
53 BL, Add. MSS 55393, Macmillan to Freeman, 10 March 1873, 14 March 1873, and Macmillan to Thompson, 11 March 1873 and 12 March 1873.
54 BL, Add. MSS 55393, Craik to Thompson, 26 March 1873.
55 BL, Add. MSS 55078, Thompson to Macmillan, 16 December 1900.
56 Thompson, *History of England*, p. 236; Edith Thompson, *History of England* (London: Macmillan, 1901), pp 337–8.

57 BL, Add. MSS 55392, Macmillan to Freeman, 8 May 1872, 19 May 1872 and 11 July 1872; Macmillan to Thompson, 11 July 1872 and Malcolm Macmillan to Green, 12 July 1872.
58 Green to Freeman, 27 June 1871, in Stephen, *Letters*, p. 304; BL, Add. MSS 55049, Freeman to Macmillan, 11 July 1871.
59 Hesketh, *Science of History*, pp 115–28.
60 Green to Freeman, 27 June 1871 and 30 December 1872, in Stephen, *Letters*, pp 303–5, 340.
61 BL, Add. MSS 55394, Macmillan to Adolphus Ward, 21 November 1873; Howsam, *Past into Print*, pp 5–6.
62 JRL, FA1/8/31–60, Freeman to Green, 14 March 1876; HHC, U DX/9/78, Freeman to Thompson, 27 May 1879.
63 HHC, U DX/9/133, Freeman to Thompson, 29 July 1885; HHC, U DX/9/166, Freeman to Thompson, 14 October 1888.
64 Powicke and Millican, 'Norgate', *ODNB*.
65 Kate Norgate, *England under the Angevin Kings*, vol. 1 (London: Macmillan, 1887), p. vii.
66 [G. W. Cox], 'Kate Norgate. *England under the Angevin Kings*', *Edinburgh Review* (October 1887), 466.
67 [Anon.], 'Miss Kate Norgate', *The Times* (6 May 1935).
68 Edward A. Freeman, 'Kate Norgate, *England under the Angevin Kings*', *English Historical Review*, 2:8 (1887), 774–6.
69 HHC, U DX/9/155, Freeman to Thompson, 4 September 1887; HHC, U DX/9/172, Freeman to Thompson, 29 September 1889; HHC, U DX/9/180, Freeman to Thompson, 7 December 1890; HHC, U DX/9/185, Freeman to Thompson, 19 April 1891; HHC, U DX/9/189, Freeman to Thompson, 20 July 1891.
70 HHC, U DX/9/8, Freeman to Thompson, 14 July 1869; HHC, U DX/9/27, Freeman to Thompson, 2 April 1871; JRL, FA1/8/31-60, Freeman to Green, 4 August 1875.
71 HHC, U DX/9/183, Freeman to Thompson, 15 February 1891.
72 HHC, U DX/9/198, Thompson's draft to the editor of *Land & Water*, 22 November 1919.
73 BL, Add. MSS 55078, Thompson to Macmillan, 16 December 1900.
74 Thompson was terrified about the damage a scandalous court case against another Edith Thompson could do to her name. The other Thompson, together with her lover, was convicted of murdering her husband. She found the publicity around the 'wretched' Edith Thompson case 'offensive' and 'likely to do my book harm'. BL, Add. MSS 55078, Thompson to Macmillan, 30 March 1924.
75 BL, Add. MSS 55078, Thompson to Macmillan, 16 December 1900; Elise Garritzen, 'Revise, edit, and improve: writing and publishing history as an unending process in Victorian Britain', *Clio*, 45:3 (2016), 308–12.
76 BL, Add. MSS 55078, Thompson to Macmillan, 7 December 1900; Thompson, *History of England* (1901).
77 BL, Add. MSS 55078, Thompson to Macmillan, 30 August 1916 and 22 April 1923; Vicky L. Morrisroe, '"Sanguinary amusement": E. A. Freeman, the comparative method and Victorian theories of race', *Modern Intellectual History*, 10:1 (2013), 31–40.
78 BL, Add. MSS 55375, Macmillan to printer Clay, 10 April 1923.
79 Edith Thompson, *History of England* (London: Macmillan, 1923), p. 1.
80 BL, Add. MS 55078, Thompson to Macmillan, 12 March 1924.
81 Herman Paul, 'The virtues of a good historian in early Imperial Germany: Georg Waitz's contested example', *Modern Intellectual History*, 15 (2018), 681–709.
82 Camille Creyghton *et al.*, 'Virtue language in historical scholarship: the cases of Georg Waitz, Gabriel Monod and Henry Pirenne', *History of European Ideas*, 42:7 (2016); Schnicke, *Männliche Disziplin*.

CHAPTER 6

Interpretative and investigative: the emergence and characteristics of modern scholarly personae in China, 1900–30

Q. Edward Wang

A worthy son-in-law like you with talent and learning and a reputation extending far and wide does not need to flaunt a PhD. But your father passed the Manchu second-degree examination and therefore it seems only fitting that you become the foreign equivalent of the third-degree holder, following in your father's footsteps and even surpassing him. Then I too would share in your glory.[1]

Introduction

This was a letter that Fang Hung-chien, a protagonist in Qian Zhongshu's (1910–98) acclaimed novel *Fortress Besieged* (1947), received from his father-in-law while he was sojourning in Europe. Apparently, Fang's father-in-law enjoined Fang to obtain a doctoral degree from a foreign university, which Fang had not been seriously pursuing. To satisfy his father-in-law, who had generously supplied the funding for his overseas study, Fang eventually bought a diploma from an obscure institution and returned to teach in China.

But the letter tells us more. By way of encouragement, Fang's father-in-law compared a PhD with "the Manchu second-degree examination," or the degree a successful candidate like Fang's father would have earned in the civil service examination administered by the Manchu/Qing dynasty (1644–1912). That is, during the 1940s when Qian was writing *Fortress Besieged*, a PhD from a foreign institution had become equal to the triumph of a candidate in the civil service examination in imperial China. When did this happen? How could a foreign degree in higher education have become *de rigueur* for anyone who wished to teach in a college in 1940s China? And if this had become a sort of required qualification, how did it influence the development of modern scholarly personae in China? In writing this chapter, I define and consider scholarly personae on three levels. The first is the external requisite, such as an advanced degree, whether earned domestically or from overseas, and whether or not the scholars under investigation worked at a modern institution of higher education. The second is a shared agreement in a given scholarly community on certain models of virtue a scholar should embody and display in his/her research. The third is an internal and intrinsic disposition a scholar demonstrates in her/his research that is not necessarily a result and/or a reflection of his/her own conscientious choice. In this regard, I am indebted to Hayden White's exploration of the types of narrative modes and, especially, his consideration of the "preconceptual" and the "prefigurative" nature of the work of the historian.[2] I also agree with Herman Paul that scholarly personae are "contested and unstable." The contestation and instability, as Paul elucidates in his article and as I will describe below using the cases in China, are often caused by historical change, resulting in the appeal of a particular, alternative persona during a given period.[3] Meanwhile, I observe that scholarly personae are also contested because, while accepted as a model of virtue at a particular time, their appeals to a scholar are often qualified and negotiated with her/his predisposed interest in and inclined aptitude for scholarship.

In the following pages, I will discuss the transformation of scholarship in early-twentieth-century China by looking at the education and career of four scholars who lived through the era. My general observation is that it was at the turn of the twentieth century that scholarly life in China began to experience a marked change and that this change impacted two generations of scholars, whose lives and careers helped shape modern scholarly personae in China. As all this took place in a relatively short time, the personae that emerged in the period bore complex and contested characteristics, marked in the main by the mingling and mixing of traditional and modern elements. The differences and complexity were demonstrated not only in *how* these scholars conducted scholarly activities in historical research and writing but also in *where* they conducted research and how their scholarly pursuit demonstrated sociopolitical virtues while living through this transitional age in Chinese history. With regard to the external requisite of their scholarly persona, the first two of the four began their scholarly activities outside an academic institution while the other two, who were a generation younger, established their careers in a modern university. And of the first two, one later joined a research institute at a university while the other remained in a private academy throughout his career. The focus of my writing, however, is on the development of the two models of intellectual virtue and how those models reflected the complex interactions between conformity and conflict, the traditional and the modern, in China's emerging academic community.

Before we proceed to discuss these scholars, I believe a brief description of the tradition of Chinese scholarship is in order. Such description is necessary because the careers of the four scholars I am to sample here invariably formed an intrinsic relationship with the Chinese scholarly tradition. But this is by no means an easy task, for the tradition evolved over the course of two millennia, from approximately the so-called "Age of Confucius (551–479 bce)" to the late nineteenth century. While Confucius was commonly recognized as the master of Chinese culture, he nonetheless admitted himself that he merely "transmitted rather than created" the tradition. In other words, before Confucius, there already existed a tradition of a culture he truly cared about and wished to carry on. Indeed, thanks to Confucius's effort in transmission, the Five Classics, for instance, were preserved to this day, even though the validity of some of their content remains debated. What Confucius accomplished was exemplary – in the centuries afterward, many scholars in the Confucian tradition carried on the same task, to extend the ancient tradition. This backward-looking approach, which was conservative in nature, played an important part in helping preserve the mainstay of Chinese civilization, one example of which was that, up till the early twentieth century, educated Chinese could read and comprehend most ancient texts from the days of yore, such as those from the Age of Confucius. This was rather uncommon among other historical civilizations.

Meanwhile, significant changes also took place in the tradition of Chinese scholarship prior to the twentieth century. During the Han dynasty (206 bce–220 ce) when most ancient texts had been transmitted by hand in manuscript forms, scholars engaged in debates about their accuracy and authenticity, which led to several different schools of interpretation as well as the development of exegetic criticism; both would help form the Chinese tradition of hermeneutics that continued through the subsequent centuries.[4] The decline and fall of the Han in the third century paved the way for Buddhism to enter China, which, through the period of division that lasted for four centuries following Han's fall, established a strong foothold in the Chinese populace and became a constant feature of the Chinese cultural scene. By absorbing Buddhist elements in both doctrines and practices, Confucian scholars launched a counterattack from the twelfth century, which resulted in a new form of Confucian learning known in the West as Neo-Confucianism. To a great extent, the Neo-Confucian movement was an intellectual revolution in that, by supplying a new set of texts (e.g. substituting the Five Classics in schooling pupils from then onward) which its advocates believed represented and delivered the real essence of Confucian teaching, it offered a new reading and interpretation of classical Confucianism. Neo-Confucianism flourished during the Ming dynasty (1368–1644), which marked a revival of Chinese rule after near a century-long Mongol conquest and rule in the country. Yet the Ming fell in the mid-seventeenth century, causing another wave of intellectual change in the succeeding Qing dynasty. Neo-Confucianism, while receiving endorsement from the Manchu rulers of the Qing, became a target of criticism during the eighteenth century. Its critics advocated a return to the Confucian Classics of earlier times, for which they revived and improved the skills and techniques of exegetic studies. Known as evidential learning, this new intellectual trend left a lasting influence throughout the twentieth century as China groped its way to embrace modernity.[5]

Statecraft vs seeking truth

The intellectual tradition and its vicissitudes in Qing China, the dynasty that marked the end of the country's long imperial period, were an important backdrop against which we will discuss the four scholars and their varied contributions to the development of modern scholarly personae, for all of them, in early childhood, were reared and schooled in that tradition. At the same time, all of them also had sufficient exposure to the modern scholarship from the West, sometimes via Japan; at least in comparison with their peers. In the face of Western incursion, which they experienced firsthand, they developed different attitudes toward their early education, or the political and cultural legacy of imperial China, which consequently influenced their pursuit of intellectual work and sociopolitical goods demanded by the challenging times.

The nineteenth century was a tumultuous time for Qing China. To the ruling Manchu emperors and most of the educated class, China's loss to Britain in the Opium Wars (1839–42 and 1856–60) was a shock, for half a century earlier the mighty Emperor Qianlong (1711–99) had effectively rejected Lord Macartney's request for trade and diplomatic relationships. But for others, such as Gong Zizhen (1792–1841), the grandson of an acclaimed evidential scholar, such danger was not totally unforeseen. While he had received a solid training in evidential learning when young, Gong later developed more interest in statecraft scholarship, for which he advocated the study of China's frontier geography. That is, while most Chinese were indulging themselves in the "prosperity" passed on to them by Emperor Qianlong's six-decade glorious rule, Gong foresaw the danger the celestial empire was about to encounter, as its borders had come under pressure from Russia in the northwest and Britain and France in the southeast.

Compared with evidential learning, which was an eighteenth-century phenomenon, *jingshi zhiyong* ("statecraft learning") was a term dating back to the late seventeenth century when the Qing dynasty had just been founded. But the underpinning idea, or the emphasis on applying knowledge to practical use, had a much longer and richer tradition.[6] The establishment of the civil service examination under the Sui and Tang dynasties from the sixth century could be seen as an implementation of this tradition. But over time, it also attracted criticisms and concerns. To those who were more interested in pursuing scholarship for its own sake – who included the evidential scholars of the Qing period, as they tended to immerse themselves in textual criticism – this pragmatic attitude toward learning was rather discouraging and even detrimental. Seeking truth and the emphasis on statecraft, therefore, represented two models of virtue in imperial China, particularly during the Qing dynasty since evidential scholarship held a wide sway toward the end of the eighteenth century. However, the changing interest shown in Gong Zizhen suggested that a new trend was about to emerge in the first half of the nineteenth century, as the country encountered military defeat by foreign powers. This new trend would evoke and revive the statecraft emphasis in scholarship.

Let us now turn to our first two scholars: Zhang Taiyan (1869–1936) and Liang Qichao (1873–1929), as both were reared during this period and both later became prominent intellectual figures that presaged the upcoming change in China's scholarly life. I choose them as well because their lives and careers contributed to the shaping of two rather different models of scholarly virtue, in which their distinct individual dispositions, educational interests, and intellectual propensities played their parts. In their early childhoods, Zhang and Liang received almost identical education and both excelled in their studies, which were mainly in reading and understanding Confucian texts from past ages, reflecting and extending the tradition of evidential scholarship. Yet there were also discernible differences. Having suffered some sort of epilepsy, Zhang failed in his first attempt at the county level of the civil service examination and decided to quit the pursuit from then on. By contrast, within five years (1884–89), Liang, then a mere teenager, passed the examinations at both county and provincial levels. This means that he was well prepared to launch his career as a scholar-official. In 1890 he went to Beijing to take the civil examination at the metropolitan level, the highest in the examination system. He failed his attempt, which was hardly unusual among first-time candidates. On the way back, Liang visited Shanghai, one of the port cities first opened to the West after the Opium War, and saw firsthand the incursion of Western powers in China. Returning home to Guangdong from his trip, Liang had a change of mind. He decided to cease his early interest in learning the techniques of textual criticism and pursue instead a new scholarship that could prepare him better for contributing his knowledge to helping the war-ridden country. This new interest landed him in the Wanmu Caotang Academy founded by Kang Youwei (1858–1927), a radical and controversial scholar of his time. Like Liang Qichao, Kang had also had an exposure to Western learning; he had visited Hong Kong and Shanghai on his way to sit civil service examinations. After he failed the examinations, Kang Youwei established the Wanmu Caotang Academy to teach his new interpretations of Confucianism that attracted Liang Qichao and others. To his students and followers, Kang's main attraction lay in his bold attempt to appropriate certain elements from the Confucian tradition to accommodate and advocate the idea of change, or *jinhualun* ("evolutionism"), the Chinese term for social Darwinism.

In the same period as Liang Qichao turned to Kang Youwei to gain a new perspective on scholarship, Zhang Taiyan moved to Hangzhou and engrossed himself in the study of evidential learning by working with Yu Yue (1821–1907), one of the most erudite scholars of the age. He would stay there for near a decade before going to Japan seeking new knowledge in 1899. At first appearance, evidential learning was a legacy from previous centuries, which aimed to understand and fathom the meaning of ancient Confucian texts via philological methods, as well as studies of paleography, etymology, and phonology. But it could also trigger revolutionary outcomes, as Zhang Taiyan's later scholarship would help demonstrate. In fact, when it first emerged, evidential learning could be well regarded as a bold endeavor to challenge the officially endorsed Neo-Confucian tradition, for the motto that guided evidential research was seeking truth from facts, rather than following the interpretative teachings of such Neo-Confucian masters as Zhu Xi (1130–1200). By applying the methods of philology and other schools, evidential scholars hoped to attain and fix the true meaning of Confucian teaching, rather than following the interpretation provided by Zhu Xi and other Neo-Confucians. As such, evidential scholars covertly demonstrated a political disapproval of Qing rule.[7]

In sum, when China faced a serious national crisis in the nineteenth century, the statecraft idea became especially attractive to many intellectuals, for they were hoping to offer their knowledge in service to the country. Liang Qichao, for instance, was drawn to Kang Youwei because the latter's new interpretation of Confucian teaching amounted to an attempt to make the tradition anew and render it useful for changed times. But as the country's crisis deepened, the question then became to what extent did traditional knowledge remain relevant and useful? While Kang continued to make his painstaking effort to revive the Confucian tradition, others advocated a complete overhaul of that legacy. In other words, as China was forced to open its doors to the Western world, the intent to render knowledge useful to society ineluctably involved a changing attitude toward the relationship and interplay between traditional Chinese learning and modern Western scholarship. More and more *literati* developed an interest in the modern West in general, and modern Western scholarship in particular. This interest played a key role in shaping the modern scholarly personae, for after the turn of the twentieth century few scholars in China could ever hope to continue holing up in their secluded ivory tower while considering applying their knowledge to saving the world. Many of them felt instead the need to adopt and incorporate new ideas and approaches from the West to foster new models of scholarly virtue deemed necessary for the challenging time. Meanwhile, the new virtues emerging at the time related to how one viewed the past and appropriated legacies from it in order to deal with the ongoing crisis.

Interpretative vs investigative

In 1895 Qing China suffered another defeat by Japan in the Sino-Japanese War. This humiliating loss significantly changed the lives of both Liang Qichao and Zhang Taiyan, as well as many Chinese including the other two scholars we will turn to below. The fact that Japan, which was not only much smaller but had also been indebted to China for its cultural development over many centuries, was able to crush the Qing army and navy in the war taught the Chinese a painful lesson: in light of the dramatic change in world history, the country had to adjust itself to the change and remodel its government on the models from the West if it ever hoped to survive. In 1898 when Kang Youwei and Liang Qichao were making another attempt at passing the civil service examinations, they worked together with many other candidates for a petition to the Qing court, asking for political reform. Their effort resulted in the "Hundred Day Reform," so-called as it lasted less than three months before being clamped down by the Qing court. Kang and Liang both fled to Japan afterward, where they continued to plead for reform, political and cultural.

In 1902 when sojourning in Japan, Liang Qichao published a series of essays which would later become the *Xin shixue (New Historiography)*, a seminal text in modern Chinese historiography, in the *Xinmin congbao (New Citizens' Journal)* he himself edited. At the outset of his *New Historiography* Liang pointed out that, while historical writing had had a long tradition in China, the tradition contained a fatal flaw in failing to delineate the evolution of the Chinese nation over time. By focusing attention on the monarch, he lamented, all the works produced from the tradition basically served one person only, instead of the Chinese people. What Liang desired for the "new historiography" was to write *minshi* ("history of the people/nation") or national history, rather than *junshi* ("history of the monarch"). Liang's proposal for "new historiography," as well as his turn to editing the newspaper in which his *New Historiography* was serialized, was inspired by the exemplary practice of Fukuzawa Yukichi (1835–1901), a major champion of Western civilization in Meiji Japan (1868–1912). In his *An Outline of a Theory of Civilization* (1875), Fukuzawa proposed the idea of writing *bunmei shi* (the "history of civilization"), in hopes of outlining the progress of the Japanese nation over past centuries. Like Fukuzawa, Liang Qichao in his *New Historiography* also offered three definitions of the nature of history:

> 1) History must describe the phenomena of evolution; 2) History must describe the phenomena of human evolution and 3) History must describe the phenomena of human evolution in order to discover the universal laws behind the process.[8]

In advocating "new historiography," Liang Qichao encouraged his compatriots to reflect upon the vicissitudes of China's long past and offer a general interpretation of the course of such evolution.

After its appearance, Liang's *New Historiography* had a far-reaching influence in changing historical thinking and writing in twentieth-century China, for many echoed his assessment of the inadequacy of Chinese traditional historiography in dealing with the national crisis. A couple of years after Liang's *New Historiography*, a group of scholars, most of whom had either studied or stayed in Japan, founded the *Guocui xuebao (National Essence Journal)* in 1905, in which they published essays that experimented with and/or expounded on the writing of a new national history of China. For example, Deng Shi (1877–1951), editor of the *National Essence Journal*, extended Liang's criticism of monarch-centered traditional Chinese historiography to the Chinese intellectual tradition as a whole. Deng reckoned that 60 per cent of the knowledge produced by the tradition was for the monarch and the other 40 per cent for his ministers, with none whatsoever left for serving the people. Other contributors to the *National Essence Journal* also endeavored to reflect, critically and comprehensively, on China's traditions. Liu Guanghan (a.k.a. Liu Shipei, 1884–1919), a prolific writer for the journal, wrote a series of essays "discussing the development of China's political system, territory, family system, rulership, law, land ownership, school, social class, and music, which appeared in almost every issue for the entire first year."[9] Their writings, together with Liang Qichao's own (which also covered a broad range of topics), fostered a model of virtue prevalent in the time. It shaped,

I argue, an interpretative or reflective, modern scholarly persona that, politically, expressed the desire to build the country into a modern nation and, intellectually, held a stance that was critical of the past and called upon scholars to interpret anew the country's history and cultural legacy for the nation-building project.

After Liang Qichao went into exile in Japan, Zhang Taiyan followed in 1899. The two had met before. Concerned about China's dire situation facing the menace of foreign invasion, in 1896 Zhang had ended his study with Yu Yue (much to Yu's chagrin) and left for Shanghai, where he not only befriended Liang Qichao and other reformers, but also joined the editorial board of *Shiwubao (Chinese Progress)*, a newspaper that promoted Kang Youwei's and Liang Qichao's advocacy of political reform. During their stay in Japan, Zhang and Liang exchanged ideas on changing the Chinese tradition of historiography. In 1900, when Zhang published his first book *Qiushu (Words of Urgency)*, a collection of essays he had written at the time, Liang Qichao provided his calligraphy for its title, which was a traditional way of showing his endorsement. Zhang and Liang thus shared the same concern that China then needed political reform to ensure its existence and survival in the modern world. With respect to the reform of historiography, it seems that at that time Zhang also agreed with Liang that it was crucial for the modern-day Chinese to develop a general understanding of the course of development of China's past. In his correspondence with Liang, Zhang expressed his desire to write a *Zhongguo tongzhi (General History of China)* that would transcend the tradition of dynastic history, the mainstay of Chinese historiography in the imperial period. Zhang believed that, compared with the history of a single dynasty,

> General history (*tongshi*) is valuable in two aspects. One is that in the form of treatise, general history focuses on discovering the laws that explain the evolution and decline of the sociopolitical. The other is in its biographies, general history centers on raising the spirit of the people and guiding them to the future.

He also commented the works of Japanese historians and preferred the "history of civilization" promoted by Fukuzawa Yukichi over other genres in historical writing.[10]

While Zhang Taiyan clearly agreed with Liang Qichao's idea of launching a historiographical revolution in the early twentieth century, he did not embark on writing the *General History of China*, nor did he continue working with Liang and other reformers for their cause. In fact, in the wake of the Boxer Rebellion of 1900, Zhang Taiyan had made up his mind to become a revolutionary – he no longer believed in the legitimacy of the Manchu Qing dynasty in ruling China. Instead, he joined revolutionary organizations led by Sun Yat-sen (1866–1925) and criticized Kang Youwei and his supporters for their continuous attempt to uphold the Qing government. To Zhang, Sun, and the revolutionaries, the Qing court's behavior in the Boxer Rebellion had proven that the reformers' endeavor was futile and outdated because the Qing dynasty's fate was already sealed; what China needed was to end its imperial system and establish a republic on the ruins.

From 1900, therefore, Zhang Taiyan began to show a clear departure from Liang Qichao in their political views, even though Liang at the time also developed some doubts at the prospects for the reform he and his teacher Kang Youwei had started. But a clearer difference between Zhang and Liang, it seems to me, was shown in their scholarly personae. If the writings of Liang and the National Essence group helped shape the interpretative/reflective persona, Zhang, while hitherto also a contributor to the *National Essence Journal*, revived and promoted the virtue cherished by evidential scholars from the eighteenth century, which was characterized by the attempt to ascertain and fathom the meaning of words in texts via methods of philology, etymology, phonology, etc. As such, I name it the investigative or evidential persona, for its main intention was to deliver veritable knowledge via textual criticism.

Let us take Zhang's *Words of Urgency* as an example. The main reason for writing the essays collected in the book was to reflect on the challenges China faced at the time and find a solution to the crises. But in contrast to the reflective virtue Liang Qichao displayed in writing the *New Historiography*, which discussed, in broad strokes, the nature of historical writing and the tradition of Chinese historiography – the latter was described by Liang as representing *jiushi* (the "old historiography") – in *Words of Urgency* Zhang offered investigative studies of the topics selected by him as essential to the development of Chinese scholarship. As one of his earliest writings, Zhang Taiyan's *Words of Urgency* ran several editions after its initial appearance, suggesting that the investigative/evidential virtue demonstrated in it retained some appeal in the early twentieth century. These editions also reflected his change of mind from a reforming to a revolutionary view. After its first publication in the early 1900s, *Words of Urgency* was quickly revised by Zhang a few months later, with the addition of two more essays. These two essays express his harsher criticism of Qing rule. Then in 1904, he issued a new edition of the book, marking a clear change of stance toward the Qing dynasty – he had by then become a thorough revolutionary, determined to overthrow Qing rule and return the rule of China from the Manchus to the Han Chinese.[11]

While reflecting the change of Zhang's political views, the different editions of *Words of Urgency* share more or less the same structure and show an identical scholarly approach. With respect to the structure, Zhang chose to write the essays more as commentaries than as treatises, which was in stark contrast to Liang Qichao's method in the *New Historiography* and especially the *Lun Zhongguo xueshu sixiang bianqian zhi dashi (Main Trends of Change in the Chinese Intellectual Tradition)*, which Liang wrote concurrently with the *New Historiography* in 1902. But then the virtue Zhang pursued and presented was also clearly different. It was evidential rather than reflective, and investigative rather than interpretative. While he was equally concerned about the inadequacy of the tradition of Chinese (historical) scholarship, Zhang seemed uninterested in offering a sweeping critique of the Chinese intellectual tradition as Liang tried to do in the *New Historiography* and the *Main Trends of Change*. Instead, Zhang published such entries as *zunXun* ("Respecting Xunzi"), *RuMo* ("Confucianism and Mohism"), *RuFa* ("Confucianism and legalism"), and *RuDao* ("Confucianism and Daoism"), in which he discussed the evolution of the Chinese intellectual tradition, centering on that of Confucian learning. In writing these essays, he incorporated new perspectives and discussed and explained them in new and different ways. But all these terms were explained in a commentary style, the dominant form of writing adopted among evidential scholars of the eighteenth century. From a comparative perspective, Zhang's *Words of Urgency* was edited in a similar fashion to Pierre Bayle's (1647–1706) *Historical and Critical Dictionary*, a seminal work that provides criticisms of the received intellectual traditions and religious beliefs in Europe.

Zhang Taiyan's critical stance in editing *Words of Urgency* was shown in his selection of some of the essays. To contemporary readers with a similar educational background, the selection readily demonstrated, among other things, a new reading of the Confucian tradition. His decision to begin *Words of Urgency* with the essay "Respecting Xunzi," for example, implicitly raised the status of Xunzi (*c.* 313–238 bce) over that of Mencius (*c.* 372–289 bce); while both Xunzi and Mencius were important followers of Confucius, Mencius had been given higher status than Xunzi in previous ages. Zhang Taiyan, however, preferred Xunzi for the reason that in Xunzi's elucidation of Confucian learning one finds his support for the idea of change, which was a train of thought previously less emphasized in the otherwise rather conservative Confucian tradition.[12] In the revised version of *Words of Urgency*, Zhang added the essay *dingKong* ("Understanding Confucius"), in which he debated with Endô Kyuichi (1874–1946) and Shirakawa Jirô (1874–1919), two noted Japanese scholars of Chinese philosophy who had criticized Confucius's cultural legacy.[13] Zhang Taiyan's intention, analogous to that of the evidential scholars of the eighteenth century, was to offer a truer knowledge of Confucius by noting his immense and complex cultural influence (e.g. certain ideas on which Xunzi had expanded had been overlooked through the ages). Zhang's take on Confucius and Confucianism here was consistent with his effort, joined by others at the time, to identify and foreground China's National Essence as a means to heighten the national spirit among the populace. To Zhang and other like-minded souls, Confucianism constituted an integral part of the National Essence, yet they did not think the form of Confucianism endorsed by the Qing court was the authentic version, nor could it represent China's cultural legacy.[14]

If Zhang Taiyan's *Words of Urgency* reflected his intention to correct previous notions about China's intellectual tradition, he pursued this goal because he had become a believer in social Darwinism, or evolutionism. Drawing on the ideas of evolutionism, he included and discussed such terms as *yuanxue* ("evolution of scholarship"), *yuanren* ("evolution of humans"), and *yuanbian* ("evolution of changes") in *Words of Urgency*, offering his comments on how evolution and/or change were the constant in human society and history. While also a strong believer at the time in evolutionism, Liang Qichao utilized evolutionary ideas to chart the development of Chinese culture. In contrast to Zhang's evidential approach and investigative study, Liang wrote a good number of treatises, carrying such titles as *Zhongguo zhuanzhi zhengzhi shilun* ("On the history of political authoritarianism in China"), *Shengjixue yan'ge xiaoshi* ("A short history of economics") and *Lun Zhongguo guomin zhi pin'ge* ("On the characteristics of the Chinese people").[15] Liu Shipei and members of the National Essence group also attempted the same, offering comprehensive reflections on various aspects of China's legacy. In a word, at the turn of the twentieth century, when modern scholarship entered its formative period in China, Liang Qichao and others promoted the reflective/interpretative persona. With its overarching approach, it became a new and appealing model of intellectual virtue attracting many followers. Meanwhile, Zhang Taiyan hoped to extend and expand on the investigative/evidential persona from the past, while also distinguishing his version from the past model in a key way – the persona or virtue Zhang hoped to establish and propagate was not to uphold the Confucian legacy, but to winnow it thoroughly in order to find certain elements useful for modern China.

Renovation and/as innovation

In the early twentieth century, thanks to his exceptional prolificacy (the titles mentioned represent just a few samples of his expansive writings in the period), Liang Qichao was exceedingly influential. His many essays appearing at the time were widely read and were inspiring to many future leaders in China, including Mao Zedong (1893–1976), the founder of the People's Republic of China in 1949. But it was Liang's *Main Trends of Change* that drew the particular attention of Hu Shi (1891–1962), the future doyen of China's emerging academic community and the third scholar in our study. Hu recalled that while a high school student, he was eager to get the newspaper in which Liang serialized the essay. In 1910, after passing the test for the Boxer Indemnity Scholarship established by the US government after the Boxer Rebellion, Hu travelled to the USA and enrolled at Cornell University. He later studied for his PhD with John Dewey (1859–1952) at Columbia University before returning to China to become a professor of philosophy at Peking University in 1917. As one of the earliest Chinese students trained in the USA, Hu played a leadership role in launching the New Culture Movement (1915–25), propounding the iconoclastic aim of challenging and dismantling the grip of Confucian ethics and ideas on the Chinese nation. What made Hu Shi a public intellectual figure of the age was his advocacy and effort to substitute vernacular for literary Chinese, in hopes of bridging the gap between the upper and lower classes in Chinese society. Thus he differed from Zhang Taiyan in significant ways. Throughout his life, Zhang mostly wrote in literary Chinese and preferred to use difficult and uncommon words and phrases to express his ideas.

As a philosophy professor, Hu Shi published his first work in 1919, entitled *Zhongguo zhexueshi dagang (An Outline History of Chinese Philosophy)*, based on his doctoral work at Columbia University. As its title indicates, it seems to be a survey of the development of philosophical ideas in ancient China, from approximately the eighth to the fourth centuries bce. In the book, Hu intended to discuss the origin, formation, and characteristics of the Age of Confucius, though Confucius was by no means the central figure in his study. In fact, he included several of Confucius's contemporaries and discussed their accomplishments and influences. As a history of ancient Chinese philosophy, Hu also discussed Confucius's followers, such as Mencius and Xunzi. Hu believed that ancient Chinese philosophy came to an end after Xunzi, before the third century bce, after the appearance of several new trends of thoughts and practices, such as the prevalence of functionalism and alchemical exercises, which were unphilosophical in nature.[16]

In structure and style, Hu Shi's writing in the *Outline History of Chinese Philosophy* bore a great similarity to that of the many reflective essays penned by Liang Qichao in the previous decade. To some extent, the book could be viewed as a sequel to Liang's attempt at surveying the evolution of Chinese scholarship from a modern perspective. It was also perhaps for this reason that, after its publication, Hu's *Outline History of Chinese Philosophy* became an instant success, paving the way for him to become an undisputed leader of the Chinese academic community of the age. Indeed, when Hu Shi returned from the USA to China to teach the history of Chinese philosophy, many, including his students at Peking University, were initially rather suspicious of the soundness of his scholarship. They wondered how a returned student from the West could teach them about Chinese history and philosophy. But with the publication of the book and his teaching of a course with the same title, Hu succeeded in winning over his class, thanks to positive remarks made by Gu Jiegang (1893–1980) and Fu Sinian (1896–1950), two student leaders who were highly respected by their classmates for their solid knowledge base in traditional education.[17]

Hu Shi's interpretation of the development of Chinese philosophy at its formative stage might be the reason he impressed his students. Yet a closer look at his work would show that, while a seemingly representative work in exemplifying the reflective persona, Hu actually promoted and praised the investigative persona embodied by Qing evidential learning. Indeed, in the preface he wrote to the revised edition, Hu expressed his gratitude to Wang Niansun (1744–1832), Wang Yinzhi (1766–1834), Yu Yue and Sun Yirang (1848–1908) of the past age; all four were acclaimed scholars in evidential learning. Hu then thanked Zhang Taiyan, stating that Zhang was the contemporary that most deserved his appreciation.[18] In his book, like Zhang who had drawn attention to Xunzi, Hu also allocated a chapter to Xunzi's intellectual contribution. By comparison, he treated Mencius together with a few others in another chapter.

A more telling example was found in Hu's Introduction, in which he discussed the nature of philosophy, characteristics of the history of philosophy, and the tasks for historians of philosophy. Then he turned to a section called "The sources of the history of philosophy" and offered an extensive discussion. "There are three goals," Hu wrote, "for the study of the history of philosophy: 1) describe changes; 2) explain the causes (for the changes); and 3) evaluation." But before one embarks on these tasks, he hastened to add, one must first learn about and acquire *zhen'gongfu* (the "essential/real techniques") in source criticism. For these real techniques would enable one to discover and discuss "the career growth of a philosopher, the change of his ideas and their causes and the true nature of his scholarship." Hu then explained the differences between primary and secondary sources before proceeding to the methods of source criticism, which to him included examining the validity of the events described in the records, checking the languages used in the documents, analyzing the style and syntax of the language, tracing the ideas expressed in the sources and, lastly, finding corroborating evidence for the sources.[19] In the book,

Hu put these ideas into practice, for example conducting detailed research into clarifying the dates and activities of Xunzi by repudiating some earlier confusions using more credible sources.

In other words, while Hu Shi was clearly indebted to Liang Qichao in developing his scholarly interest in the Chinese intellectual tradition, his work probably embodied the investigative persona associated with Zhang Taiyan's work more than the interpretative one embraced in Liang's career.[20] To a great degree, the positive reception that Hu's *Outline History of Chinese Philosophy* had in the scholarly community was also – according to the Foreword to the book written by Cai Yuanpei (1868–1940), then president of Peking University and a respected scholar who had earned the highest degree at the Qing civil service examination – because by demonstrating his critiques of the sources, Hu succeeded in clarifying the confusion that had previously plagued the field and paving the way for further research. In Cai's opinion, besides providing a concise survey of the development of Chinese philosophy, Hu Shi's real success lay in his *zhengming de fangfa* ("method of verification").[21] In other words, Hu Shi was also received more as a scholar who excelled in source-based evidential scholarship.

As noted before, in contrast to Zhang Taiyan Hu Shi held a critical attitude toward China's Confucian past. But his research exemplified the same intellectual virtue as Zhang did – they both desired to conduct empirical and exegetical investigation, in hopes of approaching and revealing the true nature of the literary body from the past. As a student of John Dewey, who gave a lecture tour in China from 1919 to 1921 at his former student's invitation and arrangement, Hu not only propagated Dewey's theory of the modern scientific method, but also argued forcefully that elements similarly scientific to those constituting the method had been hidden in the Chinese intellectual tradition, awaiting modern-day Chinese to discover and revive them. In a succinct manner, Hu Shi believed that scientific method consisted in two parts: *dadan de jiashe, xiaoxin de qiuzheng* ("1) a boldness in setting up hypotheses and 2) a minuteness in seeking evidence"). To carry out this belief, Hu launched and led the National Studies project, centering on the campus of Peking University where he edited the *Guoxue jikan (Journal of National Studies)*, one of the first academic journals in China. In many aspects, Hu's project was a continuation and expansion of Zhang Taiyan's earlier work on China's National Essence. Hu acknowledged Zhang's contribution and also worked closely with Qian Xuantong (1887–1939), one of Zhang's disciples and professor of philology at Peking University, as well as Gu Jiegang, his own student and an upcoming front-runner in the National Studies movement.[22]

Thus, during the late 1910s and the 1920s, thanks to Hu Shi's leadership role in the National Studies Movement, we see marked progress in the development of the investigative persona. Hu set the goal of the Movement as *zhengli guogu, zaizao wenming* ("reorganizing the national heritage and recreating (Chinese) civilization"). The focus of the project was on the former, which essentially meant to examine critically the extant body of historiography from the past two millennia by means of source criticism. And the purpose of the investigation was to authenticate classical texts so that forgeries could be identified and interpolations in original texts cleansed. At the methodological level, the National Studies Movement of 1920s China could be viewed as a modern rehearsal of evidential learning of the high Qing period, for similar types of exegetical investigation had also been pursued by many Qing scholars. Yet if this constituted a revival of Qing evidential learning, it also differed from the latter in a key way – by identifying the forgeries, Qing scholars had hoped to uphold the wholesomeness of the traditional body of literature whereas Hu Shi and his followers desired to expose its trumped-up foundation and replace it with a new and solid one on which they could rebuild the Chinese identity and history.

The strengthening of the investigative persona in 1920s China, as it were, successfully overshadowed the development of the interpretative persona that had begun in the previous decade. So much so that during the period Liang Qichao, after assuming a professorship first at Nankai University and later in the Research Institute of National Studies at Tsing-hua University, two leading institutions of higher education in China, also chose to offer his contribution. From 1921 to 1927 Liang wrote the *Zhongguo lishi yanjiufa (Historical Methods for the Study of Chinese History*, hereafter *Historical Methods)* and its sequel, which turned out be another important text in charting the development of modern Chinese historiography. Known for his erudition, Liang was well noted for his willingness to change his previous position; or in his own words, challenge *jiuwo* (the "old me") with *xinwo* (a "new me"). Different from the *New Historiography*, for instance, Liang's *Historical Methods* aimed to offer his investigative studies of the accomplishments of Chinese historians of the past in the field of historical methodology. But he also offered a new definition of the task of the historian. Different from his previous belief in the function of historical writing as a useful tool for nation-building, in the *Historical Methods* Liang became much more modest. He no longer considered the elucidation of national evolution as the paramount task. Instead, while discussing "The meaning and scope of historical study" in the first chapter, he provided his thoughts on the four aspects that the work of the historian should cover: "1) the manifestation of (human) activities; 2) the continuous activities of human society; 3) the assessment and analysis of the activities and their causal relations; and 4) lessons for the people of today."[23] The word "evolution" disappeared from the all the above; in 2), it seems Liang deliberately avoided the word and substituted "continuous activities" instead.

This change, it seems to me, enabled Liang to reevaluate the tradition of Chinese historiography, for if the description of human activities, instead of the explanation of their evolution, became the primary task for the work of the historian, then traditional Chinese historians had accumulated ample experience in the area. From the Han dynasty, if not earlier, when Sima Qian (*c.* 145–86 bce) penned his *Shiji (Records of the Grand Historian)*, biography writing had constituted one of the main forms of history writing. After Sima Qian's *magnum opus* was established as an exemplary model for official historical writing, Chinese historians in the imperial era continued to use the same style to churn out two dozen of the so-called *zhengshi* ("standard histories") before the nineteenth century. Liang in *Historical Methods* lauded the accomplishments of past historians in this area, including the court historians appointed by the rulers, and urged his contemporaries to emulate their predecessors' successes. To Liang, past historians had developed sophisticated methods in source criticism and evaluation, which were not only useful for modern historians but also enabled the latter to compare the scientific methods advanced by modern Western historians with their own comparable model. In this regard, Liang Qichao shared with Hu Shi the belief that scientific elements had already been developed in the Chinese historiographical tradition, worth the effort of modern-day historians to access, assess, and magnify.[24]

Liang's investigation of the historical methods in both China and the West, however, was not limited to the area of written sources. In chapter four of the *Historical Methods*, where he discussed the types of historical sources, he stated that there exist generally two types of source: non-written and written ones. And clearly, it was to the first, the non-written sources, that Liang hoped to draw readers' greatest attention, which to him included "extant relics, oral testimonies, and excavated artifacts."[25] As such, one could argue that Liang's *Historical Methods* was not written simply to rehabilitate the imperial tradition of official historical writing, which had been built mostly on written records. He also hoped that his contemporaries would go beyond the tradition. Indeed, Liang's attention to material evidence helped expand the scope of the National Studies Movement led by Hu Shi and Gu Jiegang, for Hu and Gu's focus had hitherto been on scrutinizing the literary body of historical sources. But this shortcoming would soon be overcome.

Interpretation via investigation

Writing the *Historical Methods* alone had not changed Liang Qichao's original endeavor to construct the interpretative persona for, in the same decade, he also wrote *Qingdai xueshu gailun (Intellectual trends in the Qing period)*, a highly explanatory and reflective study of intellectual development during the Qing period. Yet without question, thanks to Hu Shi's leadership of the National Studies Movement the 1920s saw the strengthening of the investigative persona in modern China. And if Hu Shi, who lacked training in archæology and anthropology, appeared insufficient to push the Movement further, he was aided by Fu Sinian, his other student and the fourth figure in our study. After graduating from Peking University, Fu went to Europe to further his studies in 1920. While in Europe Fu pursued a broad range of interests, ranging from psychology to geology. But he also had a general purpose in mind, which was to find a scientific method that could later aid him in gaining a better understanding of ancient China. While at Berlin University, he took a strong interest in the philology-based yet interdisciplinary study of the ancients, or *Altertumswissenschaft*. When he returned to China in 1927, Fu established the Institute of History and Philology in 1928, which remains a respected historical research institution in Taiwan today.

Born into a *literati* family, Fu Sinian received an excellent education in classical culture. During his college years, he was given the title "Confucius's successor" by his classmates, in praise of his wide and solid knowledge base. Before meeting Hu Shi, Fu had studied mostly with Huang Kan (1886–1935), a disciple of Zhang Taiyan known for his expertise in philology. Hu convinced Fu of the need to renovate the Chinese cultural tradition with the help of scientific method. During his search for the method in Europe, Fu learned about the National Studies Movement and became greatly impressed with its accomplishment. By exposing many forgeries from the past, for example, Hu Shi and Gu Jiegang – Fu's classmate and erstwhile roommate at Peking University – questioned the historicity of ancient China. Hu and Gu essentially declared that the history of early China, or the periods before the Age of Confucius, was untrustworthy, for the sources on which the history was based were by and large unreliable.

As a convert to the ideals of the New Culture Movement, Fu Sinian was just as iconoclastic as his teacher and classmates. Yet armed with new knowledge acquired on his European trip, he also hoped to conduct more scientific investigations, using the methods of anthropology and archæology. No sooner had he founded the Institute of History and Philology than Fu sent an archæological team to Anyang, in Henan Province, where the team excavated ruins believed to date from the Shang dynasty (1600–1046 bce), one of the three dynasties that supposedly constituted the beginnings of ancient China but that the National Studies Movement had questioned. The discovery was rather encouraging: the Shang ruins produced sufficient material evidence, ranging from soil type and scope of the dwelling structure to traces and fragments of various workshops, to suggest the existence of a once flourishing civilization. The implications of the excavation were significant: Hu Shi, Fu's teacher, for example, began to modify his earlier stance on the invalidity of early Chinese history. Others also hoped to draw on the archæological investigation and develop a new understanding of the history of ancient China.

At the end of the 1920s, when Fu launched the archæological investigation, the need to gain a comprehensive and scientific interpretation of the course of Chinese civilizational development was especially appealing to the emerging academic community, for China was facing the increasing menace of Japan's invasion. Fu's investigation proved to many that, historically speaking, Chinese civilization had experienced a continuous course of development, which existed not only in literary sources but also in material remains. Moreover, Fu's leading of the Institute of History and Philology, together with Hu Shi's early leadership of the National Studies Movement on the Peking University campus and Liang Qichao's writing of the *Historical Methods* while teaching at Tsing-hua University during the last days of his life, were all exemplary in marking the growth of Chinese higher education. It was indeed during the 1920s that academic study became professionalized in the country, marked by the organization of professional societies and the publication of professional journals in different fields. Another sign of such development, as remarked at the beginning of this chapter, was the general requirement of its practitioners to acquire an advanced degree, preferably from an overseas institution, before receiving a teaching position in China's colleges and universities. By contrast, Zhang Taiyan had not taught at a modern university, nor did he show a particular interest in doing so throughout his life.

Hu Shi's National Studies Movement and Fu Sinian's archæological dig in Anyang were important events in the emergence of China's higher education. Thus viewed, the development of China's academic community and life coincided with the enlargement of the investigative persona, which was promoted and perceived by many as a model of academic virtue for anyone aspiring to join the community. Yet this by no means suggests that the interpretative persona had become irrelevant or unattractive. In fact, a significant change was to come as the 1930s began. On September 18, 1931, in the Mukden Incident, Japan took military action against China, which resulted in its conquest of Manchuria. Adopting a policy of non-resistance, the Chinese government appealed to the League of Nations for justice.

To aid the petition, Fu Sinian embarked on the writing of *Dongbei shigang (An Outline History of Northeast China)*. As indicated by its title, *Outline History of Northeast China* is an overview of the history of Manchuria and its connection and interactions with the rest of China. Needless to say, Fu's calling it "northeast China" aimed to prove that Manchuria historically had been an integral part of China.[26] Yet to handle such a broad subject, aiming to interpret a history that spanned several centuries, was not characteristic of Fu's disposition, nor was it in line with his belief in the nature of the historical study of modern times. After returning to China, in support of Hu and Gu's emphasis on source criticism, Fu had made a well-known statement that, in modern times, "historical study was equivalent to the scrutiny of historical sources." Of course, as shown in his investigation of the Shang ruins, Fu did not want to equate the study of history simply to the study of written historical sources. Rather, his establishment of the Institute of History and Philology exercised his plan to expand one's understanding of historical sources and adopt a more interdisciplinary approach.[27]

But Fu's writing of the *Outline History of Northeast China*, which he seldom mentioned later, was nonetheless quite telling; it epitomised the change of intellectual life in 1930s China. After the Mukden Incident, Japan continued to nibble at China's territory until it embarked on a full-scale invasion in July 1937, which started World War II in Asia. The escalation of the tension between China and Japan, which to some extent had begun as early as the late 1920s, contributed considerably to altering the direction of China's intellectual life and the valuation of sociopolitical goods cherished and pursued by its intellectuals. While Hu Shi, Gu Jiegang, and Fu Sinian remained exemplary scholars in the academic community, highly respected for their exact scholarship and painstaking research, more and more of their peers and students had already become increasingly doubtful of and disbelieving in their significance and implication. The Social History Discussion was a good example: it began in 1927, thus paralleling Fu Sinian's archæological investigation, and intensified in the early 1930s. With few exceptions, participants in the Discussion, some of them were Marxists and/or future Marxists, offered their reflective opinions on how to interpret the nature of Chinese history in the past and Chinese society at the present, in hopes of figuring out whether or not a sociopolitical revolution was needed and if it was, what kind of a revolution was most appropriate. That is, in the heyday of the enrichment and fortification of the investigative persona, the interpretative persona also received more and more attention among the educated class, even though many of them might not necessarily be associated with a research institution or a university. All the same, a new context was emerging, largely due to the deepening of China's national crisis from the late 1920s and the early 1930s. Arif Dirlik (1940–2017), who wrote an early book in English on the subject of Chinese Marxist historiography, offered the following observation:

> In its new context, Marxist historiography represented an unprecedented understanding to root history in social structure, revolutionizing the conceptualization of China's past. The proliferation of social-economic history of an unmistakably Marxist bent by the 1930s pointed to the ascendancy of historical materialism in Chinese historical studies.[28]

This new situation, needless to say, would foster a new scholarly persona from the 1930s onward, one that neither the four scholars we examine here, nor Fang Hung-chien, the fictional character in Qian Zhongshu's *Fortress Besieged*, were able to foresee, much less associate with. The topic, therefore, deserves another study.

Notes

1. Qian Zhongshu (Ch'ien Chung-shu), *Fortress Besieged*, trans. Jeanne Kelly and Nathan K. Mao (Bloomington, IN: Indiana University Press, 1979), p. 10.
2. Hayden White, *Metahistory: The Historical Imagination in Nineteenth-century Europe* (Baltimore, MD: Johns Hopkins University Press, 1973), pp 1–42. White's discussion of the "preconceptual" and the "prefigurative" illustrates the determinant literary modes of representation whereas my consideration is more inclusive.
3. See Herman Paul, 'What is a scholarly persona? Ten theses on virtues, skills, and desires', *History and Theory*, 53 (2014), 348–71, especially 365–7, and 'The virtues of a good historian in early Imperial Germany: Georg Waitz's contested example', *Modern Intellectual History*, 15 (2018), 681–709.
4. See Ching-i Tu (ed.), *The Hermeneutic Traditions in Chinese Culture: Classics and Interpretations* (New Brunswick, NJ: Transaction Publishers, 2000) and Ching-i (ed.), *Chinese Hermeneutics in Historical Perspective: Interpretation and Intellectual Change* (New Brunswick, NJ: Transaction Publishers, 2005). For a focused study of manuscript culture in ancient China, see Guolong Lai and Q. Edward Wang (eds), 'Manuscript culture in early China', *Chinese Studies in History*, 50:3 (2017).
5. There are a number of studies in Chinese of the evidential learning in the Qing period. For English readers, Benjamin Elman's *From Philosophy to Philology: Intellectual and Social Aspects of Change in Late Imperial China*, rev. ed. (Los Angeles, CA: UCLA Asian Pacific Monograph Series, 2001) remains a valuable guide.
6. A search in the database of Scripta Sinica finds that, separately, *zhiyong* was used as early as the Han period whereas *jingshi* first appeared in the Tang period (618–907), but the use of the two words together did not appear until late in the imperial period.
7. There have been discussions of the relationship between evidential scholarship and the Manchu rule in the Qing period. Qi Yongxiang, for instance, draws attention to the Qing policy of censorship as a cause for the rise of evidential scholarship. See his

QianJia kaojuxue yanjiu (Study of evidential learning in the Qianlong and Jiaqing reigns) (Beijing: Zhongguo shehui kexue chubanshe, 1998), pp 68–81. In his revised edition of *From Philosophy to Philology*, Benjamin Elman offers a nuanced discussion of the subject, as a response to his critics: pp ix–x. Readers may also be interested in reading R. Kent Guy's *The Emperor's Four Treasuries: Scholars and the State in the Late Ch'ien-lung Era* (Cambridge, MA: Harvard University Press, 1987).

8 Liang Qichao, *Xinshixue (New historiography)*, in *Liang Qichao shixue lunzhu sanzhong (Liang Qichao's three historical works)* (Hong Kong: Sanlian shudian, 1980), pp 10–14.
9 See Q. Edward Wang, 'China's search for national history', in Wang and Georg Iggers (eds), *Turning Points in Historiography: A Cross-Cultural Perspective* (Rochester, NY: University of Rochester Press, 2002), pp 185–208, especially pp 193, 189.
10 Zhang Taiyan, *Zhang Taiyan shengping yu xueshu zishu* (Zhang Taiyan's autobiographic accounts of his life and career) (Nanjing: Jiangsu renmin chubanshe, 1999), pp 47–8.
11 See Zhu Weizheng's preface to the *Zhang Taiyan quanji (Zhang Taiyan's complete works)*, vol. 3 (Shanghai: Shanghai renmin chubanshe, 2014), pp 7–9.
12 Zhang Taiyan, *Qiushu (Words of urgency)*, in *Zhang Taiyan quanji*, vol. 3, pp 7–8.
13 Zhang, *Zhang Taiyan quanji*, vol. 3, pp 134–5.
14 Wang, 'China's search for national history', in Wang and Iggers (eds), *Turning Points in Historiography*, pp 185–208. In his *Zhang Taiyan de sixiang (Zhang Taiyan's Ideas)* (Shanghai: Shanghai renmin chubanshe, 2012),Wang Fansen notes that Zhang tends to consider Confucius on a par with other philosophers of the age: pp 26–35.
15 All these treatises are included in Liang Qichao, *Liang Qichao quanji (Liang Qichao's complete works)*, vols 2 and 3 (Beijing: Beijing chubanshe, 1999).
16 Hu Shi, *Hu Shi wenji (Hu Shi's writings)*, vol. 6 (Beijing: Peking University Press, 1999), pp 382–419.
17 Q. Edward Wang, *Inventing China through History: The May Fourth Approach to Historiography* (Albany, NY: State University of New York Press, 2001), pp 58–9.
18 Hu, *Hu Shi wenji*, vol. 6, p. 157.
19 Ibid., pp 172–6. I have offered a more focused discussion of the revival of evidential scholarship in the early twentieth century and its impact on modern historical scholarship in China in Q. Edward Wang, 'Beyond east and west: Antiquarianism, evidential study, and global trends in historical study', *Journal of World History*, 19:4 (2008), 489–519.
20 In a study of the development of modern scholarship in China, Chen Pingyuan chooses to focus on Zhang Taiyan and Hu Shi in his *Zhongguo xiandai xueshu zhi jianli: yi Zhang Taiyan, Hu Shi weizhongxin (The establishment of modern Chinese scholarship: Centering on Zhang Taiyan and Hu Shi)* (Beijing: Peking University Press, 1998).
21 Hu, *Hu Shi wenji*, vol. 6, pp 155–6.
22 Besides acknowledging his debt to Zhang Taiyan in the preface he wrote to the *Outline History of Chinese Philosophy*, Hu Shi also gives a fuller assessment of Zhang's accomplishments in another long article, 'Wushi nianlai zhi Zhongguo wenxue (Chinese literature over the past half century)', in *Hu Shi wenji*, vol. 3, pp 200–63. More discussions of Zhang Taiyan's relationship with the New Culture Movement are found in Wang Rongzu (Wong Young-tzu), 'Kang Youwei Zhang Taiyan helun (A joint discussion of Kang Youwei and Zhang Taiyan)', *Zhongyang Yanjiuyuan Jindaishi yanjiusuo Jikan (Bulletin of the Institute of Modern History*, Academia Sinica*)*, 15 (1986), 115–70; Ren Fangqiu, 'Zhang Taiyan yu Wusi xinwenhua yundong (Zhang Taiyan and the May Fourth/New Culture Movement)', *Zhongzhou xuekan (Journal of Zhongzhou)*, 2 (1993), 105–9; and Q. Edward Wang, 'Confucius in the May Fourth era', in Paul Goldin (ed.), *A Concise Companion to Confucius* (Hoboken, NJ: Wiley Blackwell, 2017), pp 330–51, especially pp 342–6. For Gu Jiegang's leadership role in the National Studies Movement, see Laurence Schneider, *Ku Chieh-kang and China's New History* (Berkeley, CA: University of California Press, 1971) and Wang, *Inventing China through History*, pp 64–7.

INTERPRETATIVE AND INVESTIGATIVE

23 Liang Qichao, *Zhongguo lishi yanjiufa (Historical Methods for the Study of Chinese History)*, in *Liang Qichao shixue lunzhu sanzhong*, pp 45–7.
24 There have been a number of studies of Liang Qichao's *Historical Methods* in Chinese, which are hard to cite for reasons of space. For a more detailed discussion in English, see Wang, *Inventing China through History*, pp 103–11.
25 Liang, *Zhongguo lishi yanjiufa*, in *Liang Qichao shixue lunzhu sanzhong*, pp 85–91.
26 At the outset of the *Outline History of Northeast China* Fu Sinian explains why he chose to use "Northeast China" instead of "Manchuria." See Fu Sinian, *Dongbei shigang*, in *Fu Sinian quanji (Fu Sinian's complete works)*, vol. 2 (Changsha: Hunan jiaoyu chubanshe, 2000), pp 371–498.
27 Fu, *Fu Sinian quanji*, vol. 3, pp 12–15. For a more detailed study of Fu Sinian's scholarly career and his nationalist position, see Wang Fan-sen, *Fu Ssu-nien: A Life in Chinese History and Politics* (Cambridge: Cambridge University Press, 2000).
28 Arif Dirlik, *Revolution and History: Origins of Marxist Historiography in China, 1919–1937* (Berkeley, CA: University of California Press, 1978), p. 1.

CHAPTER 7

Coalescence and conflict: historians and their personae in the Portuguese New State

António da Silva Rêgo

Introduction

So far, the framework of scholarly personae has mostly been applied to centres of historical production such as nineteenth-century Germany and Britain. This chapter, by contrast, deals with a more peripheral case: the professionalization of history in early-twentieth-century Portugal, where the identity of the historian was as much a matter of concern as it had been in nineteenth-century Britain or Germany. In Portugal, the professionalization of history took place later than in most other European countries. Starting in the 1910s, it was clearly discernible only by the 1940s. It was in this period that historical activity transformed from a relatively solitary activity, practiced by 'men of letters', into a more collective enterprise, with historians working together in a 'professionalized' discipline. At the same time, in 1926, a military dictatorship was established, which in 1933 turned into the New State, a fascist regime that lasted until 1974.[1] Characterized by a mixture of nationalism, corporatism, conservatism, Catholicism and traditionalism, the New State regime nonetheless propagated the ideal of a 'New Man',[2] which it described in language in which virtues and vices featured quite prominently.

In this chapter I argue that scholarly personae offer a helpful lens for understanding the professionalization of history in Portugal. I define a scholarly persona as a constellation of *commitments to goods*, embodied through the cultivation of *virtues* and the honing of *skills* and *practices*, which together characterize the way in which groups of people *cooperate* as scholars, in a professionalized discipline. As the word suggests, a 'constellation' is more than a list. The often intricate ways in which commitments relate to each other are fundamental to understanding the dynamics within a discipline. To that end, I explore two types of personae. First, I examine an overarching persona, characteristic of the discipline as a whole.

Secondly, I zoom in on two sets of conflicting personae, corresponding to diverging paths within the discipline. These paths led historians to cultivate different virtues, skills and practices, thereby changing the constellations even if the terminology remained the same.

Because of its focus on practices, virtues and goods, the approach of scholarly personae as developed by Lorraine Daston, Otto Sibum and Herman Paul can do justice to the epistemic, political and moral aspects of historical scholarship, while building a bridge between the personal and the collective.[3] This is particularly relevant for the Portuguese case, given that Portuguese historiography in the New State has primarily been interpreted in political terms. Thus, one of the most important works on this subject, 'History in times of dictatorship' by Luís Reis Torgal, has an eye only for the relationship between historians and the regime, thereby ignoring the historian's epistemic and moral aspirations altogether.[4] This, in turn, makes Portuguese historiographical studies hardly comparable to historiographical traditions elsewhere. Studying historical scholarship in the New State through the lens of scholarly personae tries to correct this exceptionalism. Without depoliticizing historical studies, it seeks to offer a more balanced assessment of what Portuguese historians were doing at the time.

In the first half of the chapter, I will analyse the overarching persona – a baseline model that was embodied by the overwhelming majority of historians in Portugal between the 1930s and the 1960s. This persona was characterized by (1) a commitment to knowledge, displayed in virtues of scientific explanation and virtues of philological analysis; (2) a commitment to the nation, which corresponded to virtues of patriotism, justice and reverence for tradition; and (3) a commitment to unity, not only of the nation, but of the discipline, too. Subsequently, I will discuss two conflicts which are best interpreted as clashes of competing personae: (1) a conflict between men of letters and academics and (2) a conflict between the persona of the curator and the persona of the nation builder.

A discipline coalesces

In the 1920s, there was a great deal of diversity among Portuguese historians. Some of these historians were very notable amateurs; others were teaching at recently created departments of letters that functioned as *loci* of professionalization. Consequently, the term 'historian' was subject to a high degree of polysemy. This was particularly visible in the formation of the Portuguese Academy of History (APH: 1936–38), an institution created by the government of the dictatorship, and consisting of twenty-five founding members. These included people like Júlio Dantas, a writer and playwright, Alfredo Pimenta, a prominent man of letters, Abel Fontoura da Costa, a military colonial administrator, law professors like Paulo Merêa and Marcelo Caetano, publicists such as Manuel Múrias, and traditional historians like António Baiao (director of the National Archive), Damião Peres (former high school teacher and university professor) and António de Vasconcelos (a priest, university professor and president of the Academy).[5] The question arises whether a group with such varied occupations could ever truly function as a profession.[6]

Initially, the Academy aimed less for professionalization of the discipline than to pursue political goals. Without much corporate identity, it was supposed to serve as a body with which the state could discuss the national past, with the aim of reinforcing and shaping a Portuguese collective memory. Gradually, however, the Academy took on professional status and, as a result of this, gained some institutional identity. This had notable impact on the meaning of the term 'historian'. Increasingly, 'historians' distinguished themselves from 'men of letters', mainly by emphasizing three characteristic commitments: to acquiring knowledge, to nation and to unity. I will discuss these commitments in turn, starting with the aim of deepening knowledge of the past. In relation to that aim, two types of virtue became visible: virtues of scientific explanation, on one hand, and virtues of philological analysis on the other.

Virtues of scientific explanation

The scientific attitude of Portuguese historians during the first half of the century reveals clear traces of positivist influences, which can be dated back to the nineteenth century. However, while nineteenth-century positivists in Portugal had been deeply concerned with philosophical aspects of historical thinking – they reflected extensively on determinism and evolution[7] – Academy members in the 1940s were more interested in probabilistic models of historical interpretation. Gastão de Matos's 1944 argument in favour of probabilistic historical explanations, for instance, is reminiscent of Carl Hempel's covering-law model of explanation (a way of thinking about history that stresses its methodological unity with the natural sciences).[8] Something similar can be observed in Alfredo Pimenta. Addressing a fellow member of the Academy, he maintained:

> It is not with *what could be* or could not be that we ground ourselves for our scientific positions: it is on what has been ascertained... Everything we conclude is provisory. Nor does science have the pretention of the definitive. And it does not, precisely because it knows that tomorrow is the correction of yesterday.[9]

Another notable example is Júlio Dantas, President of the Academy of Sciences of Lisbon and member of the Portuguese Academy of History:

> Whatever may be the definition of the concept of history, and as great as the divergences between historians, philosophers and sociologists may present themselves to be in terms of the nature, objective, content and methods of this science, it cannot be contested that its fundamental element is the 'fact' – in its triplicate contingent, necessary and logical expression – and that, not only in the investigation of historical facts, but in the consequent operations of the erudite synthesis and the scientific synthesis (deduction of laws), the historian aspires, above all else, to the knowledge of the truth about the events of the human past.[10]

Virtues of scientific explanation are also discernible in historians' style of writing, particularly in how they structured their narrative explanations. On one hand, the use of single-cause explanations was quite dominant, which led to long chains of causes and effects. On the other hand, categorization and essentialization were also employed quite often, which resulted in narratives that relied on abstract schematization and classification. These practices showed the importance attached to virtues of *clarity* and *simplicity*, especially in historical explanations.

Virtues of philological analysis

Historians' commitment to careful study of historical documents, by contrast, could be seen, first and foremost, in the auxiliary sciences that they developed at the time. These auxiliary sciences included numismatics, paleography, archæology, diplomatics and even 'hagiography in rigorously scientific ways'.[11] Connecting virtues of scientific explanation with virtues of philological analysis, the auxiliary sciences made diligence, patience and thoroughness essential virtues for working historians. These virtues were practised in the course of historical work, but also in discussions about source criticism, for instance in the weekly meetings of the APH, where serious disagreements between Academy members sometimes erupted. Alfredo Pimenta, for instance, criticized Rui de Azevedo's interpretation of the medieval terms *Infans*, *Princeps*, and *Rex* on philological grounds.[12]

Great value was attributed to primary sources. Most publications of the APH were editions of source material, and others often included many sources as annexes. Indeed, at the time, it was common practice even for brief research articles to include *all* sources, sometimes covering hundreds of pages, by way of appendix. Consequently, the APH spent most of its budget on source editions, many of which focused exclusively on a particular document or specific archive. Even wide-ranging studies like the

History of Portugal edited by Damião Peres included many reproductions of archival source material.[13] Such photographic reproductions might suggest that APH members cherished the virtue of 'mechanical objectivity' as defined by Lorraine Daston and Peter Galison.[14] However, the most striking aspect of APH source publications was, in fact, their ambition to categorize and reproduce as much archival material as possible. With the presentation not only of a few important documents, but what can often be described as 'excess', came a sense of the sublime.[15] More than demonstrating the detachment characteristic of mechanical objectivity, these materials (collections, lists) showed a desire for accumulation.

Often, these works of accumulation – products of diligence, thoroughness and patience – were so exhaustive that they went well beyond what was essential to understand the topic at hand. For that reason, these works sometimes functioned as *Wunderkammern*, which showed the reader all the marvels that Portugal had accomplished or discovered.[16] This is especially true of Peres' *History of Portugal*, which included photographs of primary sources,[17] a range of diagrams, maps and technical drawings,[18] as well as twentieth-century paintings of mythologized scenes from Portuguese history.[19]

Historians were not merely presenting tokens of the past in order to accumulate them, they also wanted to share the excitement of the archive, just as nineteenth-century Romantics had done. At the same time, they wanted to show, in good scientific fashion, that they had a panoptical overview of the source material available. In a sense, these historians thus combined two fantasies: the Romantic fantasy of immediate contact with the past and the scientific fantasy of the panopticon.[20]

This phenomenon did not diminish during the New State period. If we compare the two greatest works of the 1930s and the 1960s, Damião Peres' *History of Portugal* and Joel Serrão's *Dictionary of Portuguese History*, we encounter the ambition to encompass everything, including much that even scholars would not need to know.[21] (Consequently, both works are voluminous: more than 7,000 pages in the first work, more than 3,500 in the second.) However, while the former wants to tell a story about the past, the latter (a dictionary) more resembles a list, created with much diligence, patience and thoroughness.[22]

The nation

Portuguese historians were also deeply committed to their nation.[23] This was most apparent in the significance attached to virtues such as patriotism, justice and reverence for tradition. Not only was the APH created as an organ for national history, it also had a mission to justify the inalienable rights of Portugal,[24] which contributed to historical legitimization of the state and its empire overseas. Patriotism implied more concretely a research focus on periods that ought to be remembered, such as the 'foundation of the nationality' in 1139,[25] the Portuguese discoveries and expansion and the restoration of independence in 1640. Not only was the Academy engaged in commemorating the past, historians themselves also played important roles in civic commemorations.[26]

Regarding justice, historians believed themselves to have a duty to rewrite the history of those events that, in their view, had not been done sufficient justice in existing historiography. These moments included the eighteenth-century monarchy, which was seen as having suffered from mistreatment by nineteenth-century liberals and later republicans also. Consider these remarks by Father Garcia de Vasconcelos, President of the APH, about King João V (1706–50), a man whom he claimed

> worked so much for the aggrandizement of Portugal, who supported and propelled the Arts and the Letters so much and with maximum effort... An entire century of criminal demolition, of revolting misrepresentation of History was necessary to dim the intense brilliance of his reign. Today, fortunately, through insistent and laborious investigation of the sources, History is being purified, and justice is done to the magnanimous chief of the Nation that was D. João V.[27]

Historiographical judgements like these belonged to a project outlined in one of the official aims of the APH: to promote 'historical truth in the national interest'.[28] Although this project had clear moralistic and didactic overtones, it would be mistaken to assume that historians working within the APH engaged in the kind of propaganda produced by cultural functionaries at the time.[29] As they were *also* committed to deepening historical knowledge, they were historians as well as propagandists, in different combinations. Precisely at this point, the concept of scholarly personae becomes relevant. Only by examining the *constellations* of commitments, virtues and skills that guided these historians can one avoid overemphasizing a single aspect of their persona. This is particularly welcome in the study of Portuguese historiography, given that existing studies often focus narrowly on historians' political agendas, thereby ignoring their epistemic aspirations.

Unity: empowerment vs independence

Thirdly, Portuguese historians were committed to unity. This means not only that historians were supposed to identify with the entire nation (as discussed above), but also that they were expected to further the unity of their discipline. Unity was seen as badly needed for an institution like the APH, an organization that saw itself, and was seen by the state, as a body important enough to be represented in the Corporative Chamber (one of two parliamentary chambers). Unity also mattered to collective enterprises such as Peres's *History of Portugal* and the historical conferences that were organized by the government, such as the Congress of the Portuguese World (1940).

Unity was an especial priority in the 1930s and 1940s, with the establishment of the Academy, which created a rift between men of letters and Academy members. Backed by a state-sponsored institution, the latter were truly *disciplined* to the extent that they began to adopt shared vocabularies, standards and practices. These practices included the convention of making decisions unanimously, irrespective of how much discussion had preceded them. The government consultation of the Academy on the issue of when and where the battle of Vale-de-Vez had taken place was a paradigmatic example of this culture.[30] Although the issue was not very politically sensitive, the historians of the Academy pretended, despite three days of discussion and disagreement, that they had reached a unanimous conclusion. This showed how much unity and its corresponding consensual virtues, such as not criticizing others too openly, mattered to historians in the Portuguese New State.

Yet in addition to consensual virtues, historians were expected to respect hierarchy. When the APH was created, it was provided with a small Academic Council supposed to chair the sessions and to answer to the Minister of National Education.[31] However, the Council quickly acquired significant amounts of power, to such an extent that the members were now at the service of the Council, even if this was not exactly what the APH rules stipulated. What respect for hierarchy concretely implied became visible in 1938, when Alfredo Pimenta was asked by the Council to participate in a Commission for the Centennial of the Foundation of the Nationality. Pimenta refused this on the ground that

> [t]he Council does not have statutory competence to deliberate on these matters, and the Academy has not provided it for them... The Academy is not formed by children or serfs, to whom the Council may give, without further appeal, orders, or point out services that are to be rendered... I have my work plan. I am waiting for the Academy to come together in order to present [my work] to [the plenary] – because it is to [the plenary] that I must present [my work], not to the Council, separately.[32]

This challenge came from a man of means, with sufficient social capital to write in newspapers, to be heard in the public space and even to correspond personally with Salazar.[33] Pimenta did not need the Academy in order to be published or to reach large audiences.

As the conflict unfolded, it became clear that it revolved around two distinct personae: the modern academic and the man of letters. While the former was paradigmatically (but not exclusively) embodied in members of the APH, the latter had acquired status and reputation near the end of the monarchy and during the Portuguese First Republic. While the academic could be found at universities, the man of letters inhabited the public space, for example around Chiado, the literary district of Lisbon where most of the newspapers could be found, and the cream of Portuguese literary life met to drink coffee and discuss politics and arts.[34]

The power struggle between Alfredo Pimenta and the APH culminated in the marginalization of two men of letters from the Academy. As he continued to defy the Academy over the following few years, Pimenta was eventually expelled. Caetano Beirão, another historian who can be considered as embodying this persona of the man of letters, came to his defence and resigned from the Academy.[35] Pimenta found himself having to resort to his own government connections, and his cultural and social capital, to be reinstated.[36] His membership of the Academy was ultimately restored to him via a ministerial dispatch, but he was never able again to do serious work within the APH.

As the commitment to unity became more important, it became apparent that a schism was in the making: the overarching persona mentioned above was falling apart. The issue in question was not historical interpretation, but the virtues that were supposed to mark a good historian: consensual virtues or virtues of independent thinking. Alfredo Pimenta did not want the historian's expertise to be tied to the ability to serve the discipline's institutions. He wanted to preserve historians' negative liberty, so to speak – their freedom from interference by fellow academics, including especially Council members.[37] The Academy, in contrast, was perceived by several members as offering historians the positive liberty to cooperate with others, thereby allowing them to become more productive as scholars and, individually as well as collectively, more relevant to the nation. This, then, was a conflict about conflicting goods and sets of virtues: independence and courage, on one hand, and cooperation and conciliation on the other.

Conflicting personae: the curator vs the nation builder

During the early New State regime (1930s and 1940s), most Portuguese historians privileged mono-causal explanations, thereby offering clear, relatively uncomplicated accounts of the past. This clarity, however, often went hand in hand with a readiness to exclude facts that were perceived as not very meaningful. As the discipline coalesced, two other styles of writing began to develop, both of which slowly undermined the consensus on how history should be understood and explained, while challenging the historians' overarching persona.

On one hand, some historians began to consider conventional historical narratives insufficient for conveying a sense of the true greatness of the Portuguese past. Introducing metaphors and hyperbole that had previously been unacceptable, they began to write more vivid narratives that were openly patriotic in identifying the 'spirit of the nation' in its historical development – a project that more 'realistically' inclined historians rejected as incompatible with true scholarship. Indeed, these new historians openly declared that they aimed for more than realist representations of the Portuguese past: they wanted to engage in the more ambitious and more difficult task of pointing out what was truly great and meaningful in it. In a technical sense, their works might therefore be classified as specimens of anti-realist history.[38] On the other hand, another segment of the discipline started to abandon mono-causal explanations in favour of multicausal ones, without trying to sort out which of the causes was most important. They broke away from linear narratives that could be easily apprehended by the reader in order to be as faithful as possible to the complexities of historical source material.

These ideals corresponded to two very different ways of being a historian: one that allowed the scholar's world view to shape historical interpretations and one that deliberately sought to avoid this. Of course, few historians unambiguously belonged to either of these categories. The two personae – I shall call them the *curator* and the *nation builder* – should be understood as ideal types between which historians positioned themselves in word and/or deed. Many historians sometimes worked for a while in proximity to one persona, while moving closer to the other on another occasion. Few historians, indeed, consistently commit themselves to a single persona. This should come as no surprise, as human beings can be professional in various ways, cultivating different skills and virtues, as Herman Paul has suggested of nineteenth-century German historiography.[39]

The term curator refers to the aim of presenting historical artefacts as they reached the historian, instead of integrating them in convenient narrative templates. Characteristic of the curator was, in the first place, its commitment to not portray the past as something simple or familiar. This was achieved through multicausal explanations, narratives with many twists and turns, and a systematic avoidance of straightforward conclusions. Virtues of clarity and simplicity were thus, to a greater or lesser extent, exchanged for virtues of precision and completeness. Curators presented complex narratives, which conveyed as much historical source material as possible.

Paulo Merêa, for example, a law professor and historian of the Middle Ages, was so concerned with not projecting anything back upon the past that he refused even to accept his own terminology. Writing about the political regime in Portugal during the Middle Ages, he described it by defining it, while calling into question the very terms that structured his account ('feudalism' and 'manorialism'):

> The state of war in which life was permanently lived kept firm the authority of the crown, as we previously noted, while on the other hand a considerable mass of free men, especially since they were constituted into municipal *nuclei*, served, so to speak, as a counterweight against the nobility. It was this considerable mass of free men and small land owners that, together with the fact that kings had a rich patrimony at their disposal, made it possible for the latter to solve the problem of access to cavalry without making use of the system of the Frank monarchs. Many centuries would have been necessary, as Albornoz observed, for the state of things in the peninsular countries to convert itself into a complete and finished feudal system. But before that transformation could be realized, the renaissance of Roman law renovated the classic conception of the State, forever interrupting that evolution and not even allowing the manorial regime to develop completely.[40]

Instead of providing the reader with a clearly identifiable form, Merêa led his readers along meandering possibilities and concepts found in texts of the time. Instead of telling a neat story, he wanted to do justice to everything he had found. This occasionally led to interesting contradictions, as can be seen in the following passage, which argues that liberation of the servile classes coexisted with these classes being subjected to obligations that reinforced their servile condition:

> Several causes acted with effect towards the liberation of the servile classes, and among them, with particular intensity and efficacy, the multiplication of the charter letters, in such a way that, with this evolution, serfdom converted itself into another economic-juridical form of settlement: the free or voluntary settlement, in which settlers possessed the essential freedom, the freedom of movement, while in fact many of them were to find themselves subjected to obligations that would more or less approximate them to the servile condition.[41]

Not all curatorial writing took this form, though. Virgínia Rau, professor at the University of Lisbon, often directly showed her readers a selection of artefacts from the past: lists of ships and the commerce they engaged in, enumerations of farm objects and lists of agricultural output.[42] Yet instead of adding these lists as appendices to historical narratives, Rau allowed the lists to draw their readers into narratives of their own. Thus, in her studies of agrarian explorations in Portugal, Rau did not tell a narrative, but presented sources from which readers could conclude for themselves that agricultural explorations at the time were small. This was her version of not interfering with historical source material.[43]

Clearly, then, there was an aspect of sobriety to the work of these authors that came close to asceticism. Rau's and Merêa's fidelity to their sources was such that they did not want to write narratives. If these are relatively extreme examples, illustrating the persona of the curator in near ideal fashion, many historians engaged in similar, curator-like practices in hesitating to formulate hypotheses and shrinking back from making themselves visible in their texts.[44] To varying degrees, they dissociated themselves from clarity and simplicity as leading virtues, thereby challenging the overarching persona.

The persona of the nation builder, by contrast, was that of a historian who did not hesitate to draw on popular myths and images in giving narrative shape to Portuguese history. By doing so, the nation builder presented the national past in a form easily recognizable to most Portuguese readers. If this required rearrangement or removal of historical facts, the nation builder preferred narrative effect to historical accuracy. This is why the second persona that Portuguese historical studies saw emerge was committed to what one might call anti-realist history writing (anti-realist in the sense that it did not require the historian's account to be 'a genuine re-presentation of that past as it actually happened').[45]

This ideal type is usually associated with historians like João Ameal. While Ameal did not positively define his style of writing, he did distinguish his practice both from what he called 'small historicism', with its almost fetishist focus on facts, dates and places, and from 'immoderate obedientiaries of historical parallels'. Ameal preferred history to be a 'patrimony of valid experiences and a gallery of models worthy of being preserved in the collective memory'.[46] It entailed a clear evaluative component that implicitly gave shape to the past – a shape that could not be accidental, as it was eminently moral in nature. An example of this approach can be found in a passage introducing the history of the Saint João de Brito, a seventeenth-century missionary:

> In what state do we find Portugal, in the middle of the 17th century? In a state of permanent tension – creative, struggling, reconstructive tension. We could say that, all over the country, new energies vibrate. We can feel a unanimous will to face the obstacles, the dangers, the difficulties which have accumulated – and to draw, beyond, new ample roads, worthy of the traditions of national greatness.[47]

If Ameal had been the only one to embody this persona – today he is seen more as a propagandist and political thinker than as a historian[48] – then the significance of this persona would be limited. Despite belonging to the APH, he was an amateur (in the sense that he was never truly professional, despite his commercial success). However, if we recognize that personae can be embodied to varying degrees, then many historians at the time were indebted to the figure of the nation builder, even though there was a tendency for more curatorial approaches to develop in academic and university circles, with anti-realism gradually decreasing in popularity during the 1950s and 1960s.

Although, for example, Damião Peres and David Lopes, two historians that were more highly respected in the academic community than Ameal, predominantly used causal and categorical explanations, they occasionally engaged in explanations that can be associated with nation-building historians. In the *History of Portugal* he edited, Peres wrote that no Portuguese man died or was wounded in the battle of Aljubarrota (1385).[49] This was obviously false, as Peres most likely knew, or could have known at least. So either this was gross negligence or Peres's idea was to convey some kind of truth through a 'non-fact' – a statement that, although historically inaccurate, sought to convey that the battle had been a total victory for Portugal. Another good example of anti-realistic representation can be found in David Lopes's account of the preparations for the Portuguese conquest of Ceuta:

> Everything was obtained without violence. All the copper and silver that could be had was gathered, in the kingdom and outside it, with which much coin was minted, without recourse to any condition that would oppress the nation, and without declaring the objective of the enterprise, about which secrecy was desirable. Everyone wanted to serve the king.[50]

Although this was a quite simplistic way of telling the story, the idea this passage conveyed was that relative consensus had existed with regard to conquering African territory.

Writing history like a nation builder did not necessarily imply that historians became propagandists. It is important to realize that historians forcing their facts into a convenient narrative could *also* be committed to serious scholarly practices. So, again, the question is *to what extent* did historians abandon faithfulness to their sources and cultivation of virtues like precision and diligence? In so far as they privileged story telling over historical accuracy, the historian as nation builder posed just as serious a threat to the overarching persona as did the historian as curator. While the curator was abandoning clarity and simplicity, the nation builder abandoned virtues of philological analysis. So, through both developments the overarching persona came under serious pressure.

What is most interesting, then, in studies of Portuguese history-writing during the New State is that, despite professionalization, the history community retained quite some variety or even pluralism. This is all the more surprising given the limitations on free speech in the New State, most notably through censorship. How, then, was this possible? The answer is that, at the time, concepts like 'objectivity' were rather diffuse. Unlike Germany, for example, Portugal had no tradition that associated objectivity with asceticism.[51] Many Portuguese historians could therefore talk about 'objectivity' and 'distance' without actually engaging in ascetic scholarly practices. The suppression of patriotic feeling in particular was firmly discouraged by most historians shaping the field.

Equally interesting, but less surprising, is that authors most reluctant to make their own voice heard in their texts were scholars who most depended on their academic status. Merêa and Rau, for instance, were professors in Coimbra and Lisbon, respectively, and therefore establishment figures with much cultural capital. However, they had not nearly as much social capital as Ameal. The persona of the historian as nation builder was more prominent among people who enjoyed social standing outside the Academy.

Conclusion

Following the creation of an academic infrastructure for historical studies in the early decades of the twentieth century, Portuguese historical studies became professional. In the course of this process, an overarching persona emerged, constituted by three complex commitments: to knowledge, to the nation and to unity. The latter was especially important as the profession developed from a collection of individuals into a more corporate entity. In the course of this, the man of letters was gradually replaced by the academic, even though the former never completely disappeared. The commitment to knowledge also caused disagreement among historians. While scientific explanation and philological analysis initially were aims that many historians shared, increasingly the profession became divided between two new personae: the curator, who wanted to be as faithful as possible to historical artefacts, even if that meant abandoning clarity and simplicity as guiding virtues, and the nation builder, whose identification with the greatness of the Portuguese past was such that ignoring historical facts for the sake of dramatic narrative was not necessarily perceived as problematic. As this chapter has argued, these conflicting personae could develop because of a lack of shared understanding of what a historian was.

The personae approach adopted in this chapter allows us to improve our understanding of Portuguese historiography during a period when conformity was the norm (notwithstanding exceptional figures like Oliveira Marques and Magalhães Godinho). Without underestimating the political dimension of historical writing under the New State, the personae approach allows us to understand that historiography cannot be reduced to its political aspect or to the regime under which it developed. It draws attention to historians' aspirations that were influenced by broader cultural and intellectual developments, while recognizing that these aspirations often existed in the plural and in tension with each other.

Notes

1. Debates abound over the degree to which the regime was actually fascist. Some historians assert that it should indeed be qualified as fascist, while others argue that the term should be reserved for more aggressive and violent regimes, calling the New State a corporatist-conservative regime. I use a fairly broad conception of the term, referring not so much to the structure of the regime as to the sociocultural environment that supported it.
2. Fernando Rosas (ed.), *O Estado Novo* (Lisbon: Editorial Estampa, 1998), pp 179–83.
3. Herman Paul, 'What is a scholarly persona? Ten theses on virtues, skills, and desires', *History and Theory*, 53 (2014), 348–71.
4. Luís Reis Torgal, 'História em tempo de ditadura', in *História da História em Portugal, Sécs. XIX–XX*, vol. 1, ed. Fernando Catroga, José Amado Mendes and Luis Reis Torgal (Lisbon: Temas e Debates, 1998), pp 273–310.
5. Academia Portuguesa da História (APH), *Boletim: Primeiro e Segundo Anos, 1937–1938* (Lisbon: Editorial Ática, 1940), pp 65–6.
6. For more on the relation between history as a discipline and the phenomenon of professionalization, see Robert Townsend, *History's Babel: Scholarship, Professionalization and the Historical Enterprize in the United States, 1880–1940* (Chicago: University of Chicago Press, 2013), pp 1–10.
7. Fernando Catroga, 'Positivistas e Republicanos', in Catroga, Mendes and Torgal, *História da História em Portugal*, vol. 1, pp 106–8.
8. APH, *Boletim, Oitavo Ano, 1944* (Lisbon: Oficinas Gráficas da Casa Portuguesa, 1945), pp 93–4; Carl G. Hempel, 'The function of general laws in history', *Journal of Philosophy*, 39 (1942), 35–48.
9. Alfredo Pimenta, [untitled text] (1939), file of Alfredo Pimenta, APH, pp 1–2.
10. Júlio Dantas, *Congresso do Mundo Português*, vol. 19 (Lisbon: Comissão Executiva dos Centenários, 1940), p. 84.
11. APH, *Boletim, Sexto Ano, 1942* (Lisbon: Oficinas Gráficas da Casa Portuguesa, 1944), pp 87–90.
12. Alfredo Pimenta, 'Notas críticas às observações do Sr. Dr. Rui de Azevedo' (1939), in file of Alfredo Pimenta, APH, pp 1–8.
13. Damião Peres (ed.), *História de Portugal, Edição Monumental Comemorativa do 8º Centenário da Fundação da Nacionalidade*, 8 vols (Barcelos: Portucalense Editora, 1928–37).
14. Lorraine Daston and Peter Galison, *Objectivity* (New York: Zone Books, 2007), pp 115–90.
15. Umberto Eco, *The Infinity of Lists* (New York: Rizzoli, 2009), p. 223.
16. Ibid., pp 201–5.
17. Peres, *História de Portugal*, vol. 2, pp 90, 200.
18. Peres, *História de Portugal*, vol. 1, pp 136, 142, 145, 164.
19. Ibid., pp 8–9; Peres, *História de Portugal*, vol. 2, pp 344–5.
20. Jo Tollebeek, '"Turn'd to dust and tears": revisiting the archive', *History and Theory*, 43 (2004), 237–45.

21 Joel Serrão (ed.), *Dicionário de História de Portugal* (Lisbon: Iniciativas Editoriais, 1963–71).
22 Eco, *Infinity of Lists*, pp 245–54.
23 For more on the discussion whether the nation can be considered a 'good', see António da Silva Rêgo, 'History in times of fascism: discipline and practices of history during the beginning of the Portuguese New State' (MA thesis, Leiden University, 2015), pp 45–6.
24 António Carneiro Pacheco, 'Regimento da junta nacional de educação', in *Diário do Governo*, I Série nº 116, de 19 de Maio de 1936, Decreto nº 26.661, art. 39º; Carneiro Pacheco, 'Estatutos da Academia Portuguesa da História', in *Diário do Governo*, I Série nº 177, de 31 de Julho de 1937, Decreto nº 27.913, art. 2º.
25 Augusto Costa Veiga, 'Ourique – Vale de Vez', in *Anais da Academia Portuguesa da História, Ciclo da Fundação da Nacionalidade*, vol. 1 (1940), pp 13–154; Alfredo Pimenta, *A Fundação e a Restauração de Portugal, Conferencia proferida na Sessão Solemne da Camara Municipal de Guimarães, em 2 de Junho de 1940* (Lisbon: Câmara Municipal de Guimarães, 1940).
26 For examples, see APH, *Boletim, Quarto Ano, 1940* (Lisbon: Oficinas Gráficas da Casa Portuguesa, 1942), pp 82–8; APH, *Boletim Sétimo Ano 1943* (Lisbon: Oficinas Gráficas da Casa Portuguesa, 1942), p. 61; APH, *Boletim, Décimo Ano, 1946* (Lisbon: João Pinto, 1947), pp 68–9, 87–93.
27 APH, *Boletim 1937 1938*, pp 172–3.
28 Pacheco, 'Estatutos', art. 2º.
29 For example, see the case of Costa Brochado in Luís Reis Torgal, *Estados Novos, Estado Novo: Ensaios de História Política e Cultural*, vol. 2 (Coimbra: Imprensa da Universidade de Coimbra, 2009), pp 106–16.
30 APH, *Boletim 1940*, 82–8.
31 Pacheco, 'Estatutos'.
32 Alfredo Pimenta, [Carta enviada ao Exmo. Snr. Conde de Tovar], 22.5.1938, in file of Alfredo Pimenta, APH, pp 1–2.
33 Manuel Braga da Cruz (ed.), *Salazar e Alfredo Pimenta: Correspondência, 1931–1950* (Lisbon: Verbo, 2008).
34 Luís Trindade, *O Estranho Caso do Nacionalismo Português: O Salazarismo entre a Literatura e a Política* (Lisbon: Imprensa de Ciências Sociais, 2008), pp 75–130.
35 Caetano Beirão, [Letter to the APH renouncing his position], in file of Caetano Beirão, APH.
36 We can find Pimenta's account of what happened in Alfredo Pimenta, *Para a História da Academia Portuguesa da História* (Lisbon: Author's edition, 1948).
37 This can be seen in the defence of Alfredo Pimenta by João do Amaral in the National Assembly; *Diário das Sessões*, IV 61 9 December 1946, pp 46–7.
38 Anthony Jensen, *Nietzsche's Philosophy of History* (Cambridge: Cambridge University Press, 2013), pp 141–8. For a more in-depth discussion of this term as applied to the present setting, see Rêgo, 'History in times of fascism', pp 113–15.
39 Herman Paul, 'The virtues of a good historian in early Imperial Germany: Georg Waitz's contested example', *Modern Intellectual History*, 15 (2018), 681–709.
40 Paulo Merêa, 'Terceira parte – organização social e administração pública', in Damião Peres (ed.), *História de Portugal, Edição Monumental Comemorativa do 8º Centenário da Fundação da Nacionalidade*, vol. 2 (Barcelos: Portucalense Editora, 1929), p. 470.
41 Merêa, 'Organização social', p. 448.
42 Virgínia Rau, 'A grande exploração agrária em Portugal a partir dos fins da Idade Média', in *Estudos de historia económica* (Lisbon: Ática, 1961), pp 15–32.
43 Ibid., pp 24–5.
44 See, for example, Damião Peres, 'Sétima parte – a reconquista Cristã', in *História de Portugal, Edição Monumental Comemorativa do 8º Centenário da Fundação da Nacionalidade*, vol. 1, ed. Damião Peres (Barcelos: Portucalense Editora, 1928), pp 435–6.

45 Jensen, *Nietzsche's Philosophy of History*, p. 142.
46 João Ameal, *Perspectivas da História* (Lisbon: Livraria SamCarlos, 1960), pp 7–10.
47 João Ameal, *João de Brito, Herói da Fé e do Império* (Lisbon: Edições SPN, 1941), p. 5.
48 Torgal, *Estados Novos, Estado Novo*, vol. 2, pp 83–8.
49 Damião Peres, 'Capítulo XXIV – a crise da nacionalidade', in Damião Peres (ed.) *História de Portugal, Edição Monumental Comemorativa do 8º Centenário da Fundação da Nacionalidade*, vol 2. (Barcelos: Portucalense Editora, 1929), p. 370.
50 David Lopes, 'Capítulo III – os portugueses em Marrocos: Ceuta e Tânger', in *História de Portugal, Edição Monumental Comemorativa do 8º Centenário da Fundação da Nacionalidade*, vol. 3 (Barcelos: Portucalense Editora, 1931), p. 385.
51 Paul, 'Virtues of a good historian', 698.

CHAPTER 8

The emergence of the English Marxist historian's scholarly persona: the English Revolution debate of 1940–41

Sina Talachian

Introduction

Otto Sibum and Lorraine Daston define a persona as 'a cultural identity that simultaneously shapes the individual in body and mind and creates a collective with a shared and recognizable physiognomy... creatures of historical circumstance; they emerge and disappear within specific contexts'.[1] The Marxist historian is one such persona or social species which emerged within specific contexts, such as France and the Soviet Union in the 1920s and 1930s. My focus will be on one of its most influential iterations, which defined its semantic content in Britain by the 1960s when the persona became a viable one to adopt there. It originated in the Communist Party Historians' Group (CPHG), founded in 1946 and dissolved in 1956. My aim in this chapter is to delineate the emergence of this English Marxist historian's persona by looking at the debate that precipitated the Group's founding. This debate came to define not only the Group's main research agenda, but by extension also the basic contours of the persona that was being fashioned within it.[2] Although the debate continued until 1948, when a majority view came to be established, I will focus here on the initial and most decisive stage of it, in 1940 and 1941.

It was the outcome of this phase, beginning with the publication of Christopher Hill's 'The English Revolution: 1640' in 1940,[3] that opened up the possibility within the Communist Party for a Historians' Group to be formed in 1946. The basic contours of this Marxist historian's persona that was being invented are revealed by the various participants in the debate, in particular those who advanced Hill's thesis and founded the Historians' Group along with him: Maurice Dobb, Dona Torr and A. L. Morton. Moreover, the historiography that the debate produced came to be one of the chief calling cards for this Marxist historian's persona while it was being cultivated and disseminated, from the Group's founding until the 1960s and 1970s, when it came under increasing scrutiny and its influence in academia began to wane.[4]

In 1940 Hill's thesis was novel and bursting with explanatory power that was intended to bring to an end the dominance of 'bourgeois' historiography and displace the persona of the 'bourgeois' historian.[5] By relying on meticulous study of primary sources and eschewing overly reductive economic determinism, as was common among his classical Marxist predecessors,[6] Hill and other members of the Group active in academia had abided by the epistemic virtues promulgated within the discipline. However, at the same time they also maintained a commitment to distinctively Marxist epistemic, moral and political goods and the virtues required to obtain them. These constitute the basic elements that went into the making of the English Marxist historian's persona as exemplified in the English Revolution debate. They consisted of the epistemic commitment to obtaining a dialectical and historical view or understanding of history, the moral commitment to the emancipation of the proletariat and the political commitment to Communism of the Soviet variety as espoused by the Communist Party of Great Britain (CPGB).[7] The obtaining of these commitments required the exercising of appropriate virtues, such as employing dialectical and historical materialist methods, engaging in class analysis and maintaining loyalty to the Communist Party.[8] These virtues in turn implied an opposition to vices, which members of the Historians' Group believed that 'bourgeois' historians lacked.[9] However, as shall be seen in the discussion of the debate, there was also a struggle over the proper interpretation of these commitments and virtues, one that played out within both the Historians' Group itself and the wider Communist Party.[10]

Constellations of commitments and the concept of distorted desire

While Daston and Sibum provide a useful basic definition of 'persona', the analytical framework for persona analysis that I employ in this study, with some minor adjustments, is the one developed by Herman Paul. The terminology of virtues and goods is derived from his helpful elaboration of the concept of personae as consisting of 'constellations of commitments to goods (epistemic, moral, political, and so forth), the pursuit of which requires the exercise of certain virtues and skills'.[11] These virtues and skills are in turn 'rooted in desires, which are shaped by the examples of others as well as by promises of reward',[12] and I would add by threats of punishment. As with Daston and Sibum, personae are collective templates transcending individual variation, which is why they ought to be perceived as archetypal models of scholarly selfhood, to be found in an intermediary level between the micro and macro levels of analysis.[13] The notion of desire helps illuminate a distinguishing feature of the English Marxist historian's persona relating to the unusually politicized and hierarchical environment in which it was fashioned, namely the CPGB. Naturally, there were also hierarchies and politics in the academy, but as deeply committed Party members the historians in the CPGB had to contend with a different *degree* and *kinds* of manipulation than was and is seen in English academia more generally. In order to capture and highlight this I employ the concept of *distorted desire*, which occurs in settings wherein forces external to scholarly concerns interfere with and manipulate those concerns in ways that go beyond the general manipulation of desire one sees in relatively autonomous academic contexts.[14] The concept is not intended to be normative, implying the existence of a natural state of scholarly selfhood with a purely autonomous kind of desire free from any outside influence or manipulation. I agree with Paul that desire is always open to and affected by influence and manipulation in academic environments that are relatively autonomous.[15] It is *this* desire that is distorted as a result of a scholar's presence in environments wherein an extraordinary degree of manipulation occurs as a natural state of existence. To take an example discussed in the following section: when in 1932 Maurice Dobb put forward a nuanced conception of classical Marxist categories that went against Party orthodoxy, rather than merely being reprimanded by his colleagues and superiors in ways one might see when committing a *faux pas* in academia he was branded a class traitor and enemy, threatened with expulsion and being ostracized from his social circle. Still, remarkably enough, he recanted and remained in the Party, though a different man than he had been before this episode. The concept of distorted desire is aimed at capturing this distinctive phenomenon, which I believe is crucial in understanding the making of the English Marxist historian's scholarly persona.

As shall be seen in the discussion of the English Revolution debate, the CPGB was an environment in which distorted desire was the norm. Although there were fluctuations in the extent to which desire was distorted by doctrinaire party *apparatchiks* prior to and during the existence of the CPHG,[16] it remained an ever-present feature of its members' lives and activities as historians. It is not surprising that it came to be an increasing source of conflict within the Party, particularly among those in the Group who were also active in the academy and were acutely aware of the lack of such an external censor, and the space it afforded to cultivate commitments to goods and virtues that would allow them to flourish as scholars. This tension, exacerbated by events that shocked the Communist world in the early 1950s – in particular Khrushchev's de-Stalinization speech and the brutal crushing of the Hungarian uprising in 1956 – ultimately led to the Group's dissolution, when in particular the younger academics in it had enough of subjecting themselves to the whims of the Party bureaucracy.[17] While the conclusion of the initial stage of the English Revolution debate led to the formation of the Historians' Group, it also exhibits omens of its eventual dissolution through the looming presence of distorted desire.

Why did the debate that led to the emergence of the CPHG begin in the first place? To be able to answer this one must first look at the preludes to the debate in the early 1930s, and the main figures involved in it who went on to found the Group after it concluded: Torr, Dobb, Morton and Hill. After a brief discussion of each of them leading up to the debate in 1940–41, I shall move to the debate itself, which reveals how they joined together to begin the invention of the English Marxist historian's persona.

The Historians' Group's founders

Dona Torr, who at 63 was the oldest member of the Group upon its founding in 1946, was born into a well-to-do family in 1883 at Carlett Park, Eastham, Chester, the third daughter in the family of four daughters and two sons.[18] Her father was an Anglican priest and the Canon of Chester Cathedral, which together with her private education at home instilled in her a lifelong passion for the history of religion, in particular of Methodism, which she took up as one of her areas of expertise in the Historians' Group.[19] She went on to study in Heidelberg and at University College London, where she read English and Greek Philosophy, and after a decade of involvement in various left-wing and anti-war causes was a founding member of the CPGB in 1920.[20]

Victor Kiernan, one of the members of the Group who knew her well, recalls that while she was '[u]nassuming on her own account, she could be a stickler for observance of party rules when she felt they were being neglected'.[21] In the twenty-five years before the founding of the Group she was active overseas for the Comintern, though little is known about what exactly she did during this time, and worked on translating various German Marxist texts into English, most notably some of the writings of Marx and Engels.[22] It was during this time that she built her status as a reliable and excellent communist, and became very close to Party luminaries like the general secretary Harry Pollitt. In later years she would use the authority emanating from the social capital she had acquired to protect some of the younger communist historians when they veered too far from Party orthodoxy.²³ While the Historians' Group did have some female members, with the exception of Torr and Dorothy Thompson their contributions are nearly invisible. (Thompson, along with her husband Edward, came to prominence with her work only after the Group's dissolution.) This is the case not only in the secondary literature,²⁴ but remarkably also in the archives, revealing the gendered nature of the Group.²⁵

Torr never became involved with academic historiography, which in practical terms meant that she never published in professional journals nor had the desire to. 'That fine Communist scholar Dona Torr, working ten hundred miles outside of academia', was how E. P. Thompson described her years later.²⁶ The fact that Torr was able to play a leading role in the Historians' Group and the Communist Party is a testament to her great skills and abilities as a historian and activist, and she deserves recognition as a central figure in the narrative of the Group's founding and the emergence of the English Marxist historian's persona. As shown by her role in the English Revolution debate discussed below, she was indispensable to both.

Like Torr, A. L. (Leslie) Morton remained a lifelong member of the CPGB who embodied a commitment to a more doctrinaire interpretation of Communism and prioritized Party loyalty to a great extent.²⁷ Born into a family of farmers in 1903, he was educated by governesses at home and later on attended grammar and public schools before leaving for Cambridge University in 1921. In his first two years he studied History and in the third he took up English, all the while being politically active in the University Labour Club.²⁸ As recalled by Maurice Cornforth, an acquaintance of his and fellow member of the Group, it was during the 1920s that he moved further to the political left:

> At that time, the immediate post-war years of the early twenties, intellectuals who felt concern about society and politics had to stand up and be counted as to whether they were for or against the Russian Revolution, for or against the strike demands, particularly of railwaymen and miners, and for or against taking industries into national ownership and starting up measures to relieve poverty and unemployment, and for a more equal distribution of wealth. Leslie found himself in the Labour Club among those who were 'for' – a very small minority in the University.²⁹

After three years at Cambridge, he became a general teacher at a grammar school in Sussex before losing his position after participating in a strike. After being unemployed for some months and having to borrow money from friends to make ends meet, he found employment as a teacher at another school, the progressive Summerhill, where he worked for a year. Then he moved to London in 1928 to run a bookshop and joined the CPGB. In 1934 he became the proprietor of the Party's *Daily Worker* publication – successfully winning a legal case brought against it for inciting violence by calling for protests against Mosley's fascists – while also contributing to it as a reporter and editor. He participated in and reported on the 1934 Hunger March, and throughout the 1930s he worked for the Party in advancing its cause through such activism, as was the case with Torr.[30]

Another noteworthy aspect of Morton's intellectual activities in this period was his engagement with literature, which Hobsbawm noted was a common theme in the Historians' Group and one of the reasons why they were averse to crude economic, reductionist and determinist historical thinking of the Soviet kind:

> As I read my diary of 1934–5, it is perfectly clear that its writer was getting ready to be a historian. What I was trying to do above all else was to elaborate Marxist historical interpretations of my reading. And yet I was doing so in a way I almost certainly would not have done, had I continued my education on the continent. The 'materialist conception of history' was, of course, central to Marxism. However, Britain in the 1930s was one of the rare countries in which a school of Marxist historians developed, and I think this was partly due to the fact that on the arts side of British sixth forms literature took the space left vacant by the absence of philosophy. British Marxist historians began, more often than not, as young intellectuals who moved to historical analysis from, or with, a passion for literature: Christopher Hill, Victor Kiernan, Leslie Morton, E. P. Thompson, Raymond Williams and indeed myself.[31]

To conclude Morton's story in the lead-up to the debate, in 1938 he published *A People's History of England*,[32] which became the Party's official textbook of English history and garnered him the reputation of its principal historian. After the book's publication he threw himself into Party activism, and he served in the Royal Artillery during the War, though he remained stationed in England.[33] In 1946 a conference was organized to discuss Morton's book and help improve it ahead of its reprinting.[34] It was out of this conference that the idea came to form the Historians' Group, becoming one of the formal Party Groups under the umbrella of the National Cultural Committee.[35] Yet this was only made possible by the outcome of the English Revolution debate of 1940–41.

Unlike the traditional story that is told in the secondary literature concerning the origins of the Historians' Group, the English Revolution debate was born out of a long, protracted period of internal turmoil and strife, of which this debate was but the latest episode. This is personified in the figure of Maurice Dobb, a key player in the debate. Dobb joined the Communist Party in 1922, a mere two years after it was founded.[36] As Hobsbawm later recalled, the Party was not 'used to such notably well-dressed recruits of such impeccably bourgeois comportment'.[37] Born in London in 1900 and growing up as a precocious youth in a relatively well-to-do household – his father was a successful merchant – he became radicalized over the course of 1919, after a brief but intense youthful flirtation with the Christian Science movement.[38] This was shortly before he took up a scholarship to study History at Cambridge.[39] After a year he switched to Economics, and began producing scholarly work that impressed his fellow academics (like his supervisor Keynes) and communists alike.[40] While he was a loyal Party member throughout the 1920s, he fell foul of the Party orthodox when he published the pamphlet *On Marxism Today* in 1932. He had neglected to cite Stalin or praise the Communist Party and, worst of all, he failed to appreciate the scientific and immutable nature of Marxism. Public repudiations of him in Party journals ensued. R. Page Arnot, a leading Party member and respected activist, argued in the Party's leading Political Committee that '[w]e should make it clear that not only should he [referring to Dobb] not write articles in journals, but that comrades should not publish books without reference to the Party'.[41]

Following this pressure, Dobb profusely apologized internally and sent a letter of apology to the Party journal for public repentance. It was deemed insufficient by hardliners in the Party, and he continued to be harassed for months after. The attacks were often deeply personal: '[Dobb] does not simply use arguments addressed to the *petit bourgeoisie*, or approach critically their problems and assumptions in order to reach a Marxist basis; he adopts their outlook as if it were his own'.[42] The recently set up Cambridge Party branch, which he had helped form, had to pass judgement as well, as Dobb formally fell under its jurisdiction. They wrote a report diagnosing the causes of Dobb's sins, mirroring those that had already come out in the attacks in the communist press: 'a lack of contact with the proletariat', '[his] class origins and bourgeois surroundings', for which the cure was to engage in 'the real practical work of the Party' for 'only continual participation in this work can provide the necessary background for a writer of propagandist literature'.[43] Dobb made a vain attempt to defend himself at the branch meeting where this report was read. By one account he ended the day by vomiting in a toilet.[44] Dobb's travails during this time did not go unnoticed by his fellow Party members, most notably Hill. Though blessed with a less affluent background, Hill too was saddled with the baggage of an elite education and immersion in the world of academia, in his case centred around Oxford rather than Cambridge. He knew he had to tread carefully if he was to avoid drawing the ire of the Party orthodox and be reprimanded and forced into submission, as had happened to Dobb when he dared proclaim a Marxism that was moving in a less reductive and teleological direction.[45]

Born in York in 1912 Hill too was a precocious child, and he too was brought up in a Christian family (in his case Methodist). Although not particularly wealthy, his household was a stable one, with his father being a reasonably successful solicitor.[46] At the age of 16 he was recruited by Oxford dons Vivian Hunter Galbraith and Kenneth Bell, who had marked his examination papers at Balliol and were highly impressed by his talents. They went to visit him in York to offer him a Brackenbury scholarship in person to try to dissuade him from further pursuing his application to Cambridge.[47] The mission was a success, and Hill matriculated at Balliol College in 1931 to begin his study in Modern History. It was around this time, at the age of 19 (as was the case with Dobb) that he started to become radicalized. The first spark of politicization occurred during an extended holiday in Freiburg shortly before arriving at Oxford. There he witnessed the increasing growth of the Nazi Party and the fierce opposition to it by the Communists, and he chose sides accordingly. Hill went on to win the prestigious Lothian prize in 1932 and earned a first-class bachelor's degree in 1934, finishing the year with a fellowship at All Souls College.[48] It is unclear when exactly he joined the Communist Party of Great Britain, but in any case it was before 1935, when he moved to the Soviet Union and lived there for a year while recovering from illness. While he enjoyed Russian life he developed an antipathy to Soviet politics with its many contradictions – instilling in him the first germs of the cynicism which others in the Historians' Group like Dobbs and Hobsbawm would come to embrace as well.[49] Upon his return to Britain in 1936 he worked as assistant lecturer at University College for two years before returning to Balliol College as fellow and tutor.

Before joining the Army in June of 1940 he published the essay 'The English Revolution, 1640', the arguments for which he had partly developed through conversations with Torr and Morton, who encouraged him to write it. It was written in an iconoclastic, polemical vein, meant to be his testament were he to perish in the war, which he was convinced he would.[50] This was to be a pivotal moment for historians in the Communist Party in the years to come, for Hill had managed to write an unorthodox history that initially was vehemently opposed by Party leaders, sparking the initial phase of the English Revolution debates that lasted until the following year; and he came out of them victorious.[51] As Torr would later remark, '[w]e all owe it to him in the first place and it was a victory for politics as well as theory'.[52]

The English Revolution debates

Beginning in 1940, with Hill's proposed thesis, produced in collaboration with Torr and Morton and critically taken up and defended by Dobb,[53] the English Revolution debates extended into 1948, dominating the first two years of the Group's activities. As I shall now elaborate, they reveal the emergence of a distinctive, socially recognizable Marxist historian's persona, and how the space that allowed it to develop in the first place by placing limits on the Party's political interference and imposition of ideological orthodoxy was fought for and won. In other words, this is the story of how the pervasive presence of distorted desire in the 1920s and 1930s was fought against so as to establish relative autonomy for the historians in the Party – the necessary condition for the Historians' Group's founding in 1946, marking a crucial step in the making of the English Marxist historian's persona.

Shortly after Hill's essay was published as a booklet in 1940 the German *émigré* economist Jürgen Kuczynski, who was also a leading member of the Communist International and an orthodox-minded Party ideologue, wrote a scathing review of it under the pseudonym 'P. F.' in the Party's outlet *The Labour Monthly*, sparking an intense internal debate among supporters and detractors of Hill.[54] This was a transparent attempt to enforce Party orthodoxy and maintain the enforcement of distorted desire by the Party leadership against its academic members. The orthodox *apparatchik* Rajani Palme Dutt had encouraged Kuczynski's attack, and as Dutt had recently replaced Harry Pollitt as General Secretary of the Party Hill had a powerful foe to contend with.[55] Kuczynski's objection was aimed primarily at the particular commitments to epistemic, moral and political goods Hill embodied and represented rather than what the precise date of the English bourgeois revolution had been. What to an outsider may have seemed like a mundane dispute over chronology in fact went to the heart of the Marxist historian's nature, or rather, what its 'proper' nature ought to have been. The main problem Kuczynski identified in Hill's argument concerned Hill's supposed description of late-sixteenth-century England as being 'essentially feudal', and that it remained so until 1640 when Cromwell's class of independent gentry spearheaded a revolution to abolish feudal social and economic privileges, thereby clearing the path for capitalist development, as the French Revolution was later to do.[56] Kuczynski countered that feudal agriculture, in which lords held serfs, had already been displaced by capitalist agriculture by the end of the sixteenth century, when there was a large population of what he termed 'agricultural proletarians', and a significant manufacturing base had already been developed. He backed up his case by referencing Marx, who in *Capital* had described England's economy of the sixteenth century as being bourgeois-capitalist; and Engels, who had made similar comments. These powerful allies were enlisted as approving his thesis and, by extension, opposing Hill's.[57]

Soon after Kuczynski's review appeared Douglas Garman, a director of the Party's Lawrence and Wishart publishing house and a friend of Hill's, wrote a reply in which he made explicit the motivations behind Kuczynski's attack.[58] Hill had in fact not denied that there had been significant capitalist development before 1640, as Kuczynski claimed, but rather developed an account of the English Revolution that 'show[ed] historical development as a process, brought about by conflicting social forces; whereas [Kuczynski] can only discern a succession of neatly labelled social orders'.[59] Rather than adopting the crude and reductionist stageism that Kuczynski had learned from orthodox Soviet Marxism, in particular Plekhanov and the Soviet historian Mikhail Pokrovsky,[60] in which one mode of production succeeds another – feudalism to capitalism in this case – Hill had presented an account of sixteenth- and seventeenth-century England that contained varieties of economic and social forms, feudal and capitalist, uneasily co-existing yet doing so nonetheless until the revolution of 1640 swept away the last remnants of feudalism.[61]

Moreover, Kuczynski had neglected to say when and how the transition to bourgeois society did occur if not during the English Revolution as identified by Hill. Instead, he seemed to suggest that in fact no such revolution had occurred, and the transition had been gradual and peaceful.[62] This made him guilty of two moral and political vices alongside the already mentioned epistemic one: a lack of attention to the class struggle and indulging in reformism.[63] This was a significant charge, as the corresponding virtues of class analysis and revolutionary politics were perceived as being primary elements of a Marxist's historian's persona. The only charges of Kuczynski's to which Garman did not reply were his identification of the vices of relying on 'bourgeois' sources, and in so doing contradicting Marx and Engels.[64] Indeed, Hill had not primarily drawn on Marx or Engels for his thesis, but rather on the histories of the period produced by 'bourgeois' historians like Gardiner and Firth, whose extensive analyses of agricultural, manufacturing and other relevant records plainly supported Hill's case.[65] An even more profound influence on him was the socialist and decisively academic historian R. H. Tawney, who in the 1910s and 1920s had already begun moving away from academic orthodoxy, focusing on constitutional matters and probing the economic and social conditions of sixteenth- and seventeenth-century England.[66] Hill was later to refer to him as 'the giant upon whose shoulders all historians of the 17th century stand'.[67]

These influences are significant for they reveal Hill – and by extension those who supported the thesis he had put forward, such as Torr, Morton, Dobb and after 1948 the majority of the Historians' Group – had taken up a radically different attitude to non-Marxist academic historians from that of Party ideologues like Kuczynski, who saw any reliance on and reference to them as a vice.[68] Tawney, for example, had been a frequent object of vicious criticism in Party outlets. To give an indication of how Party ideologues perceived him in 1940 when Hill's essay was published, Allen Hutt, editor of various Party publications such as *The Daily Worker* and spokesperson of Party orthodoxy, accused Tawney in *The Labour Monthly* of endorsing red-baiting, perceived within the Party as one of the worst vices one could be guilty of.[69] Several years before, in reviewing a book Tawney had written on China, he had been maligned as a 'philistine' who favoured imperialist exploitation of colonies and produced propaganda for big business: 'Professor Tawney though a "socialist", is not a champion of the oppressed nations of the world and his Christian sympathy with the plight of the oppressed Chinese people does not prevent him from outlining a programme in perfect harmony with the idea of perpetuating its semi-colonial status'.[70] To Party ideologues and *apparatchiks* like Dutt and Kuczynski it was not only heresy to draw any lessons from obviously reactionary, 'bourgeois' academics like Gardiner and Firth, even if these only concerned apparently innocuous accounts of agricultural conditions, but also to do so from socialists like Tawney who, while being progressive politically, were not Marxist and more importantly were not members of the Communist Party. In other words, they did not share the epistemic commitments to dialectics and historical materialism, the moral commitment to the emancipation of the proletariat or the political commitment to Communism, and hence were deemed to be intrinsically suspect by the likes of Kuczynski, who themselves embodied dogmatic, schematic and crudely Stalinist interpretations of these three commitments.[71]

However, not only were such historians and their work excluded from being valued as a significant source of insight by the hard-line Stalinists, but the latter ensured that it was politically dangerous for Party members like Hill to cite these 'bourgeois' thinkers approvingly. The *apparatchik*'s watchdog mentality, always enforcing their orthodoxy on others, as shown by the reaction to Hill's essay and the experiences of others like Dobb, instilled fear in all – distorted desire was the norm.[72] As discussed in the previous section, Dobb had been rebuked by Dutt (the powerful Party ideologue) in 1932 for insufficiently praising Stalin and the Communist Party in essays he had written.[73] Now it was again Dutt who had prompted Kuczynski's attack on Hill, for the same reasons as Dobb had been targeted, for Hill also had mentioned neither Stalin nor the Party at all, and Marx was cited only once in his essay.[74] The fact that Dutt now occupied the position of General Secretary of the Party seemed only to make matters worse for Hill and his supporters.

The 1940–41 debate was to end differently from the Dobb controversy of a decade earlier, however, and it involved a variety of factors relating not only to the proper definition of particular virtues and commitments that were struggled over by both sides, but also to those relating to the social and political capital the actors involved possessed and employed. After Garman's initial article rebutting Kuczynski's criticism, Torr and Dobb entered the fray in 1941, writing articles with the aim of legitimizing Hill's thesis and delegitimizing Kuczynski's.[75] They were published in the February issue of *The Labour Monthly*, where the debate between Kuczynski and Garman had played out in December the year before, and so were carefully read by Party members and, more importantly, its leaders. At this point it was still unclear which side would be victorious in the debate, which meant winning the approval of the Party leadership so that one view became the officially sanctioned one. In order to obtain such a victory both sides relied significantly on language of virtue and vice, in line with the commitments to epistemic, moral and political goods they shared, meaning that the victorious side revealed the nature of the particular persona that was established as the norm after its victory. As we have seen, Kuczynski had identified in Hill vices of an epistemic kind – rejection of the schematic stageism contained in the former's commitment to a reductionist historical materialism – and of a political kind – Hill's supposed lack of adherence to Marx and Engels. These were seen as interrelated, emanating from Hill's reliance on 'bourgeois' sources, perhaps the ultimate vice in the eyes of ideologically orthodox Party members and the leadership.[76] Garman had countered by noting that Hill's rejection of a crude stageism was in fact one to be admired by those committed to the epistemic good of historical materialism, and it was on this point that Torr and Dobb doubled down.[77]

Torr began her piece by declaring that 'I agree with the criticisms of [Kuczynski]'s review made by Douglas Garman; I also think that [Kuczynski]'s interpretation is non-Marxist, whilst Hill's method, whether one agrees with every particular estimate or not, is Marxist'.[78] In order to prove her case she emphasized the primary Marxist epistemic good of dialectics and the virtues required to obtain it, which Hill had displayed so eloquently while Kuczynski had ignored it in favour of adopting its corresponding vices: '[Kuczynski]'s chief mistake is his mechanical conception that if capitalism has established itself as a dominant force then "bourgeois society" must be automatically established as well. He thus contradicts the fundamental law of social change.'[79] The law of dialectics was then reiterated by citing Marx's *Preface* from whence the base/superstructure distinction arose, confirming that a transformation in the economic base did not lead to an immediate transformation in the political sphere, as Kuczynski had claimed.[80] A citation of Engels on the sixteenth-century economic revolution was added as well, in which his statement directly contradicted Kuczynski's claim while endorsing Hill's thesis: '[b]ut this mighty revolution in the economic conditions of society was not followed by any corresponding change in its political structure. The State order remained feudal while society became more and more bourgeois.'[81] She concluded:

> Hill's argument is true to this dialectical distinction. New productive forces develop first in the form of relatively unorganised quantitative economic changes which can advance, not without class struggles and social changes, but without the aid of highly co-ordinated class action. Then comes first, intensified political struggle against classes identified with the old *social structure* and finally the decisive qualitative change of the *social system* which can only be brought about by the highest organised forms of co-ordinated class action demanding the supreme expression of unified will, action and leadership, e.g., Cromwell and the 'New Model' army.[82]

So Garman had been right to accuse Kuczynski of the vices of rejecting class analysis and endorsing reformism, having 'not clear[ed] himself from Garman's charge of reformism by citing a list of events which involved forcible acts', for '[t]he hallmark of reformism is its attitude, not to force as such, but to the class struggle – its refusal to recognise the way in which class struggle is the motive power of advance'.[83] Dobb took a less polemical route and focused on pointing out the importance of changes that had occurred in the mode of production, feudal and capitalist, which he believed both Kuczynski and Hill had insufficiently addressed, though Hill had at least begun to think seriously about them and had opened up the space for novel perspectives on them by rejecting the crude stageist variety of historical materialism.[84]

The most significant part of Torr's defence of Hill, which was to play a considerable part in Hill's victory, concerned reliance on 'bourgeois' sources, in particular on the Soviet historian Mikhail Pokrovsky. This aspect of the English Revolution debates composes what I have termed the 'Pokrovsky affair', the outcome of which signalled the communist historians' independence from Soviet and Communist Party (historiographical) ideology, thereby enabling the Group's formation and the fashioning of a Marxist historian's scholarly self within it. It is therefore important to pay specific attention to this affair. Rather than trying to argue that it was in fact legitimate to rely on 'bourgeois' sources to obtain such knowledge as needed for one's own, Marxist, epistemic, moral and political commitments, as Torr and other historians in the Group believed, she attacked the legitimacy of one of Kuczynski's sources, the aforementioned Pokrovsky, from whom he had learned a crude and stageist Marxism.[85] Having already demonstrated that Hill had displayed the epistemic, moral and political virtues shared by Marx and Engels, and even Lenin and Stalin regarding the importance of class analysis,[86] Torr now moved to delegitimize Pokrovsky, whose name denoted the particular constellation of virtues that Kuczynski embodied and portrayed as being the only legitimately Marxist one.[87] In her personal archives there are notes from the early 1930s, well before the Hill controversy, in which Torr described Pokrovsky as a crude, non-Marxist thinker who did not have a grasp on the dialectic, mirroring her later attacks on Kuczynski.[88] These sentiments are echoed in the archives of the sixteenth- and seventeenth-century section of the Historians' Group. In a document titled 'The Pokrovsky controversy'[89] the origins and fortunes of the particular persona represented by Pokrovsky are summarized:

> During the 1920s the best-known historian in the USSR, was M. N. Pokrovsky. Two of his works – *Brief History of Russia* and *History of Russia from the Earliest Times to the Rise of Commercial Capitalism* – were translated into English. In 1929–30, steps were taken by the CPSU [Communist Party of the Soviet Union] to expose and root out errors and weaknesses in ideology. The Academy of Science was thoroughly reorganised and a number of prominent philosophers, historians, etc., were subjected to criticism. Pokrovsky came under heavy fire for certain historical conceptions contained in his work which were said to be (a) inconsistent with facts (b) contrary to Marxism-Leninism, and (c) linked with various undesirable political tendencies. Pokrovsky himself died in 1932, but keen discussion of his work continued until 1934, when it was summed up, adversely to Pokrovsky, in a joint resolution of the CC [Central Committee], of the CPSU and the Council of People's Commissars. This resolution is held to have marked a major turning-point in the development of historical studies in the USSR... Pokrovsky's error was seen by his critics, in fact, as a fundamental error of historical method, which led his disciples into mistaken notions of current political significance regarding the nature of social revolutions.[90]

Torr's early notes on Pokrovsky were thus in line with shifting orthodoxy within the Soviet Union, but this was something of which Kuczynski and many others in the CPGB were unaware at the time of the English Revolution debates.[91] In an interview many years later Hill recalled how the initial debate on the English Revolution was resolved. After the salvoes by both sides in *The Labour Monthly* between December 1940 and February 1941, Hill and his supporters and Kuczynski's and his were summoned to take part in official Party proceedings to settle the matter, just as Pokrovsky's fate had been settled in the Soviet Union.[92] Held at the Party headquarters at 16 King Street, London, the outcome of these proceedings was to decide the fate of the historians in the Communist Party, and so also whether the Historians' Group would ever have been founded. According to Hill the decisive argument during these proceedings hinged on Torr's attack on Pokrovsky, which Hill reiterated and, crucially, demonstrated to

Party leaders by bringing with him Soviet texts in which Pokrovsky had been denounced. This convinced the Party leadership to not censor Hill's views.[93] Still, it was only after June 1941, when the Nazi invasion of the Soviet Union prompted Pollitt's return as Party General Secretary, that Hill's thesis became an acceptable, and by 1948 the majority, view, while support for Kuczynski evaporated.[94]

Torr's close relationship with Pollitt and other influential Party figures like Klugmann, head of the Propaganda and Education Department, played a significant if not critical role in assuring Hill's victory. This element had been missing when Dobb, an isolated figure in the Party, had faced Dutt about a decade earlier.[95] However, as seen the conflict went beyond the purely political, and also crucially involved a debate on the virtues and vices that a Marxist, and specifically a Marxist historian, had to possess. There was a subtle move away from the rigid categories of Stalinist Marxism, always presented as a natural evolution of the Marxist scientific method, while a relative autonomy was carved out in the Party for its historians, creating a space free from the kind of extremely distorted desire that had blocked any such creative innovation and development before. In short, Hill's victory laid the foundations for the formation of the Historians' Group, and enabled the further development of the particular constellation of virtues, or persona, that was to be cultivated within it – the English Marxist historian's scholarly persona.

Notes

1. Lorraine Daston and H. Otto Sibum, 'Introduction: scientific personae and their histories', *Science in Context*, 16 (2003), 1–8, at 2–3.
2. David Parker, *Ideology, Absolutism and the English Revolution: Debates of the British Communist Historians 1940–1956* (London: Lawrence & Wishart, 2008), pp 10–11; Dennis L. Dworkin, *Cultural Marxism in Postwar Britain: History, the New Left, and the Origins of Cultural Studies* (Durham, NC: Duke University Press, 1997), p. 267.
3. Christopher Hill, 'The English Revolution: 1640' ([1940]; published in book form: London: Lawrence and Wishart, 1955).
4. Glenn Burgess, 'Introduction', in Burgess and Matthew Festenstein (eds), *English Radicalism, 1550–1850* (Cambridge: Cambridge University Press, 2007), pp 1–16, at pp 3–7.
5. A. L. Morton, 'An important history (review)', *The Labour Monthly* (1939), 381–2; Christopher Hill, 'Our England (review)', *The Labour Monthly* (1939), 126–7.
6. I am thinking specifically of the Marxist theoreticians of the nineteenth century who dabbled in historical writing, like Karl Kautsky and Georg Plekhanov, as well as the Soviet historian Mikhail Pokrovsky – all of whom were figures the Group's members sought to distance themselves from. See Hill, 'English Revolution', pp 28–9.
7. Labour History Archive and Study Centre, Manchester (hereafter LHASC), CP/CENT/CULT/08/02, Historians' Group Papers 1940–1969, 'Stages in history', 1941, pp 1–9, at pp 1–2, 5.

8 Ibid., pp 1–2.
9 Christopher Hill, 'English history (review)', *The Labour Monthly* (1938), 449–51, at 449.
10 Owing to limitations of scope I am unable to provide a more expansive description of these commitments and virtues and how they changed over time. For the purposes of this chapter the rudimentary description provided here and elaborated on in the discussion of the founders of the CPHG and the English Revolution debate of 1940–41 should suffice to reveal the basic contours of the Marxist historian's persona that was being invented at that time.
11 Herman Paul, 'What is a scholarly persona? Ten theses on virtues, skills, and desires', *History and Theory*, 53 (2014), 348–71, at 348.
12 Ibid.
13 Daston and Sibum, 'Introduction', 2–3.
14 Though as Paul notes, with the ongoing financialization of the academy these may be coming to an end as well, if they have not ended already. See Paul, 'What is a scholarly persona?', 370–1. For a more detailed discussion of the methodology and distinctive conception of persona that I employ, which does differ in some respects from that put forward by Daston and Sibum, and from Paul's, see Sina Talachian, 'The return of the social: persona analysis as a method for intellectual history' (forthcoming).
15 Paul, 'What is a scholarly persona?', 367–9.
16 One can imagine other instances of this when investigating persona such as academia under a dictatorship.
17 John Saville and E. P. Thompson, 'The case for socialism: discussion from the British Communist Party', *International Socialist Review*, 17:4 (1956), 119–22, at 120; E. P. Thompson, 'Socialist humanism: an epistle to the Philistines', *The New Reasoner* 1 (1957), 105–43.
18 Victor Kiernan, 'Torr, Dona Ruth Anne (1883–1957)', *Oxford Dictionary of National Biography* (Oxford, 2004 – hereafter *ODNB*), online at www.oxforddnb.com/view/article/59174.
19 Dave Renton, 'Opening the books: the personal papers of Dona Torr', *History Workshop Journal*, 52 (2001), 236–45, at 237; LHASC, CP/IND/TORR/02/07, notes on religious and rationalist themes by Dona Torr, 'Methodism', n.d., pp 2–5.
20 Kiernan, 'Torr'; Renton, 'Opening the books', 237.
21 Kiernan, 'Torr'.
22 Ibid.
23 Renton, 'Opening the books', 238.
24 Hobsbawm only mentions Torr and Dorothy, and only in passing, though he admits women's history was a weak spot of the Group, without however elaborating on why this was the case. See Eric Hobsbawm, 'The Historians' Group of the Communist Party', in Maurice Cornforth (ed.), *Rebels and Their Causes: Essays in Honour of A. L. Morton* (London: Lawrence & Wishart, 1978), pp 21–47, at pp 22, 28, 37. One exception in the secondary literature is the work of Dave Renton. See Renton, 'Opening the books'; Dave Renton, 'The history woman', *Socialist Review*, 224, online at pubs.socialistreviewindex.org.uk/sr224/renton.htm (consulted 28 February 2018).
25 Aside from Torr I have not been able to find any contribution by a female member of the Group in the minutes and other documents in the archives, and Torr's presence itself is very limited. The dominant voices are the male ones. See LHASC, CP/CENT/CULT/05, *CPGB History Group (i)*; LHASC, CP/CENT/CULT, *CPGB History Group (ii)*.
26 E. P. Thompson, *The Poverty of Theory and Other Essays* (New York: Monthly Review Press, 1978), p. 115.
27 Margot Heinemann and Willie Thompson, 'Editors' preface', in Heinemann and Thompson (eds), *History and the Imagination: Selected Writings of A. L. Morton* (London: Lawrence & Wishart, 1990), pp 7–9, at p. 7; Maurice Cornforth, 'A. L.

Morton: portrait of a Marxist historian', in Cornforth, *Rebels and Their Causes*, pp 7–20, at pp 16–17.
28 Cornforth, 'A. L. Morton', pp 7–8.
29 Ibid., p. 8.
30 Ibid., pp 9–11.
31 Eric Hobsbawm, *Interesting Times: A Twentieth-Century Life* (New York: Pantheon Books, 2002), pp 97–8.
32 A. L. Morton, *A People's History of England* (London: Lawrence & Wishart, 1948).
33 Cornforth, 'A. L. Morton', pp 15–16.
34 LHASC, CP/CENT/CULT/06/01, 'Minutes of the Historians' Conference', 29–30 June 1946, pp 1–2.
35 LHASC, CP/CENT/CULT, 'The National Cultural Committee'.
36 Maurice Dobb, 'What the Communist Party has meant to me', *The Labour Monthly* (1940), 445–6, at 445.
37 Eric Hobsbawm, 'Dobb, Maurice Herbert (1900–1976)', *ODNB*, online at www.oxforddnb.com/view/article/31034.
38 He was later so embarrassed by this that he sought to erase it from his biography. See Timothy Shenk, *Maurice Dobb: Political Economist* (Basingstoke: Palgrave Macmillan, 2013), pp 9, 35.
39 Ibid., p. 11; Maurice Dobb, 'Random biographical notes', *Cambridge Journal of Economics* 2 (1978), pp 115–20, at 115.
40 Hobsbawm, 'Dobb'.
41 Shenk, *Maurice Dobb*, pp 70–71.
42 Ibid., p. 72.
43 Ibid., p. 73.
44 Ibid., pp 73–4.
45 Ibid., p. 48.
46 Robin Briggs, 'Hill (John Edward) Christopher (1912–2003)', *ODNB*, online at www.oxforddnb.com/view/article/89437.
47 Briggs, 'Hill'; Martin Kettle, 'Christopher Hill', *The Guardian* (2003), online at www.theguardian.com/news/2003/feb/26/guardianobituaries.obituaries (consulted 28 February 2018).
48 Kettle, 'Christopher Hill'.
49 Hobsbawm, *Interesting Times*, pp 191–2; Shenk, *Maurice Dobb*, p. 48.
50 Hill, 'English Revolution', pp 4–5.
51 Dworkin, *Cultural Marxism in Postwar Britain*, pp 34–5; Dave Renton, 'Studying their own nation without insularity? The British Marxist historians reconsidered', *Science and Society*, 69 (2005), 559–79, at 562.
52 Renton, 'Studying their own nation', 562.
53 Keith Tribe, *Genealogies of Capitalism* (London: Palgrave Macmillan, 1981) pp 12–13.
54 I will cite his texts under his real name: Jürgen Kuczynski, 'The English Revolution, 1640 (review)', *The Labour Monthly* (1940), 558–9.
55 Dutt replaced Pollitt in 1939 upon Britain's entry into World War II, because the signing of the Molotov-Ribbentrop pact conflicted with Pollitt's anti-German rhetoric of the years before. He was to be replaced again by Pollitt after the German invasion of the Soviet Union in June 1941. See Robert Service, *Comrades: Communism, a World History* (London: Pan Books, 2008), p. 215.
56 Jürgen Kuczynski, '"The English Revolution, 1640": a rejoinder', *The Labour Monthly* (1940), 653–5, at 653.
57 Ibid. Engels had written '[t]he feudal fetters were smashed, gradually in England, at one blow in France'.
58 Douglas Garman, '"The English Revolution, 1640": a reply to P. F.', *The Labour Monthly* (1940), 651–3.
59 Ibid., 651.

60 As discussed further on this was to play a significant role in the outcome of the debate.
61 Garman, 'English Revolution', 651; Hill, 'English Revolution', pp 28–9.
62 Garman, 'English Revolution', 652–3.
63 Ibid.
64 Kuczynski, '"English Revolution": rejoinder', 653.
65 Hill, 'English Revolution', p. 45; Christopher Hill, 'The agrarian legislation of the interregnum', *The English Historical Review*, 55:218 (1940), 222–50, at 225–6, 234–5.
66 R. Richardson, *The Debate on the English Revolution* (Manchester: Manchester University Press, 2011), pp 113–15.
67 Christopher Hill, 'Storm over the gentry', *Encounter*, 11 (1958), 76.
68 Kuczynski, '"English Revolution": rejoinder', 653.
69 Allen Hutt, 'Philistine gospel (review)', *The Labour Monthly* (1940) 251–5, at 251; Kevin Morgan, 'The Communist Party and *The Daily Worker*, 1930–1956' in Morgan, Geoff Andrews and Nina Fishman (eds), *Opening the Books: Essays on the Social and Cultural History of British Communism* (London: Pluto Press, 1995), pp 142–59.
70 G. L. Pu, 'A decade of China', *The Labour Monthly* (1933) 696–705, at 702–3.
71 Shenk, *Maurice Dobb*, p. 69.
72 Ibid., pp 70–1.
73 Ibid.
74 Hill, 'English Revolution', p. 20.
75 Dona Torr, 'The English Revolution', *The Labour Monthly* (1941) 90–2; Maurice Dobb, 'The English Revolution', *The Labour Monthly* (1941), 92–3.
76 Kuczynski, '"English Revolution": rejoinder', 653, 655.
77 Garman, 'English Revolution', 651.
78 Torr, 'English Revolution', 90.
79 Ibid., 91.
80 Ibid.
81 Ibid.
82 Ibid.
83 Ibid.
84 Dobb, 'English Revolution', 92.
85 Kuczynski, 'English Revolution (review)', 558–9; Torr, 'English Revolution', 91.
86 Torr, 'English Revolution', 91–2.
87 Kuczynski, 'English Revolution (review)', 558–9.
88 LHASC, CP/IND/TORR/03/01, Drafts of projected book on the state to have been produced by a sub-group of the CPGB, Dona Torr, 'Development toward feudalism', 1932, pp 1–13, at p. 11.
89 LHASC, CP/CENT/CULT/08, Papers re the sixteenth- and seventeenth-century section of the History Group, author unknown, 'The Pokrovsky controversy' (n.d.), pp 1–3.
90 'The Pokrovsky controversy', pp 1–3.
91 Dworkin, *Cultural Marxism in Postwar Britain*, p. 35.
92 Ibid.
93 Ibid.
94 Ibid., pp 35–6.
95 Shenk, *Maurice Dobb*, pp 70–1.

CHAPTER 9

Of communism, compromise and Central Europe: the scholarly persona under authoritarianism

Monika Baár

Introduction

What does it take to be a (good) historian under a system of institutionalized repression? What kind of professional and ethical choices are scholars compelled to make and what motivates them in reaching these decisions? What are the implications of the exposure to an oppressive regime for one's professional career and does the study of scholarly persona in 'exceptional conditions' endorse, refine or refute existing discussions on the subject? This chapter engages with these questions by interrogating the work, life and self-fashioning of one of the foremost Hungarian historians of the communist period, Péter Hanák (1921–97), whose achievements were significant in placing Hungarian history in a transnational perspective and studying it with the most up-to-date research methods. As a scholar who experienced the 'terrors of history' under two authoritarian regimes, for Hanák, history studied and history lived were inextricably linked. This can be evidenced from an anecdote which he related in his memoirs in a jocular tone. In mature years Hanák had to undergo urgent heart surgery. When the internal specialist who had examined him beforehand got to see the image emerging on the X-ray screen he exclaimed: 'Gracious heavens! On these arteries I can see the history of the entire twentieth century!'[1]

This chapter examines Hanák's choices of subjects for historical study, and it ponders to what extent his life experiences, educational background and the intellectual tradition in which he became socialized influenced those choices. All these factors contributed to the makeup of his 'scholarly DNA' which, like real DNA, in interaction with his environment made him the scholar that he became. In that context, this chapter will reveal that Hanák's persona was deeply influenced by the legacy of civic-liberal patriotism which had its origins in *fin-de-siècle* Austria-Hungary. The chapter discusses his *ars poetica* as a historian and his activities as a public intellectual. It reveals that Hanák forged his own persona by navigating his way across a range of personae. From these, he absorbed characteristics which, at first glance, might not necessarily appear to be always reconcilable with *one* distinct persona. In his work, in his historical analyses and in his life choices Hanák was first and foremost a 'compromiser', which justifies the special attention which the article pays to this notion. In a broader context, this study is also concerned with the ways in which historians interpreted national history under the communist period and asks to what extent their persona influenced their assessment. To that end, it shows that Hanák found his ideal, or, as he put it, his 'utopia', in the form of a civic, cosmopolitan patriotism. Scholarly personae emerge and disappear within specific contexts and the fashioning of a new persona cannot take place without having recourse to certain older, existing ones.

One possible advantage of the conceptualizations that take the notion of persona as their point of departure is that they appear to do less homogenizing than traditional conceptualizations that revolve around 'schools' and 'generations'. They also have the advantage of bringing to the fore divisions and fault lines within the profession. For example, such cleavages could include religious and political divides and the emphasis on specialized research versus preference for writing for the general public. These potentials render the concept of scholarly persona particularly inspirational for pondering the question whether and to what extent historians at a certain time and in a certain place share some common understanding of what it means to be a historian in the first place.[2] Studies that approach this fundamental question include short-term or *longue durée* perspectives, while geographically they mainly focus on Europe and North America.[3] The feature that they appear to share is to take as their point of departure a scholar in an unexceptional situation. This may include the historian dusting off documents in the archives or beavering away in a study. Another variant may be the historian surrounded by students at the university and becoming the founder of a 'school'. Surely, alternatives also exist: for example, historians who prefer not to lock themselves in their study, but engage in politics, or even perform public roles. The martyred historian, who paid with his/her life for insisting on her/his principles constitutes another persona; suffice it to think of Marc Bloch. Nevertheless, most often political engagement by the historian is largely a voluntary act, which certainly might involve risks, but not risking one's life. Existing conceptualizations tend to locate the notion of persona 'at the intermediary stage between the individual biography and the social institution'.[4] This study addresses the intricate connection between these levels and it investigates how they become shaped under repressive societal conditions. As such it seeks to widen existing focus primarily on 'ordinary' situations in larger and better-known academic cultures. Ultimately, it invites reflection on the question to what extent the 'core' and nature of a scholar's work may or may not be left intact by external circumstances and what agency (if at all) scholars themself possess *vis-à-vis* those circumstances.

Living with a 'stain'

To what extent and how then does the 'permanent state of exception' – the inescapability of the dictates of an authoritarian regime – become imprinted on the scholarly persona? Péter Hanák produced a vibrant autobiographical essay, *Ragaszkodás az utópiához* (*Insistence on Utopia*), first and foremost intended for his two sons, which may provide a suitable point of departure for taking a closer look into this question. As we shall see, his book was not devoid of self-justification. In fact, its main motivation was to seek justification for his enthusiasm for the communist system for a short period after World War II. During that period his ideological commitment was rewarded with important positions, from which he was able to do harm to some of his colleagues in the name of 'class struggle', something which left a stain on his reputation for the rest of his life. If the entire twentieth century was mirrored on Hanák's arteries, the essay reveals that two experiences in particular were of crucial significance: the Holocaust, in which he lost his entire family; and the 'blood-stained' revolution of 1956 which left him with an injury and cost him his university job.

Hanák was born in 1921 in Southern Hungary, in the mid-size city of Kaposvár, into a poor Jewish family. Although an outstanding pupil, who contributed to his family's maintenance by tutoring his less gifted but more affluent classmates, Hanák was denied entry to university by anti-Semitic legislation, the so-called *numerus clausus* which seriously restricted the acceptance of students of Jewish origin at universities. Instead, Hanák became a metal worker in a big factory and a trade unionist. In 1942, he was forced to enter Jewish labour service in the Hungarian army. Under adventurous conditions he succeeded in escaping and returning to Hungary, only to find that his parents had been gassed in Auschwitz and his brother had disappeared without a trace. Many young people in a similar situation chose to leave the country in the years that followed. Hanák would have been in a position to follow suit, as his father's brother, who settled down in the United States, invited him across and even offered to adopt him and finance his studies. Nevertheless, he denied the invitation. His decision to stay loyal to the country the leaders of which had sent his entire family to the gas chambers was motivated by a somewhat archaic form of patriotism.[5]

In the 'new order' that followed after the war Hanák was finally admitted to university to study History and Latin. In 1948 he was granted a one-year scholarship to undertake research in Rome on aspects of the Hungarian revolution, on its 100th anniversary. In 1949 the Communist Party achieved victory in massively fraudulent elections. In that year of the communist takeover, the 'purging' in academic life began. This entailed the victimization and marginalization of so-called 'bourgeois historians', many of whom had studied or worked in Western Europe during the interwar period. Hanák was actively involved in those purges: he observed some of his senior colleagues and produced reports on them which contributed to their victimization and elimination for a period of time from the historical profession. Hanák made several attempts to explain and justify this involvement in his biography, by repeatedly asking the question 'how could I identify with this inhuman regime?' He argued that everything in the party was subordinated to the realization of communism, and as a consequence external pressure often became internal imperative.[6] He did not deny that the fear of prison, torture or loss of status constituted coercive factors, but he found that an even more significant consideration was the fear of yet another identity crisis: he was an orphan and the party became his family. If he had given up his total commitment, that would have led to his excommunication and falling into an empty space. Hence 'this monster state was for a long time the object of my identification'.[7]

Lastly, Hanák argued that in his situation – a young man of Jewish origin – no alternative to the Communist Party existed. He claimed that when in 1945 he was walking the streets of Budapest, stumbling upon corpses, and when he saw the total bankruptcy of the old regime, joining the communists remained his only option. Other parties did not appear to be capable of preventing the return of fascism and the Social Democratic party looked old-fashioned and inefficient.[8] At that stage it was not yet visible that the new threat was arriving not from the right but from the left. To what extent was this claim self-exoneration?

One of the most accomplished *émigré* historians, István Deák (b. 1928), who became professor at Columbia University and later helped Hanák's socialization in American academia during his stays there, gave his views on this matter. Deák was very appreciative of Hanák's scholarly qualities. This however, did not exempt him from criticism. To that end, Deák noted that, while Hanák's readiness to confront his past was laudable and did not find many followers among his generation, he never managed to make the ultimate step in his self-criticism. This would have been the realization that his support of the regime was not driven merely by idealism and fear, but also by the promise of privileges and the appetite for power. According to Deák, it was not inevitable that a young, talented man would choose the Communist Party, even if he had been a victim of the previous regime.⁹

Around 1953–54, when the corpses from the show trials and the prisons of the secret police started to emerge, as tortured people were released from prison, it became more and more difficult to deal with the 'cognitive dissonance' between ideological dictates and everyday realities. But Hanák's 'awakening' only took place somewhat later, in 1956, when he found himself in the midst of revolutionary events.¹⁰ Two days after the outbreak of the revolution, his students at Eötvös Loránd University, Budapest requested that, together with the dean of the Faculty of Humanities, Hanák represent their demands for autonomy during the political negotiations. This became his *dies irae*. The streets were full of protesters who demanded the removal of the old guard of party leadership, the withdrawal of Soviet troops, a national government and complete amnesty for every participant in the events. Yet this day which started triumphantly turned into a tragic one when Soviet soldiers and Hungarian secret police members started to fire into the crowd. Hanák himself was shot in the leg, which required an operation to remove the bullet and which also 'removed' him from centre-stage in the coming events. His colleague, the dean, was shot several times in the forehead and died immediately.

Following the revolution, back at the University, Hanák refused to withdraw his statement that educational autonomy and reform were necessary at his faculty. As a result, he was expelled from the university, but could take refuge at the Institute for History of the Hungarian Academy which hosted several historians who were marginalized for political reasons. In the 1970s and 1980s the political system under the Kádár regime differed markedly from the earlier period in that the regime no longer imposed moral or existential pressure on people to *unconditionally* adjust to it. Hanák's commitment did not disappear altogether. He developed a certain distance, as he belonged to those 'reformists' who sought to change the system from within, to put a 'human face' on communism. In an interview conducted in the 1990s Hanák was asked how he thought it could be possible for many academics seemingly to have no problem whatsoever in coming to terms with the dictates of an unjust and authoritarian system and for some even to display cynical gestures of approval. In reaction he pointed out that the incidence of heart attacks, stomach ulcers and similar illnesses was exceptionally high among those people, in which he saw proof that they might have adjusted to the system from the outside, but not 'within'.¹¹ Hanák's own attempt at self-justification involved the claim that while for a short period of his life he indeed had believed in the world-saving communist doctrine and cherished the cult of smaller and larger dictators, his ideological commitment never became 'total' in the Bolshevik sense of the word.[12]

From the 1960s onwards, Hanák was allowed to travel to international conferences, among which a conference held at Indiana University in 1966 on the nationalities of the dual monarchy represented a significant milestone. In 1971 he became visiting professor at Columbia and Yale Universities, later conducted research at Princeton, in Bielefeld and in Washington. In his later years, Hanák was fortunate to experience for a second time the collapse of 'an unhuman regime that had led the country into a cul-de-sac'.[13] He had known that the system would collapse one day, but did not expect to live to see it happen. 1989 thus became an *annus mirabilis* and, like many of his colleagues, for a split second he believed that this was the 'homecoming' of his utopia: the democratic, productive and peaceful co-existence of Danubian nations. Very soon, however, a rude awakening followed: with the resurrection of conservative nationalist forces the conflicts within Central Europe and within Hungary also intensified. As he later lamented, in order to realize utopia much more self-criticism, self-knowledge and political and intellectual 'vigilance' would have been necessary.[14] If utopia – a cosmopolitan ideal sensitive to regional characteristics – remained elusive, nevertheless Hanák symbolically contributed to its transmission. In 1991 he became one of the founders of the Central European University in Budapest, so in 1997, when he passed away, the hope remained that utopia could be kept alive. It is the irony of fate that two decades later, in 2017, the University found itself in danger of expulsion from the country by an 'illiberal' Hungarian government.

Finding a *modus vivendi*: a historian of many compromises

Hanák's professional interests revolved around the following main subjects: the (re)assessment of the significance of the Austro-Hungarian Compromise; the social, cultural and intellectual history of the *fin-de-siècle* period in the Austro-Hungarian Empire and the idea of Central Europe in the past, present and future, both as 'reality' and as 'utopia'.

The Compromise between Austria and Hungary was a legal act that created the Austro-Hungarian dual monarchy in 1867. Immediately after it had been concluded, a debate on its legacy began, and the polemics continued well into the twentieth century, with widely varying verdicts. Among these was the view that the Compromise itself was a positive development, in fact the embodiment of the 'realizable' demands of the principles of the 1848 revolution. Another view held that it was a mutually destructive arrangement for both parties concerned, while according to a third the balance was negative because the Compromise made Hungarians believe that without the Habsburgs their very existence was impossible.[15] Marxist historiography of the 1950s and 1960s condemned the first, 'bourgeois' viewpoint; instead, it considered the act of 1867 the betrayal of the principles of 1848. Hanák undertook research on the basis of unexplored sources, introducing new economic and societal aspects which up to his time had remained underrepresented in these debates. The conclusion he reached was that the Compromise represented a realistic arrangement and that, despite many conflicts, the era following 1867 was one of economic and cultural development. This verdict emphasized the interdependence of the two compromising parties and the wider European context of the legal act. As such, it contradicted both Hungarian nationalist and conventional Austrian 'wisdom' on Hungary's place within the empire. The results of Hanák's research were published in German in the book *Ungarn in der Donaumonarchie* (1984). It was a sign of recognition of the strength of his interpretation that it significantly shaped the historical debate, not just in Hungary but also in Austria. There it contributed to the revision of an influential viewpoint represented by Erich Zöllner (1916–96). According to Zöllner, for Austria the Compromise was even more tragic than the defeat at Königgrätz, because it led to a permanent crisis and the loss of Austrian identity, and Hungarians created division in the hitherto unified Austrian Empire.[16]

Moreover, the emphasis on pragmatic solutions was characteristic not only of Hanák's argument on the Compromise, but also in his work, his academic conduct and the nature of his persona. With hindsight, such a way of trying to negotiate a *modus vivendi*, which was based on realizing the interdependence between the regime and its historians, may be judged in different ways, depending on circumstances. It may be condoned as a realistic attitude that seeks to bring out the best of the available opportunities, or it may be condemned as an attitude which is damaging to the historian's integrity and possibly to the quality of his work. Yet it is worth remembering once again that acting as an 'uncompromising persona' may involve much higher risks than usual under an authoritarian regime.

Hanák also employed the concept of compromise as a (self-justificatory) framework to describe the generational divides along political lines in the period immediately following World War II. He detected three distinct groups in this era. The first included those who wanted to take revenge for the atrocities they had suffered in the past and found terror an essential tool for the creation of the new world. The second category included the 'compromisers' who believed that revenge could not become the foundation for a new world. Finally there were those who formulated their ideas exclusively with reference to the future and did not relate to the past in any form. Hanák identified himself as belonging to the second group but, then, he was compelled to grapple with the problem that he had taken part in repressive acts. In his autobiographical essay he made the following attempt to come to terms with this contradiction: '*We, the compromisers* did not thus belong to the group that sought revenge. But the party which we joined showed its fist to us, there was no way to remain non-committal, because that was seen as identical with lack of loyalty.'[17]

Lastly, the different incarnations of Hanák's persona over the course of five decades of a working life were characterized not only by transformations, but by compromises. In addition to the young scholar coming 'from below' and launching his career with great ideological zeal, it later included the marginalized intellectual. With the passing of time and the change of political circumstances that aspect of his persona gradually morphed into a very different incarnation: that of the public historian and even a school maker. Hanák's commitment to Marxism also changed over time, while his European outlook, the combination of an old-fashioned sense of patriotism with cosmopolitan values and the appreciation of the Central European intellectual heritage, appears to have accompanied his entire career.

Fin-de-siècle culture

Hanák's research stays at some of the most prominent universities – Columbia, Yale, Bielefeld – in the 1970s and 1980s enabled him to familiarize himself with research topics and methodologies that extended beyond the kind of history that was full of ideological ballast and revolved around 'fundamental turning points' from a Marxist perspective. In the course of those stays he discovered the *Annales* school and the history of everyday life. He also became inspired by the German proponents of new social history emerging in the 1970s, with particular emphasis on the problems relating to *embourgeoisement*, as explored by Jürgen Kocka and his colleagues. New currents in cultural history did not escape him either, and inspired essays from him on topics ranging from urban high culture to the culture of the bourgeoisie and the history of the operetta. All these intellectual encounters were refreshing for him because, in his own words, these methods represented a more 'human' history. Instead of focusing on power, they allowed him to focus on the people. They also allowed him to reveal to his more doctrinaire colleagues and readers that, contrary to some vulgar Marxist interpretations, history was never mono-causal.[18]

The greatest impact on Hanák's work was exercised by the historian Carl Schorske, whom he befriended during his stay at Princeton. Schorske was author of the magnificent *Fin-de-siècle Vienna: Politics and Culture*, a masterful collection of seven interdisciplinary essays which earned him the Pulitzer Prize in 1981. The book offered an analysis of political and intellectual life in the city. Focusing on prominent intellectuals and artists such as Sigmund Freud, Gustav Klimt, Oskar Kokoschka and Arnold Schönberg, it revealed that their innovations required a break with the nineteenth-century liberal tradition. The inspiration provided by Schorske and Hanák's own interest in modern cities and in the comparative method motivated him to study the dynamics of the competition between Vienna and Budapest in arts, architecture and politics. The outcome was, among other things, the essay collection *A kert és a műhely* (*The Garden and the Workshop*), the English version of which was first published, with Schorske's foreword, shortly after Hanák passed away. In the book 'garden' stood as a metaphor for Vienna's aesthetic and individualistic culture, while 'workshop' stood for the busy, socially engaged and industrializing Budapest. While Hanák's book provided no equivalent to the coherence and consistence of Schorske's *tour de force* – one reviewer characterized it as a book 'more to enjoy than to study' – it was a worthy and lively contribution which discussed topics ranging from *embourgeoisement*, via urbanization and the history of the operetta, to death in Vienna and Budapest. If not in depth and coherence, in certain aspects the book did serve as a 'twin' to Schorske's *magnum opus*. In addition, the commonality of the chosen genre – the essay – what critiques described as Schorske's 'almost sentimental occupation with the Viennese center' was mimicked in Hanák's focus on Budapest. Moreover, the way Schorske somewhat idealized the image of German-Jewish cultural life which stood in marked contrast to the political sphere of the period could also be detected in Hanák's argument.[19]

It was also at this time that Hanák discovered his affinity with the intellectual generation of the *fin-de-siècle* period in Vienna and Budapest. He felt that their status on the margins of society, their falling out of public life, their existential solitude and anxiety were reverberating with his own experiences. Among those intellectuals he named in particular were Hugo von Hoffmanstahl, Béla Bartók, Robert Musil and Franz Kafka. As Hanák put it: 'I could relate to those, who could not identify themselves with anything but *l'art pour l'art*'.[20] Moreover, by positing himself as the successor to those marginalized and alienated intellectuals, Hanák also diagnosed his alienation from the Communist Party with reference to their experiences: 'I did not have a family of my own, the party became my family. Like George Lukács, Wittgenstein and Karl Kraus who got to experience the hollow nature of their own *grand bourgeois* life from within, its hypocritical nature and fake morals, I felt within my own "family" in the same way. But this alienation had to be kept secret, first even from ourselves.'[21]

This individual interest became more pronounced once it was possible to showcase that it institutionalized forms. One major event in this connection was a colloquium between Hungarian and American historians devoted to progressivism. As Carl Schorske noted, '[w]hile young American historians were preoccupied with the reanimation of the legacy of pre-Cold War progressivism and the New Deal in the conservative atmosphere of the Cold War, their Hungarian counterparts were reviving their own cosmopolitan and democratic intellectual tradition of the turn of the century'.[22] From the 1970s onwards, as the communist regime came to gradually soften, under carefully observed parameters it became possible to write about the progressive intellectual traditions of the *fin-de-siècle*, which represented an alternative to communist 'progressivism'. The members of the so-called civil radical group of *fin-de-siècle* Budapest had included Karl Mannheim, Karl Polányi and Oszkár Jászi who all had an avid interest in societal problems. Oszkár Jászi, to whose legacy Hanák dedicated a book, was an outstanding political and social analyst of the Austro-Hungarian Empire, and a proponent of Danubian patriotism. In this book Hanák argued that, contrary to interwar accusations coming from the right wing of the political spectrum, the civic radical discourse was patriotic, but its focus of allegiance had been, not the ethno-nation, but an envisioned multiethnic and democratic cultural-political community.[23]

Although this civil-radical group remained marginalized, it was significant because during their careers its members exercised intellectual critique of conservative nationalist traditions and of communist ideology in equal measure.[24] It therefore perfectly suited Hanák's ideal which was likewise critical of the nationalist legacy, while increasingly distancing itself from the Marxist legacy. In addition to the intellectual and political culture, Hanák was thoroughly influenced by the literature of the era, and in particular by Robert Musil (1880–1938) and his magnificent, though unfinished, book *Der Mann ohne Eigenschaften*. This book documented the moral and intellectual decline of *Kakania* – a label Musil coined from the famous k. und k. (*kaiserlich und königlich*) attribute – an Empire which appeared to have got stuck in a 'not entirely committed to modernization, but not entirely backward' state. What Hanák appreciated most in Musil's writings, well before they had been discovered and even become fashionable in the circles of a wider reading public, was a special sense of absurdity and the ironic distance he kept from 'big history'.

The public intellectual

Some historians find it a paramount task to produce works intended for the general public, while others feel no affinity with such a mission. The same applies for another, but not entirely unrelated type of engagement: participation in public life and contribution to political debates. In both cases, such involvement may be judged in different ways. It may be viewed as a virtue that allows the historian to descend from the ivory tower and/ or act as a responsible citizen. Alternatively, it may be frowned upon because of the potentially necessary compromise on academic standards it might involve or for alleged political partisanship. In Central and Eastern Europe at the time Hanák was working, public and political involvement by historians was often regarded as the norm, rather than the exception, especially in terms of their contribution to the nation-building process. This influential view was first advanced by R. W. Seton-Watson in his inaugural lecture 'The historian as a political force in Central Europe' at the School of Slavonic Studies in 1922. According to Seton-Watson, current political miseries acted as an incentive to revive historical studies, enabling the present to be contrasted unfavourably with past glories. In Central and Eastern Europe the historical tradition was to play an 'absolutely decisive' part, even rescuing whole nations from oblivion.[25] The validity of Seton-Watson's thesis about historians' political engagement as a Central and East European *peculiarity* is highly questionable – it is enough to think of German historians' involvement in the debates around German unification, the political roles played by members of the French liberal school (Guizot, Thierry) or Thomas Macaulay's promotion of a Whig version of history in nineteenth-century Britain. However, this does not invalidate his point about the politicized context of historians' work in the region. In that context it is worth remembering that in an unfree state the contours between the 'professional' and the 'public' realms and the notion of the '(a)political' are not only elusive but also constantly evolving. Under certain conditions even 'silence', the *absence* of political commitment or withdrawal from the public may qualify as 'political', particularly when commitment is dictated by the authoritarian regime.

Throughout the mature stage of his career, Hanák consciously engaged with the public and thanks to his public appearances in the media he became a household name in Hungary. In performing that role, utilizing the intellectual capital that he had been accumulated, he often found himself in a position to articulate provocative ideas that were one step ahead of the officially accepted viewpoints. This in turn further increased the weight of his public performances in the unfree political sphere. It was not so much, therefore, the professional content of his message, but the 'productive tension' created in this way that made his popular performances notable. As his fellow *émigré* historian, István Deák, noted shortly after his death: if Hanák had been born in the United States or Western Europe, he would only be remembered by his historian colleagues. However, 'to his fortune or misfortune', he was born into a small Central European city which predestined him to a life with tragic experiences, but also afforded him the chance to perform a role as a highly influential public intellectual.²⁶ Hanák was aware that not all members of the profession were appreciative of that role; from an elitist stance, some of them considered his participation in TV programmes as a 'light' and 'diluted' version of scholarship. In contrast, he believed it to be historians' and other intellectuals' task to take responsibility for shaping the consciousness of their community and he even dedicated a reflective essay to the subject.²⁷

At the same time, he was sympathetic to some of his colleagues' reservations. In the field of history, the boundaries between the 'professional' and the 'amateur' scholar are not as precisely delineated as for example in the medical profession. The naive belief that history is first and foremost 'storytelling' and hence that everyone is an expert in history motivates some amateurs to fashion themselves as 'popular historians'. They express views that compromise the members of the historical profession who find themselves compelled to debunk some of the more illusory ones. For Hanák, the difference between these two categories had nothing to do with formal qualifications – a degree in history, experience in research. In his essay 'A történész lelkiismerete (On the historian's conscience)' (1995) he argued that the factor distinguishing the professional historian from the amateur is that the former's most important 'companion' is self-doubt, whereas the latter has difficulties separating the 'what happened' from the 'what should have happened', the *sein* from the *sollen*.²⁸

Hanák also reflected on the intricate relationship between history writing and politics. He was aware that the discipline of history is often accused of being the servant of politics. Among numerous formulations he referred to Arthur Koestler, who characterized history (writing) in the image of an 'unscrupulous master builder' who constructs a building using mortar mixed from lies, blood and mud. He saw the greatest danger in the kind of history that assumed the function of national pedagogy. Rather than asking intellectually provoking and challenging questions, its representatives turned history into a static, legitimizing discipline, carefully guarding the national historical heritage, 'an untouchable' possession. According to Hanák, 'for the people of East-Central Europe, during the long centuries of dependence and subordination, the national heritage was evoked as consolation, and also as the legitimation of political demands yet to be made'.²⁹ The pathos which characterized the cult of anniversaries was the antithesis of critical public scholarship. It evolved from the tragic events of the past, the constant fight for survival. It was pious and judgemental, leaving space neither for alternative narratives, nor for doubt and humour. Hanák thus concluded that the historical discipline was badly in the need of realistic and responsible rethinking of national issues.

While he was critical of these nationalist tendencies, he also understood their roots. One moment of revelation came when, in the early 1980s, he went to see a historical musical in New York. Its title was *1776* and it revolved around the dramatic moments of the war of independence and the American Declaration of Independence. The musical abounded in songs and dances, which were not at all of patriotic nature:

> For a while I was surprised as I asked myself what would be the reaction if a musical related the story of the Hungarian revolution of 1848, casting in the role of national heroes actors who are jumping, dancing and singing on the stage. Scandal! Our historical thinking does not tolerate music, dance or humour. But there is a big difference here: George Washington, Benjamin Franklin and Thomas Jefferson died peacefully and after full lives. Our heroes of the revolution either died on the battlefield, or committed suicide or ended up in lifelong exile. Our relationship with history is different here, in the Danubian region.[30]

Lived reality and utopia: Central Europe

This 'different relationship' with history was at the core of Hanák's engagement with Central Europe. As we have seen, his civic patriotism was indebted to the *fin-de-siècle* legacy, but he detected its roots even further back: 'my personal utopia, that of Danubian patriotism, dates back to 1848'.[31] The revolutionary days of 1848 saw the 'marriage' of liberalism and nationalism, with demands including equality before the law, and freedom of expression and of religion. In aligning himself with the liberal tradition of 1848, Hanák was able to contest the belief that the cultivation of national consciousness (for example the heritage of the revolution) was the privilege of conservative, right-leaning scholarship. In addition, his engagement with the idea(l) of Central Europe was also part and parcel of a series of vibrant discussions that started in the early 1980s. These discussions conveyed an ideological message alongside others: they sought to distinguish the Central European satellite countries from the Soviet space. Contributors to these debates resided in various countries of the region and even in emigration. What connected them was a stance that can be described as 'critical patriotism': the search for an alternative to the ethno-nationalist tradition that was gaining increasing prominence in the final years of the Cold War.

The revival of the idea of Central Europe, buried during the Cold War, had promise to deliver a counter-narrative to the 'realized utopias' of the twentieth century. It also became Hanák's tangible utopia. Among the numerous authors who engaged with the cultural and geopolitical aspects of the Central European dream (and reality) two writers' ideas became particularly resonant: those of the Czech Milan Kundera and the Polish *émigré*, Nobel-Prize-winner Czeslaw Milosz. Kundera's prominent essay 'The tragedy of Central Europe' insisted on Central Europe not as a 'state formation', but as culture or fate.[32] It pointed out that its borders were imaginary and constantly changing with the historical situation. At the core of Kundera's essay was the argument that Central Europe belonged to the realm of Western 'rationalism' and not to Eastern 'irrationalism'. Attractive as such a claim might have been, its proponent quickly fell under criticism for having perpetuated a false dichotomy. Another aspect of Kundera's ruminations about Central Europe that received critical reactions was their selective nature: anti-Semitism and Nazism were core experiences in the region but were not themes he chose to focus on. Interestingly, the same applies to Hanák's historical research: despite – or perhaps precisely because of – having experienced its impact on his own skin, he undertook no attempt to engage with the 'darker' shades of the intellectual legacy of the *fin-de-siècle*.

While appreciating Kundera's views on Central Europe, Hanák found that his own approach particularly resonated with Czeslaw Milosz's observations on the nature of literature in Central and Eastern Europe. According to Milosz:

> The most striking feature in Central European literature is its awareness of history, both as the past and the present... personae and characters who appear in these works live in a kind of time which is modulated in a different way than is the time of their Western counterparts: events of the political decade in which the characters live, of decades which formed and marked them, but also those of their parents' lifetime, constantly lurk in the background and add a dimension rarely met with in Western works. In the latter, time is neutral, colourless, weightless, it flows without zigzags, sudden curves and waterfalls. In the former, time is intense, spasmodic, indeed practically an active participant in the story. This is because time is associated with a danger threatening the existence of the national community to which a writer belongs.[33]

Hanák found Milosz's point applicable in a much broader context and that it was precisely this 'tangibility' of history in every aspect of life, the outcome of constant catastrophes endangering national existence, that constituted the core of a Central European mindset.[34] He also agreed with Milosz's claim that in this region 'imagination always comes from the collective memory and from a sense of menace'. Still, it was precisely these conditions that shaped its intellectual heritage and that made it attractive enough for Hanák to insist on an awareness of history. During the communist period, imagination provided a counter-narrative which retained 'the dream'. In an essay written in 1984 Hanák asked the question '[w]hat would our brave new world be in 1984 without dreams and utopia?'[35]

A sign of Hanák's insistence on his utopia was that he continued to cherish it even in the 1990s, when it started to lose its intellectual currency and become a target of criticism.[36] He regretted that for many it became the new edition of the German *Mitteleuropa* plans or of anachronistic nostalgia for the lost empire, or even worse, revanchism. In an essay reflecting his debate with Eric Hobsbawm on this theme he pointed out that, just as it had been an obligatory pious gesture among Western intellectuals to lament the loss of Central Europe in the 1950s, then become enthusiastic about it in 1956 and in 1968, the intellectual fashion of the 1990s was to express disappointment with it. From this new vantage point it became the land of eternal troublemakers and of Kafkaesque castles. Reacting to Hobsbawm's claim that Central Europe was not a reality but a value judgement, and that it had more affinity with politics than with geography, Hanák asked: 'So what? Is perhaps the notion of the West devoid of any value judgement?'[37]

The many personae hiding in one historian

What predictable and what somewhat counter-intuitive observations can be made on the basis of Hanák's life-work and persona about existing categorizations, definitions and discussions of the subject? To what extent did the conditions under which he worked exercise an impact on his work or, to put it differently, which traits of his persona appear to be (more) fundamental to the historical profession and which ones appear to be peculiar to the situation in which he lived and worked? Could the limitations of an authoritarian system at times be inspirational, allowing the historian to make virtue out of necessity? To what extent can the role of 'nature', i.e. one's scholarly DNA, be influenced or even overwritten by 'nurture': one's own choices and intellectual development beyond the early scholarly stage?

As we have seen, Hanák negotiated various personae in the course of his long working life. He started his academic career as an overtly ambitious scholar who was at the same time a committed cadre of the Communist Party. To some extent his youthful persona appears to have shared certain similarities with some Italian and British Marxist historians of that period, such as Francesco Renda and Eric Hobsbawm. Nonetheless, in 'acting out' this persona, it did make a considerable difference that a 'young Marxist' in one of the western Iron Curtain countries did not enjoy the support of the dominant regime, but formed part of a small academic subculture. In the period after the revolution of 1956 Hanák became a marginalized historian, who could nevertheless use the silence to which he was 'sentenced' for undertaking productive research in the secluded environment offered by the archives. Archival work is a quintessential constituent of a historian's profession, so the question may arise whether it makes sense to specify it as part of a distinct persona. However, in an authoritarian context, 'research in the archives' usually acquired a new connotation. Archives and libraries often served as 'refuges', as hiding places for scholars who had lost their positions at universities or had just been released from prison. At times, the notion of the archive also operated as a metaphor for professional research based on authentic and validated sources, which could be contrasted with the ideologically motivated, superficial kind of research undertaken by historians whose ideological commitment overwrote professional and ethical standards. Although not himself employed in the archives – he held a position in the Institute for History of the Hungarian Academy – during the late 1950s and early 1960s Hanák was able to relaunch his academic career as part of the 'archival subculture' of marginalized intellectuals. He succeeded in making virtue out of necessity in using this period to excavate hitherto unknown sources on which his reinterpretation of many Austro-Hungarian events became based.

The stain on Hanák's persona that derived from his malicious actions towards some of his 'bourgeois' colleagues forever disqualified him from acquiring the position of the 'heroic intellectual' (in the eyes of those who opposed the regime). Yet it gave him access to another possible persona: not the 'virtuous', but the 'fallible' historian with a 'human' face, who was not exempt from certain vices and who was trying to perform his work as effectively as possible in full knowledge that he had to observe certain 'rules of the game' if he hoped to see his work published. As we have seen, during the 1970s and 1980s, being able to draw on the intellectual capital that he accumulated as a respected and popular historian and a public intellectual, Hanák found himself able to afford the expression of critical and moderately provocative ideas that were one step ahead of the officially endorsed frameworks. As his popularity grew, and as students assembled around him in increasing numbers, he even found himself being considered a 'school-maker' and his open-mindedness and cosmopolitanism proved attractive for many members of the new generation. In addition to his charisma, there was something contagious about his enthusiasm for any of his subjects, and two decades after his death it is evident that he succeeded in transmitting many constituents of his scholarly DNA to the next generation of researchers, both in Hungary and beyond.

While the shades of Marxism were gradually fading in Hanák's work and became reduced to occasional, obligatory lip service to the works of Marx and Engels, something appears to have remained an unalienable constituent of his persona, something in which he, 'the compromiser' knew no compromise: the effort to safeguard the national heritage against chauvinism by placing that heritage in a regional and European framework. This was the legacy and mission that he inherited from his intellectual role models, the Danubian patriots of the nineteenth century and the civic radicals of the *fin-de-siècle* period, and this was what he later transmitted to his students. Moreover, the importance of that mission was corroborated by his own, tragic, life experiences. In fact, often the divide between those Hungarian historians who eagerly pursued the 'discipline' of national pedagogy and those who warned against its dangers proved more decisive than the degree of their commitment (or lack thereof) to communist ideology. Moreover, this divide between the 'saving the nation from danger/extinction' stance and 'saving the nation from ethno-nationalist excesses' was replicated in the circles of *émigré* historians who had not fallen under the dictates of communist ideology and whose work was not subject to censorship. In that sense, Hanák's cosmopolitan persona showed similarities with that of another *émigré* historian I have mentioned, István Deák, even though Deák remained critical of Hanák's youthful, communist 'excesses'. This is not to say that reserving a distinct persona for *émigré* historians could not be meaningful. However, the physical distance and the freedom from the authoritarian regime were perhaps less important factors than could be presumed on the basis of common sense.

From the comfortable distance of mainstream scholarship, the historiographical production of the former 'Eastern bloc' may appear homogeneous, undistinctive and permeated with communist ideology to an extent that completely undermines professional quality. It may therefore seem somewhat counter-intuitive that communist and nationalist historiography were eminently compatible: from the 1970s nationalist–exclusivist populist rhetoric gained more and more influence in the historians' community and at times was even supported by the government. With hindsight, in the different incarnations of Hanák's persona, the significance of the communist context appears to be less decisive than one would expect. Rather, the lasting legacy of his persona, a message that he passed on to his students, was the need to critically engage with myopic nationalism and to find alternatives to it, even if one knows full well that those alternatives may forever remain in the realm of utopia.

Notes

1. Péter Hanák, 'Töredék fiaimnak', in Hanák, *Ragaszkodás az utópiához* (Budapest: Liget, 1993), p. 91.
2. Herman Paul, 'What is a scholarly persona? Ten theses on virtues, skills and desires', *History and Theory*, 53 (2014), 351.
3. Lorraine Daston and H. Otto Sibum, 'Introduction: scientific personae and their histories', *Science in Context*, 16 (2003), 2.
4. Ibid., 1.
5. István Deák, 'Hanák Péterről', *Budapesti Negyed*, 22 (1998), 7.
6. Hanák, 'Töredék fiaimnak', p. 37.
7. Ibid., 39.
8. 'Szétszakadt nemzedék. Mihancsik Zsófia beszélgetése Hanák Péterrel', *Budapesti Negyed*, 22 (1998), 15.
9. Deák, 'Hanák Péterről', 8.
10. This is described in detail in Hanák, *Ragaszkodás*, pp 47–61.
11. 'Szétszakadt nemzedék', 24.
12. Hanák, 'Töredék fiaimnak', p. 74.
13. Ibid., p. 88.
14. Hanák, 'Reálpolitika és utópia Közép-Európában', in *Ragaszkodás*, pp 224–5.
15. Péter Hanák, *1867 európai térben és időben* (Budapest: Historia, 2001), pp 175–7.
16. Ferench Glatz, 'Bevezetés', in Hanák, *1867 európai*, p. 9.
17. Hanák, 'Szétszakadt nemzedék', 15.
18. Hanák, 'Töredék fiaminak', p. 86.
19. Scott Spector, 'Marginalizations: politics and culture beyond *fin-de-siècle* Vienna', in Steven Beller (ed.), *Rethinking Vienna 1900* (New York: Berghahn, 2001), p. 136.
20. Hanák, 'Töredék fiaminak', p. 86.
21. 'Szétszakadt nemzedék', 18.
22. Carl. E Schorske's foreword to the translation of Hanák's book *A kert és a műhely* (*The Garden and the Workshop*) (Princeton, NJ: Princeton University Press, 2014), p. 10.
23. Péter Hanák, *Jászi Oszkár dunai patriotizmusa* (Osiris: Budapest, 1985).
24. György Litván, *Magyar gondolat, szabad gondola: Nacionalizmus és progresszió a század eleji Magyarországon* (Budapest: Magvető, 1978).
25. R. W. Seton-Watson, *The Historian as a Political Force in Central Europe* (London: School of Slavonic Studies at the University of London King's College, 1922), p. 27.
26. Deák, 'Hanák Péterről', 7.
27. Péter Hanák, 'Közép Európa: a bomlás alternatívája', in *Ragaszkodás az utópiához*, pp 291–2.
28. Péter Hanák, 'A történész lelkiismerete', and 'A történetírás: birtokper', *Budapesti Negyed*, 305, 294.
29. Péter Hanák, 'Reflexiók a századelő kultúrájáról', *Budapesti Negyed*, 234.
30. Hanák, 'A történetírás: birtokper', 296.
31. Péter Hanák, 'Ragaszkodás az utópiához', in *Ragaszkodás az utópiához*, p. 129.
32. Milan Kundera, 'The tragedy of central Europe', trans. Edmund White (from the French), *New York Review of Books*, 26 April 1984, 33–8.
33. Czeslaw Milosz, 'Central European attitudes', *Cross Currents: A Yearbook of Central European Culture*, 5 (1986), 101.
34. Hanák, 'Közép-Európa: a bomlás alternatívája', p. 297.
35. Ibid., p. 133.
36. Péter Hanák, 'Az alapítások kora', in *Ragaszkodás az utópiához*, p. 261.
37. Péter Hanák, 'Temetni veszélyes', in *Ragaszkodás az utópiához*, p. 280.

Chapter 10

What is an African historian? Negotiating scholarly personae in UNESCO's *General History of Africa*

Larissa Schulte Nordholt

Introduction

Scholarly personae have been studied, so far, almost exclusively in European and North-American contexts. Given the recent 'global' turn in historiography and the social dynamics of in- and exclusion present in the history of historiography, this is remarkable.[1] This chapter therefore aims to study the emergence of African history as a (sub-)discipline in the second half of the twentieth century, to illuminate how templates of scholarly personae might have emerged outside a strictly European context. To do this, I will look at UNESCO's *General History of Africa*, a project in which historians actively sought to create a new way of looking at the African continent's history during a time that the discipline of African history was establishing itself as a reputable scholarly activity.

Studying scholarly personae through the prism of UNESCO's *General History of Africa* allows us to enrich existing literature in another way, too. Scholars employing the persona concept have mostly adopted micro or meso perspectives of historical scholarship, and focused on specific scholars and their ideals of virtue and vice and on cross-disciplinary comparisons of virtue catalogues, respectively.[2] African historians engaged in the *General History of Africa*, by contrast, invite us to adopt a macro perspective, given that they dissociated themselves from 'the' Western historian, no less, in its multiple, Eurocentric, incarnations. What could it mean for the study of scholarly personae to move to such a macro level and scrutinize a moment in the history of historiography that purposefully sought to combat existing models of 'good scholarship' from a decolonizing perspective?

The postcolonial actors who wrote history in this moment were caught in a paradoxical negotiation of the historical difference between their societies and the need to deal with Western projections of modernity on those societies. This led them to regard western historiography, at least as it pertained to the history of Africa, with scepticism. Therefore, whilst they were still embedded in a Western system of academia, they simultaneously agitated against that system. As a result the ideals they formulated were partly based on the antithesis of something as considerable as the 'Eurocentric historian'. The question this chapter asks is what these actors imagined that antithesis would look like? What, in other words, was an 'African' historian in the context of African historical studies in the second half of the twentieth century, according to various African historians and Africanists?

In this chapter I will discuss the shared commitments and ideals that were part of the scholarly persona of historians working on a postcolonial history project funded by the United Nations Educational, Scientific and Cultural Organization (UNESCO), the *General History of Africa (l'Histoire générale de l'Afrique)*, which I will introduce in a more detailed way in the following section and refer to as the GHA. I will illustrate how the framework of the scholarly persona may be used to interrogate the paradox of 'double-consciousness', or working with different perspectives, within the GHA and how the historians working on the GHA constructed a shared vision of what a scholar should not be: a persona *non grata*. I will do so first by discussing the GHA's system of peer review for the various chapters that were part of the multi-authored eight-volume work. The reports of the so-called reading committees show how historians in charge of the work meant to shape its content and by extent its authors. Secondly, I will look at a small *casus* of obituaries of eminent GHA historians to show the virtues and character traits that were used to praise them and fit them into the mould of an Africanist hero. Finally, I will discuss some cases where these constructed ideals became contested in order to illustrate the multiplicity of perspectives within the GHA and the difficulty of creating a postcolonial history and a postcolonial (or decolonial) scholarly persona that was completely free from vices belonging to the persona *non grata*.

The *General History of Africa*

African historical studies in the second half of the twentieth century emerged from a longer tradition of eighteenth- and nineteenth-century African and black intellectual traditions. These traditions stemmed from resistance against the all-encompassing racism that had accompanied the European imperialist penetration of the continent and the Americas.[3] In the twentieth century the focus of some intellectuals shifted from political philosophical tracts to the production of historical works.[4] These historical works were meant to prove that Africa had a history that was worth telling and that it was not an image of eternal stillness, as it had been depicted by European intellectuals.[5] As a result, during the period of political decolonization 'doing' African history became associated with the retaking of control from the West. 'Mental decolonization', the effort to free not only the colonial body, but also the mind, therefore became tied to the production of African historiography. This need to move away from Western explanations within histories of colonized pasts has been a key problem within postcolonial thought.[6] Relating specifically to African 'gnosis' (methods of knowing) Valentin Mudimbe has analyzed the creation of an African 'alterity'. He made it clear that the translation of historical difference in the context of African historiography is situated in a long tradition of othering Africans and their history, while Africa has simultaneously played a crucial role in the creation of a Western epistemological system of superiority. He has described how the 'idea of Africa' in modernity had essentially been created mostly by Europeans, and some Africans, from the fifteenth century onwards, using Western epistemological systems, culminating in the creation of a colonial library, a constellation of Western mythologies concerning the 'dark continent'.[7] Mudimbe argued that invariably the West had also been influenced by the colonial library and therefore by Africa, but that it was always Africa and 'the African' that ended up in a position of inferiority and otherness.[8] It was this colonial library that African intellectuals in the nineteenth and twentieth century had to position themselves towards and that they were reacting against when writing a history of the continent seeking to position itself as different from the library.

In 1964 UNESCO, the United Nations Educational, Scientific and Cultural Organization, became the vessel through which a group, mostly of African intellectuals, put into practice this need to move away from a colonial library and officially embarked on what the Nigerian historian J. F. Ade-Ajayi later dubbed 'the climax' of Africanist historiography: the production of an eight-volume *General History of Africa*.[9] The *General History of Africa* was to provide the whole continent, including North Africa, with a synthesis of the written academic history it so far lacked. Work on the GHA lasted for over three decades, from 1964 until 1998.[10] The project was pluralistic in its historiographical outlook and expressly stated that it wanted to avoid the vice of dogmatism. The GHA is usually seen as an expression of Africanist historiography, associated with the Ibadan school of history in Nigeria, from which Ade-Ajayi also hailed. But authors who have been situated in different historiographical schools, such as the Dar Es Salaam school of 'useful', Marxist-inspired history or the Parisian creed of *engagé* historians, also contributed.[11] Like most historians of Africa working in the early postcolonial years, the GHA was more concerned with the content than the context of historiography.[12] As such the work can be seen as a genuine sample of African historical studies in the second half of the twentieth century. In line with pan-African ideology, moreover, contributing authors came from all parts of the continent as well as the diaspora.[13] The pan-Africanism practised in the GHA included Arabic North Africa. The historians who led the project came together as the 'International Scientific Committee for the drafting of a general history of Africa' (ISC). This ISC was thirty-nine members strong, two-thirds of whom were Africans or of African descent. I will use the GHA as a case study to explore how scholarly personae can be used as a framework to interrogate African historiography and vice versa, how the GHA might help broaden the scope of the framework of the scholarly persona.

Reading committees

As mentioned above, the contributors to the GHA made use of a system of peer review to edit chapters. I will use the reports of reading committees for volumes IV and V, dealing with Africa from the twelfth to the sixteenth, and the sixteenth to the eighteenth, centuries, to show how these reading committees actively helped regulate what Afrocentric history looked like. It was stated in the GHA statutes that all chapters had to be approved by a multitude of different readers. A *rapporteur* was assigned to each reading committee and had to collate the various comments made, both by members of the committee and other members of the ISC.[14] *Rapporteurs* could come from inside or outside Africa. The ISC and the reading committees wielded a considerable amount of power over the scholarly atmosphere within which these authors and editors functioned. As a consequence, the international epistemic community of historians working on the GHA was regulated by a set of implicit rules set both by the ISC and by the various reading committees, which were mostly staffed by ISC members.

A big issue *rapporteurs* had to deal with was the use of outdated terminology. Reading committees consistently resisted the use of what they saw as racist and outdated terms to describe Africa or its inhabitants. These were often colonial terms that had originated in the West's long history of othering Africans and African history. The reading committee for volume IV identified the words and phrases 'natives', 'dark continent', 'bushmen', 'hottentots', 'animism', 'magic' and 'black African specialists' as problematic in its first report. Moreover, the Kenyan historian Bethwell Ogot, the only African member of this particular reading committee, noted that the word 'tribe' had been 'overused'.[15] The reading committee for volume V also objected to a myriad of words. ISC members David Chanaiwa and Isaria Kimambo both objected to the use of *'noir'* [black] and *'continent noir'* [black continent].[16] Moreover, readers objected to the use of words such as *'sorcellerie'* [sorcery]. F. A. Albuquerque Mourao, a member of the ISC from Brazil, stated that 'to interpret any incantation, any secret ritual as *sorcellerie* would be to inverse reality' and went on to argue that these rituals needed to be explained with greater care so as to not perpetuate a lack of understanding of African culture.[17] Moreover, Adu Boahen, editor of volume VII, suggested that references to cannibalism should be deleted 'since it will feed the stereotype of a universal practice rather than a desperate reaction to catastrophe'.[18] The avoidance of perceived racist and colonial terminology signifies the ongoing positioning of historians within the GHA *vis-à-vis* other historians, and *vis-à-vis* the colonial library. Moreover, it provides a glimpse into the kind of values and (political or moral) ideals that denoted the 'right' kind of historian of Africa. It seems that a willingness to go against the grain in order to challenge Eurocentric ideas of African historical and racial inferiority was a key characteristic of the scholarly persona of historians within the GHA. The French historian Jean Devisse, who acted as a *rapporteur* for the seven-member body that regulated the GHA's everyday business (the Bureau), also fulfilled these criteria, when he confessed to being shocked at times at the use of what he dubbed outdated and racist terms.[19]

Eurocentrism became the biggest error that the reading committees sought to correct. This was abundantly clear in all the reading reports, where Eurocentrism was often used to disqualify chapters.[20] In the reading report on volume V the discussion regarding chapter two reveals a difference of opinion: 'Boahen finds the chapter most unsatisfactory and totally unacceptable. Slater finds it a beautiful piece of work, which reaches a very high level of scholarship indeed.' Boahen thought the 'spirit and Eurocentric stress run counter to the spirit of this history'. Henry Slater, a historian from Dar Es Salaam, stated regarding the chapter, conversely, that 'Africa's place in the world is masterful'.[21] The rest of the committee and the ISC agreed with Boahen that the chapter was Eurocentric and therefore bad. In a summary of another reading report for the same volume, the charge of Eurocentrism surfaced again.[22] Slater's opinion seems to have been somewhat of an anomaly. However, the kind of Afrocentrism that was espoused by the ISC throughout most of the GHA was not necessarily commonplace in Africanist circles.[23] Although Slater was never a key player within the GHA, the anecdote shows that it was not always clear what writing African history 'from the inside' looked like within the somewhat amorphous ranks of the GHA.[24]

It was clear, however, to Ivan Hrbek, the Czech *rapporteur* for the reading committee for volume IV, what African history should *not* look like, when he enforced the replacement of an author who had produced a sub-par chapter. He wrote that the chapter 'does not give the impression of being written by a modern scholar', thereby placing the author outside accepted scholarly discourse.[25] Hrbek was especially unhappy with the use of outdated literature, which referred to the much hated Hamitic hypothesis as a valid theory to understand and explain African history. The Hamitic hypothesis has had various incarnations, but usually refers to the idea that agricultural and civilizational progress in African history stemmed from outside the continent.[26] Hrbek's dismissal of the chapter was largely based on the author's use of this theory. He summarized his dissatisfaction with the continued reliance on Hamitic theories as follows:

> When will there be an end with all these strange hybrid and mixed peoples coming from Arabia, Egypt and other parts of the world and crossing the Sahara to and back founding states and dynasties and then changing their colour, names, customs, religions, languages so that nothing is left?... Let us finish once forever with all this even if some traditional accounts tend to support it.[27]

The last sentence is, of course, especially telling as it shows how important it was to get rid of seemingly racist theories. Hrbek was not the only one within the reading committee for volume IV who found the chapter problematic because of its use of the Hamitic 'curse'. In his reaction to the various reports on volume IV, the editor, Djibril Tamsir Niane, seemed to share Hrbek's annoyance with the attribution of external influences as an explanation of historical facts in Africa: '[l]a tendance est souvent manifeste chez les uns et les autres d'attribuer une influence par trop grande aux influences extérieurs et aux recherches des écoles historiques extra-africaines [it is often perceivable that people attribute too great an influence to exterior forces and to research of historical schools outside Africa]'.[28] In the end the author was indeed replaced. Eschewing 'Hamitic theories', which were seen as racist and unscientific, not just because of the lack of evidence for them, but predominantly because of their focus on extra-African factors, was another important point of Afrocentric positioning within the GHA.

As all of the above shows, the reading committees exerted a high degree of control over the final product and the authors of the *General History of Africa*. Through their commentary the reading committees implicitly created a set of rules and guidelines for authors to abide by and therefore set the standards for what was needed to be a good and effective scholar within the project: a commitment to Afrocentrism and therefore a condemnation of Eurocentrism and racism, in other words a willingness to change perspectives on African history and position oneself as the opposite of a Eurocentric historian. The aims connected to these commitments were activist in nature. The circumvention of Eurocentric and colonial perspectives through, for instance, the removal of certain terms – or indeed authors – showed what was important to the editors of the GHA not just on an epistemic, but also on moral and political levels. Nonetheless, a certain conformism with Western scholarship is also evident from the way in which some readers worried about chapters being intelligible to the non-initiated.

Social-justice scholarship

Scholarly activism was an inevitable part of historical work aimed at changing the way historians and others perceived African history. Nevertheless, GHA historians were embedded in the culture and practices of the historical discipline, in which they sought to carve out a place for African history. This shows all the more obviously in the plethora of scholarly obituaries that were written for some of the 'greats' of the GHA. The obituaries provide us with a clear picture how members of the ISC, such as Adu Boahen, Jan Vansina and Joseph Ki-Zerbo, as well as the somewhat more controversial political scientist Ali Mazrui, were presented to the outside world. What tropes surfaced in that presentation and in how far is there a sense of repetition across different obituaries? These are pertinent questions because scholarly obituaries are not just a description of scholars' lives; they are a scholarly genre as well. They are part of a system of scholarly justification aimed towards other scholars. Obituaries therefore are interesting source material when it comes to the study of scholarly templates. They can serve as models of what a scholar should or should not be like and they sometimes conform the life of the dead to set standards.[29] This is precisely why obituaries are so worthwhile when we want to know more, not about the actual life of the scholars portrayed, but about the ideals (or faults) they embodied. Scholars who are outliers, who do not necessarily fit a mould, are all the more interesting in this respect. Mazrui, for instance, functioned as the editor of volume VIII and was chosen to do so despite the fact that he was not, strictly speaking, a historian.[30] Although he was a respected political scientist and a historical thinker in his own right, his ideas concerning African history, or rather the way it should be written, did not necessarily fit with those of other members of the ISC. In a similar vein, the obituaries written for the pioneering European historian Jan Vansina, who passed away recently (February 2017), are interesting as well. Vansina, as a European within a group of Africans, did fit the mould of African historical scholarship within the GHA, despite the fact that the

GHA aims had stated that the project would privilege Africans writing African history over Europeans.

The eldest of the four scholars mentioned above, Joseph Ki-Zerbo, born in the Upper Volta in 1922, was one of the first Francophone intellectuals who concerned himself with black African history, publishing a monograph on the history of Africa as early as 1964. He spent his entire career engaged in both scholarship and politics, serving as both professor at the University of Ouagadougou and as a member of parliament. When he passed away in 2006, *Présence Africaine* devoted a special issue to his memory. In it, Pathé Diagne, who was also involved in the writing of the GHA, celebrated Ki-Zerbo's intellectualism, his patience and his insistence that African history needed to be treated with precision in a time of passionate history. But he also noted that Ki-Zerbo was known as 'Joseph Ki, le militant [Joseph Ki, the advocate]'. Moreover, 'Joseph Ki amait convaincre [Joseph Ki loved to convince]', Diagne wrote when referring to Ki-Zerbo's work for the GHA as the editor for volume I.[31] In another obituary, which appeared in the same issue of *Présence Africaine*, similar virtues were attributed to Ki-Zerbo. He wanted to change things and, along with other prominent Francophone African historians who were active in the GHA, such as Cheikh Anta Diop, Ki-Zerbo thought intellectuals should be engaged in politics and public debate. But the writer of this obituary, Mangoné Niang, also mentioned Ki-Zerbo's clear mind and strict work ethic.[32] Another *Présence Africaine* obituary writer, Adame Ba Konaré, situated Ki-Zerbo within the historical discipline, by calling him the 'father of African history'. She praised his commitment and precision in advocating oral tradition as valuable sources with which to research African history. However, she also meaningfully emphasized that Ki-Zerbo's way of dealing with African history did not mean he was not preoccupied with questions of objectivity towards the facts.[33] What all three of these obituaries show, however, is that the most important quality the writers awarded Ki-Zerbo was his engagement in politics and advocacy for African history. Nevertheless, they also emphasized characteristics such as precision and the ability to stay objective, in order to position Ki-Zerbo as what Hrbek would have called 'a modern scholar'.

Adu Boahen was likewise celebrated, even more so than Ki-Zerbo, as an activist scholar. In 1959 he had been the first Ghanaian to receive a PhD in history and in 1967 the first to chair the department of history at the University of Ghana Legon. Like Ki-Zerbo, he had been active in both the political and the scholarly spheres. In an editorial in the *Journal of African History* he is described as '[a] scholar-activist' who 'demonstrated a consistent opposition to dictatorial rule and military regimes that earned him stints in prison'. Boahen, moreover, was 'a prolific scholar', whose work earned him numerous prizes.³⁴ In 1992 he became the presidential candidate for the New Patriotic Party and ultimately he lost the controversial election to Jerry John Rawlings. Mazrui commented on this, in a letter to a UNESCO representative, Monique Lesueur, stating that Boahen's presidential campaign might have hampered his ability to work for the ISC somewhat.³⁵ Scholarly activism, then, could be hampered by actual political activity – at least according to Mazrui. It seems there was a difference between the way Mazrui (or Vansina) engaged simultaneously in scholarly activism and public intellectualism and the way Ki-Zerbo and Boahen actually functioned as elected representatives. It is not surprising, therefore, that Boahen's obituary writers emphasize his ability to combine scholarship with political activity.

Nevertheless, Mazrui himself was also praised for his activist work, in the *Journal of Pan African Studies*:

> Defining features of Mazrui's intellectual legacy include courage and controversy. A principal theme of his work was to identify and criticize abuses of political, economic and military power, whether by colonial or imperial nations, including the United States, or by leaders of developing countries, including African nations.³⁶

Mazrui had been born in Kenya in 1933 to a family of Islamic scholars. He earned a DPhil at Oxford University in 1966. He would later become a critical postcolonial thinker, who was somewhat controversial both in the West and in Africa. As the editorial obituary by the *Journal of Pan African Studies* states, he was a fierce debater. Nevertheless he strived to treat all people with respect and dignity. Mazrui, moreover, was a dedicated teacher who went to great lengths for his students. His 'great humanitarian' qualities caused him, like Boahen, to put himself at risk for causes he truly believed in. 'Mazrui also risked his reputation, even when not his life, by taking positions of principle that generated sharp criticism and condemnation.'³⁷ Another commemoration of the professor emphasized his transition from 'universal scholar' to 'Pan-Africanist political activist', caused by his period in the 'belly of the anti-black, anti-Muslim imperial beast of the United States'. This commemoration also described him as a pioneer, who, through the GHA, engaged in a 'methodological subversion [of] Eurocentrism' in the volume he edited for the GHA. It also noted his commitment to social justice caused by a mind that was 'increasingly agitated by oppression in all its forms'. It gave him the title *griot*, meant for storytellers in West Africa, thereby connecting him to oral traditions and the core methodological battle of early African historical studies.³⁸ Both obituaries described here painted a picture of Mazrui as larger than life, an example for others to live up to. It is made abundantly clear that Mazrui fought against the oppression and obscurity of Africa.

This theme is also present in the obituaries for Jan Vansina. Vansina stood for social justice in his scholarship, writes David Schoenbrun, but he did not let his identification with the oppressed hamper his scholarship: he was also critical.[39] Schoenburn thereby emphasizes the importance of 'social-justice scholarship' while simultaneously normalizing it by connecting Vansina's activism to a well-known historical virtue. The obituary written about him by Michele Wagner for the African Studies Association highlights the same combination of Vansina's critical judgement and passionate scholarship. Vansina, Wagner writes, was committed to research that he was passionate about. He was a pioneer who gave voice to those who had previously been ignored in historical research. Wagner moreover echoes Vansina's own semi-autobiography, *Living with Africa*, when she describes the arduous journey Vansina undertook in order to be able to earn a PhD in history, owing to his unconventional dealings with oral source material. She also, again echoing the autobiography, connects Vansina's identification with the oppressed of the world to his own oppression as a Flemish boy in Belgium during the early twentieth century.[40] Wagner, and Vansina himself too in his autobiography, describes Vansina as intellectually open and committed to combatting Eurocentrism out of a need to uncover hidden pasts. None of these virtues or character traits are either completely epistemic, or completely moral or political, therefore blurring the boundaries between the personal, the academic and the political.

What this small collection of obituaries might show is that in the twentieth century a commitment to 'social-justice' scholarship was seen as an important part of the character of Africanist scholars. Unsurprisingly so, since, as has been established, African history was not yet a recognized and reputable (sub-)discipline. The obituary writers recognized the ability to advocate for the field and, more broadly, for the recognition of the history of African peoples, as something positive and something necessary in order to be a good historian of Africa. Even so, the writers also realized that in order for politically charged activism to be recognized as sound scholarly behaviour, they had to situate it squarely within the boundaries of what was perceived as acceptable scholarship. They did this by emphasizing GHA historians' critical thinking, objectivity, hard work, responsible handling of source material and didactic qualities, alongside their activism or political activity. That is not to say that such qualities were not to be found in traditional African ways of dealing with the past, nor that these qualities belong exclusively with the West, but rather that they were attributed to institutionalized Western historiography.

Ideals in practice

The reading committee reports and the obituaries both show that engagement in activist scholarship was a key characteristic of the scholarly persona of Africanists. However, the reports also show that it was not always clear what that meant in the context of the GHA. The obituaries discussed, moreover, not only show which character traits and virtues were idealized, but also emphasize the difficulty of attaining an institutional position such as Vansina's or Ki-Zerbo's. Although the point of these obituaries is surely to emphasize the capacities of their subjects, they also advance a point concerning the (institutional) circumstances in which early historians of Africa worked. It is not without reason that many of the leading GHA historians received the label 'pioneer' and it was undoubtedly harder for black Africans to reach a particular position than for Europeans. It has to be emphasized here that the axis of the scholarly persona as a tool of analysis is only one point of understanding when it comes to the historiography of the GHA. Likewise, when answering the question why ideals of mental decolonization within the GHA were sometimes difficult to realize, more than just the framework of the scholarly persona needs to be taken into account. Yet that very framework, by emphasizing the actual doings of historians, might put some flesh on the bare bones of a political analysis. Simultaneously, adding political undertones to the persona analysis might enrich the latter as well.

One reason why mental decolonization was difficult to realize was because it was hard to decide which African perspectives should carry the most weight. The effort to allow marginalized histories to be heard and to liberate oppressed people by endowing them with modern history went beyond a simple dichotomy between 'African' and 'European' perspectives and interests. The GHA aimed at including neglected identities and histories within smaller geographic spaces than the enormous philosophical concept of 'Africa'. During the writing of what would eventually become chapter seven of volume V, dealing with Africa from the sixteenth until the eighteenth century, a conflict emerged concerning one of Africa's most heated political struggles during the twentieth century; the divide between north and south Sudan. The original author, the North Sudanese Professor Yusuf Hasan, and the editor of volume V, the well-known (Kenyan) Bethwell Ogot, had a difference of opinion that was based upon questions of inclusion or exclusion of marginalized histories. Ogot had altered Hasan's chapter in order to include the history of non-Arab South Sudanese ethnic groups. This angered Hasan. He deemed it a distortion of history and, gravest of historiographical errors he thought, a projection of twentieth-century political problems back into a sixteenth-century past.[41] Ogot, however, had included South Sudanese history in the chapter in order to avoid writing history from a single perspective.[42] The heart of the conflict between Hasan and Ogot, therefore, had to do with different views of what exactly constituted the history of the Sudan and how it should be written. The ISC favoured a diversity of views and the inclusion of a more pan-African point of view and therefore chose to include the alterations made by Ogot. Nonetheless, both Boahen and Maurice Glélé, the UNESCO official in charge of the GHA, urged Ogot to try to make amends in order to salvage Hasan's authorship.[43] Ogot needed considerable diplomatic skills in order to pacify and convince Hasan to change the chapter, which carried the latter's name. The conflict apparent in the writing of politically sensitive histories made it necessary for Ogot to possess skills that were more than academic. In an effort to contribute to mental decolonization and practice scholarly activism, he had to push against an existing historical hierarchy, in this case that of the Arabic predominance in the existing historiography about the Sudan.

A difference in interpreting which issues were important or not sometimes caused problems when European voices were raised. Even though the project aims had made it clear that the GHA had to be written predominantly by African authors, this proved to be difficult to realize at times. Unsurprisingly, the subsequent dominance of European authors and therefore European points of view – for origin was inextricably linked to epistemic convictions – led to critique both from participating African historians and, ironically, Europeans.[44] In 1979, a Ugandan Professor, a specialist in the history of Madagascar and member of the ISC, Phares M. Mutibwa, wrote a letter of complaint to the Director-General of UNESCO, the Senegalese Amadou-Mahtar M'Bow. In the letter he identified several ongoing problems with the GHA. The influence of European points of view was one of them. The reconstruction of African history could potentially be undermined by the presence of too many Europeans because their concerns did not necessarily reflect African concerns and because they were ideologically motivated along Cold War lines. This was specifically problematic for the writing of volume VIII, which dealt with African history from 1935 onwards.[45] The already marginalized history of African peoples could be at risk of being silenced or distorted by European voices once again, Mutibwa argued:

> Whatever may be our shortcomings, we cannot abdicate our responsibility of reconstructing our history and in the way we want to project that history. Here I do not wish to suggest that we should bend or alter history to fit our own wishes; but I hold it to be true that while others can assist us in the reconstruction of our past, it is we ourselves, in the last resort, must decide

what we were... In short, while we should have as contributors non-African historians, who moreover have greater resources than we ourselves have in carrying out research and even writing, the new General history of Africa should principally be written by Africans regardless of the paucity of their experiences and resources.[46]

Mutibwa put the responsibility for creating an Africanist historiography in African hands, rather than argue that Europeans had to leave the project altogether. Europeans, he relented, had been instrumental in making the writing of African history possible. The professor had accepted that the involvement of Europeans was inevitable owing to institutional difficulties. Mutibwa understood that Africans and the African past did not have the same amount of institutional and ideological power as Europeans and their historiography, even when it came to shaping the African past. This, however, he decided was all the more reason to guard against a predominance of Europeans in the GHA and, as Africans, to take responsibility in the writing of African history.

Institutional difficulties concerning the writing of African history are also described in the autobiography of Bethwell Ogot and the account that Jan Vansina wrote of his life as a historian of Africa. In his autobiography Bethwell Ogot described an arduous journey to earn a PhD in the 1950s. During this time he had been continuously thwarted in his aims as a result of a lasting conviction amongst predominantly European historians that African history, or at least history of Africa before the arrival of Europeans, did not exist.[47] As described above, Vansina told a similar tale concerning his PhD in his semi-autobiographical book. There was unwillingness in Belgium, where he earned the degree in 1957, to classify his work on the Kuba as history, and instead it was constantly relegated to the realms of ethnography.[48]

To return to Mutibwa's letter: he also wrote that African historians should not become too wrapped up in matters of political administration, lest their scholarship evaporate. Not all scholars involved in the GHA necessarily thought that political activity was virtuous behaviour. Combined with Mazrui's comments concerning Boahen's political activities, it seems that for some GHA scholars the virtue of political or social 'engagement' ought not to be carried to its logical conclusion by actually becoming a scholar-politician.

However, it could be difficult to decide where activism employed to reach a decolonized history stopped and political subjectivity started. This was the case when the drafting of volume VIII, and thereby of the whole GHA, came to an end in the late 1990s. Upon completion of the volume Mazrui had written a postscript because a considerable time gap opened between the writing of the final chapter and publication of the work. As a result important historical moments in African history, such as the end of apartheid or the Rwandan genocide, had not been discussed or even mentioned in volume VIII because they occurred after the chapters were drafted. The postscript was not a great success amongst the ISC members who still bothered to involve themselves with the GHA in 1997; Vansina stated:

> tout cela est beaucoup trop actuel et superficiel pour mériter une inclusion dans ce volume – Il ne faut pas donner une arme capitale aux détracteurs en puissance de cette histoire de l'Afrique qui sont tentés de l'accuser d'être partisane et un outil politique, ce que la commission et sons bureau ont en général évité depuis 25 ans! [all of this is much too current and superficial to merit inclusion in this volume – one should not provide a lethal weapon to powerful critics of this history of Africa, who are inclined to accuse it of being partisan and a political tool, which is what the Committee and its Bureau have generally avoided for twenty-five years!][49]

Evidently, Vansina had done his best to aid the GHA in walking the fine line between scholarly activism aimed at making African history known and actual political advocacy. Mazrui had crossed this line in the wrong direction. Vansina's statement that the postscript was not historical enough also sheds light on his criticism. Mazrui was a political scientist and not a historian and had evidently crossed a boundary between disciplines. Another ISC member, Dioulde Laya, was unimpressed by Mazrui's postscript, calling it 'très subjectif au plan scientifique, très erroné au plan politique, et nocif au plan intellectuel [scientifically very subjective, politically very erroneous, and intellectually harmful]'.[50] Although Boahen was decidedly more positive about the postscript, he too was not without criticism. Tellingly, however, his critique was more focused on what political issues Mazrui had left out.[51] Evidently not all ISC members agreed on what constituted 'virtuous' behaviour when it came to the writing of the postscript. Mazrui's tendency to favour a political science-oriented approach over a historical one had also created problems when the table of contents for his volume had to be prepared. Social-justice scholarship could be interpreted differently by different types of scholars.

Inescapably, then, the ideals and goals sketched in the sections above were not uncontested. The historians working on the GHA ran into a multitude of difficulties whilst trying to achieve their goals. A paradox plagued the GHA. It functioned within a European system and therefore had to conform to certain scholarly standards and practices established in the West. This, among other things, meant that the presence of Europeans in the GHA was hard to avoid, as Mutibwa reluctantly admitted in his plea for African responsibility in the creation of an African past.

The paradox of African history

As has become clear in this chapter, writing African history from an Afrocentric perspective in order to prove the existence of a past of great value was partly motivated by feelings of moral and political indignation. As such, the historians who worked on the GHA set out to write African history partly because they were convinced that it was the right thing to do and partly because they wanted to right a wrong. Owing to this focus on historiographical justice the scholarly persona, with its virtues and vices that transcend the scholarly sphere, seems an apt framework within which to regard this emergence. Scholarly persona in this chapter could be read as what Herman Paul has dubbed an 'embodied image of a regulative ideal', from which 'contrastive models of virtue' emerged.[52] GHA authors and what they wrote were regulated by an ISC that was invested in managing the gaze from the outside; after all, they were concerned with how 'the West' might perceive topics such as cannibalism or magic. In the obituaries of scholars, the templates used for the subjects were adjusted ever so slightly to fit ideals of 'Western' or 'modern' scholarship, while simultaneously moving away from those very archetypes. One of the key critiques by GHA historians of Western historiography was the West's false assertion of objectivity when it came to African history. As such, the ideal that was crafted was mostly contrasted against and around the ideal of 'the Western historian'. Moreover, the writing of the GHA almost coincided with the emergence of African history as a (sub-)discipline. Boundary work, the need to demarcate the emerging field of study from other fields of study, was therefore an important part of the everyday work of the International Scientific Committee that was in charge.[53]

The emergence of new ideals of scholarly personae were influenced by, first, an emphasis on identity as a key organizational factor within the GHA and, second, being situated within a Western academic system and, more specifically, the discipline of history, which had been developed in nineteenth-century Europe. It is important to stress that the experience of Europeans within the project was different from that of Africans. It is also necessary to stress that the GHA was, first and foremost, a top–bottom initiative and, on top of that, its authors were almost exclusively male. Although the project aims had stated that the volumes were to reach a large audience on the African continent, the Africans who worked on the GHA were invariably highly educated.[54] The need to conform to scholarly standards taught in European and North American universities, and the epistemic virtues that accompanied those standards, such as a particular Eurocentric ideal of objectivity, sometimes collided with the need to express an African identity through history and develop distinct character traits and virtues that belonged to the emerging (sub-)discipline for the African historians that worked on the project.

This collision of worlds has been described by many African, Caribbean and African-American intellectuals in the nineteenth and twentieth centuries. W. E. B. Du Bois called it a 'double-consciousness', by which he meant the need of African-American people to always regard themselves through the eyes of white folk in order to survive.[55] Frantz Fanon, moreover, related it to the writing of history specifically in his *Les Damnés de La Terre*. He observed the estrangement of native intellectuals, as he called them, from their own soil and their subsequent wish to learn more about their own traditions and history.[56] African historians working on the GHA were enmeshed in this estrangement; they experienced a constant need to refer to two different epistemological frameworks. Ali Mazrui too recognized this dilemma as it pertained to the GHA specifically when he reflected on the project in a paper delivered as part of a symposium about the methodology of the GHA. Strikingly, he argued that the ability to combine a Western education with a 'view from within' would lead to better scholarship. 'The very initiation into Western academic culture, and the power of comparative observation linked to his familiarity with both the West and his own society, provide the requisite exposure to discover salience and appreciate significance in Ibo society', Mazrui wrote, hypothesising an imaginary Nigerian Ibo historian. The combination of a Western education with an insider view was in line with academic ideals in the field of anthropology, Mazrui stated, thereby acknowledging the ties between African history and the emergence of the discipline of anthropology, which Mudimbe has described as well. Having a double consciousness was an epistemic virtue, which was acknowledged by the academy through anthropology, Mazrui theorized.[57]

Conclusion

As this chapter has shown, the idea of the scholarly persona can be used as a critical perspective from which to regard the frame-of-mind in which scholars active within the GHA saw their work. In an effort to legitimize their perspective on African history as a valid historical exercise they clothed their commitment to social-justice scholarship and a historical liberation of African peoples in scholarly virtues such as objectivity or the need to be critical. The scholarly persona inherent in the GHA was to a certain extent a reflection of the location of the emerging discipline itself: it moved between the wish to create a new Afrocentric history that would do away with racist theories, such as the Hamitic one, and the wish to make the continent's history legible to educated elites and Western readers. This was reflected in the emerging template for scholarly personae. My hypothesis that the African intellectuals within the GHA possessed a 'double-consciousness' or needed to obtain one, seems to be confirmed by these challenges. Obtaining such a double consciousness, or the skill to navigate different epistemological environments, became a key virtue within the GHA. After all, there was a constant need to refer to both the 'new' Afrocentric history and the existing discipline of history. European intellectuals within the project, such as Vansina and Hrbek, seem to have identified with this struggle. A question for further research then might be whether Europeans (and other non-Africans) navigated the boundary work and moral questions of African history and the emerging ideals for scholarly personae differently from Africans, and if so, how and why?

What, moreover, does this tell us about the use of scholarly personae from a macro perspective? The macro perspective used here, as well as the context of protest against existing historiographical structures, presents a narrative in which historians had a clearer idea of a historian *non grata* than of an ideal-typical model of 'good' scholarship. What the GHA produced most decisively was an antithesis; as a result of the weight of the colonial library GHA historians strived to avoid the spectre of the 'Eurocentric Western historian'. 'Good' historical scholarship was contrasted against 'bad' historical scholarship – a Eurocentric approach – and it was around this antithesis that the ideal of the GHA historian was regulated and that templates of ideal-typical scholars were shaped.

Notes

1 See Samuel Moyn and Andrew Sartori (eds), *Global Intellectual History* (New York: Columbia University Press, 2013).
2 Mineke Bosch, 'Scholarly personae and twentieth-century historians', *Low Countries Historical Review*, 131:4 (2016), 33–54; Christiaan Engberts and Herman Paul, 'Scholarly vices: boundary work in nineteenth-century orientalism' in Jeroen van Dongen and Paul (eds), *Epistemic Virtues in the Sciences and Humanities* (Cham: Springer, 2017), pp 79–90; Herman Paul, 'What is a scholarly persona? Ten theses on virtues, skills and desires', *History and Theory*, 53 (2014), 348–71; Lorraine Daston, *Objectivity* (New York: Zone Books, 2007).
3 Toyin Falola, *Nationalism and African Intellectuals* (Rochester, NY: Rochester University Press, 2001), pp 26–7, 32.
4 See Kenneth Dike, *Trade and Politics in the Niger Delta 1830–1855* (Oxford: Oxford University Press, 1956).
5 See Hugh Trevor-Roper, *The Rise of Christian Europe* (London: Thames and Hudson, 1965), pp 9–11, and Wilson Jeremiah Moses, *Afrotopia: The Roots of African American Popular History* (Cambridge: Cambridge University Press, 1998).

6 Dipesh Chakrabarty, *Provincializing Europe: Postcolonial Thought and Historical Difference* (Princeton, NJ: Princeton University Press, 2000).
7 V. Y. Mudimbe, *The Invention of Africa* (Bloomington, IN: Indiana University Press, 1988).
8 Ibid., pp 1–23.
9 J. F. Ade-Ajayi, 'Africa at the beginning of the nineteenth century: issues and prospects', in Ade-Ajayi (ed.), *General History of Africa*, vol. 6 (Paris: UNESCO, 1989), p. 1.
10 The French version of the last volume, volume 8 *Africa since 1935*, was published in 1998, thereby completing the original goal of the project. However, UNESCO is currently working on a ninth volume focused on the diaspora or 'global Africa'.
11 See Horace Campbell, 'The impact of Walter Rodney and the progressive scholars on the Dar Es Salaam School', *Social and Economic Studies*, 40:2 (1991), 99–135.
12 Ibrahima Thioub, 'Writing national and transnational history in Africa: the example of the "Dakar School"', in Stefan Berger (ed.), *Writing the Nation. A Global Perspective* (New York: Palgrave Macmillan, 2007), p. 198.
13 UNESCO, *Preparation of a General History of Africa* (Paris: UNESCO, 1983), p. 6.
14 Jan Vansina, 'UNESCO and African historiography', *History in Africa*, 20 (1993), 339.
15 UNESCO Archives Paris (UAP), CC CSP 38, Report of the Reading Committee 1977, pp 7–29 and UAP, CLT CID 89, VOLUME V – READING COMMITTEE / COMITE DU LECTEURS, date unclear.
16 UAP, CLT CID 89, GENERAL HISTORY OF AFRICA – VOLUME V. First Reader's Report, June 1982, p. 3.
17 UAP, CLT CID 89, GENERAL HISTORY OF AFRICA – VOLUME V. Second Reader's Report, 15 June 1983, pp 28–30.
18 Second Reader's Report, p. 12.
19 UAP, CLT CID 89, Interim Report Volume V, chs 5, 9, 17, 18 and ch. 2 by J. Vansina, 15 January 1984, p. 1.
20 UAP, CLT CID 89, Reading Report by David Chanaiwa, date unclear, p. 1.
21 UAP, CLT CID 89, Fifth reader's report V.V, 24 June 1984, p. 2.
22 UAP, CLT CID 89, Revised Reading Report after Brazzaville, date unclear, p. 36.
23 See Chinweizu, *Decolonising the African Mind* (Lagos: Pero Press, 1987).
24 UAP, SHC/MD/10, Meeting of experts for the drafting and publication of a *General History of Africa* (Addis Ababa, 22 to 26 June 1970), p. 2.
25 UAP, CC CSP 38, Report of the Reading Committee 1977, 21.
26 Chinweizu, *Decolonising*, pp 76–80; Toyin Falola, 'Nationalism and African historiography', in Q. Edward Wang and Georg G. Iggers (eds), *Turning Points in Historical Thinking: A Comparative Perspective* (Rochester, NY: University of Rochester Press, 1999), p. 210.
27 UAP, CC CSP 38, Report of the Reading Committee 1977, 23.
28 UAP, CC CSP 38, Lettre circulaire Niane à messieurs les membres du comité de lecture du volume IV de *l'Histoire générale de l'Afrique*, 7 July 1977.
29 Anna Echterhölter, *Schattengefechte: Genealogische Praktiken in Nachrufen auf Naturwissenschaftler (1710–1860)* (Göttingen: Wallstein, 2012), pp 10, 20–1.
30 This was done because no historian could be found. Vansina, 'Unesco', 344.
31 Pathé Diagne, 'Une nouvelle image du professeur Africaine', *Présence Africaine*, 173 (2006), 23–6.
32 Mangoné Niang, 'Le veilleur du jour', *Présence Africaine*, 173 (2006), 21–2.
33 Adame Ba Konaré, 'L'histoire africaine aujourd'hui', *Présence Africaine*, 173 (2006), 27–36.
34 'Editorial: Professor Emeritus Albert Adu Boahen (1932–2006)', *The Journal of African History*, 47:3 (2006), 359–61.
35 UAP, CLT CID 99, Ali Mazrui to Monique Melcer Lesueur, 3 August 1992.
36 'Ali Al'Amin Mazrui: pan Africanist, scholar and teacher', *The Journal of Pan African Studies*, 7 (2014), 4.

37 'Ali Al'Amin Mazrui', 5.
38 'Ali Mazrui – a tribute to an intellectual *griot*', presented at the Ali A. Mazrui International Symposium, Southern Sun, Westlands, Nairobi, 16 July 2016.
39 David Schoenbrun, 'Jan Vansina (1929–2017): a founder figure in the study of Africa's past, early and recent', *Azania: Archæological Research in Africa*, 52:2 (2017), 269.
40 Michele D. Wagner, 'Obituary – Jan Vansina (14 September 1929 – 8 February 2017)', *History in Africa*, 44 (2017), 5–9 and Jan Vansina, *Living with Africa* (Madison, WI: University of Wisconsin Press, 1994), p. 5.
41 UAP, CLT CID 92, Yusuf Hasan to Bethwell Ogot, 12 August 1986.
42 UAP, CLT CID 92, Bethwell Ogot to Yusuf Hasan, 15 April 1981; UAP, CLT CID 92, Bethwell Ogot to Maurice Glélé, 24 September 1982.
43 UAP, CLT CID 92, Adu Boahen to Bethwell Ogot, 26 October 1986; UAP, CLT CID 92, Maurice Glélé to Bethwell Ogot, 26 June 1986.
44 UAP, CS CSP 39, Observations Jean Devisse, date unclear.
45 UAP, CS 1408, CC CSP 33, Phares M. Mutibwa to His Excellency Amadou-Mahtar M'Bow, 16 March 1979, p. 3.
46 Mutibwa to M'Bow, pp 3–5.
47 Bethwell A. Ogot, *My Footprints on the Sands of Time* (Kisumu: Ayange Press, 2003), pp 94–7.
48 Vansina, *Living with Africa*, pp 37–9.
49 UAP, CLT CID 103, Jan Vansina to Christophe Wondji, 8 March 1997.
50 UAP, CLT CID 103, Dioulde Laya to Christophe Wondji, 16 May 1997.
51 UAP, CLT CID 103, Adu Boahen to Christophe Wondji, 18 March 1998.
52 Herman Paul, 'The virtues of a good historian in early Imperial Germany: Georg Waitz's contested example', *Modern Intellectual History*, 15 (2018), 681–709.
53 Thomas F. Gieryn, 'Boundary-work and the demarcation of science from non-science: strains and interests in professional ideologies of scientists', *American Sociological Review*, 48:6 (1983), 781–95.
54 Meeting of Experts (Addis Ababa, 22 to 26 June 1970), pp 1–2.
55 W. E. B. Du Bois, *The Souls of Black Folk* (Chicago: A. C. McClurg and Co., 1903), p. 2.
56 Frantz Fanon, *Les damnés de la terre* (Paris: François Maspero, 1961), pp 195–8.
57 Ali Mazrui, 'Dilemmas of African historiography and the philosophy of the UNESCO *General History of Africa*', in *The Methodology of Contemporary African History: Reports and Papers of the Meeting of Experts Organized by UNESCO at Ouagadougou, Upper Volta, from 17 to 22 May 1979* (Paris: UNESCO, 1984).

CHAPTER 11

The finitude of personae: Bryce Lyon, François Louis Ganshof and the biography of Pirenne

Henning Trüper

Introduction

Among the tools that aim to explain the cultural production of 'social frames' for the 'presentation of self' (Erving Goffman) in science and scholarship, the concept of the scholarly persona is unique in its focus on the specifically *moral* nature of the frames in question. The concept is tied to the 'epistemic virtues' – and possibly some vices, too – that are thought to inform the production of knowledge.[1] Personae establish an unbreakable linkage between social norms of comportment, their internalization as virtuous moral dispositions and the emergence as well as the justification of knowledge. Personae appear to be produced through the deployment of moral norms for social distinction and individuation.

On a general level, basic posits about the epistemological functions of virtuous personae might easily appear to be unchanging. Nonetheless, the terminology was introduced precisely in order to grasp a particular *history* of changing moral norms that programmed an equally mutable self-understanding of science and scholarship.[2] Therefore, *prima facie*, it would appear plausible to assume that the historicity of scholarly personae depends on the possibility that the system that produces them has not always been, and will not always be, in place; and that perhaps it has even already come to an end. Indicators from the history of the natural sciences, as collected, if with some ambivalence, by Steven Shapin, might well be regarded as pointing in that direction. The mid-twentieth-century shift to 'big science' – large-scale laboratories, proliferating specialization and the hybridization of military, industrial and academic research – would appear to have reconfigured what a 'scientific life' is. Even if moral norms continue to impinge on the production of knowledge, they appear to apply more directly to institutional settings than to the beautiful and virtuous minds of lone geniuses.[3]

In the present chapter I pursue the question of the finitude of personae as a systemic feature of the production of knowledge in the domain of historical scholarship. More precisely, I outline the traits of an argument in favour of the assumption that the end has already occurred. At the same time, the chapter takes into account that the conditions of this argument, in the 'small'-research environment of the humanities, differ from those in big science. The finitude of personae in general, across science and scholarship alike, can only gain in plausibility if one finds ways around assigning historical agency solely, or even just primarily, to institutional change.

It may be worthwhile to add that, from a heuristic point of view, the question of finitude helps with grasping the specific merits of homing in on scholarly personae in an environment of competing analytic approaches. The disadvantage of the concept of persona would seem to be that it hinges the social production of scholarly selfhood exclusively on a bipolar relationship between knowledge and virtue. This model might however be too simple. In practice, scholarly personae can be traced only in the context of textual forms, and they appear dispersed across various types of writing.[4] For this reason, they cannot lose their moorings to textual media, and contingencies alien to the concept of persona, such as channels of communication and technologies of writing, must be taken into account. Moreover, analysis of scholarly individuation might strive to be multipolar, with other axes than that between knowledge and virtue to be taken into account. Bourdieu's concept of *habitus*, for instance, allows for a broader grasp of distinction as a systemic factor in the make-up of social groups and does not privilege moral standards.[5] Other models for analysing scholarly selfhood highlight how scientists are ensconced in practical, mediatic, material and technological networks of various kinds.[6] There remains something of a question as to how the personae approach intends to relate to these models, and whether its distinctive focus on moral histories adds to, or on the contrary subtracts from, the complexity of debates. In this chapter, I contend that the analysis of personae actually contributes distinctive insights, which come into sharper view if one considers their finitude. The study of personae, I argue, makes visible the manner in which modern scholarly knowledge is bound up with a variety of only seemingly extraneous structures, among which gender norms, traditional norms of academic honour, textual media and historical time, mortuary practices and even the anti-humanist theory revolution of the 1960s.

As a case study, I will discuss interactions of two twentieth-century medievalists, François Louis Ganshof (1895–1980) and Bryce Dale Lyon (1920–2007), in particular as concerning a third, Ganshof's deceased teacher Henri Pirenne (1862–1935), whose biography Lyon wrote in the early 1970s.[7] The chapter therefore presents a generational sequence of models of personae, with an added transatlantic complication since Pirenne and Ganshof were Belgian nationals, whereas Lyon was a citizen of the United States, who repeatedly spent time in Belgium as a researcher, for the first time in 1951–52.[8] Lyon's teacher Carl Stephenson (1886–1954) had already sought additional training in Belgium when he had studied with Pirenne, a celebrity of the discipline, at Ghent University in 1924–25. For Lyon, writing the biography of Pirenne was a matter of satisfying his considerable interest in the recent history of historical writing; but it was also a matter of indirectly commemorating his deceased teacher. As for Ganshof, he had himself contributed to the biographical knowledge about his revered master, most notably by means of an extensive 1959 article for the biographical dictionary of Belgium.[9] As Pirenne's most favoured student and successor, Ganshof was uniquely placed to provide information and contacts, such as with Pirenne's only surviving son Jacques (1891–1972), who granted Lyon access to his father's papers that were only in the process of being transferred to the archives of the Université Libre of Brussels (ULB). Jacques Pirenne also read some of the chapters in draft, but died two years before the publication of the book.

Within the very ample corpus of correspondence in the Ganshof archives, the friendship with Lyon led to exceptional forms that are remarkable for their degree of informality and intimacy.[10] The working relationship that emerged in the process of the writing of the Pirenne biography is an altogether unique occurrence in Ganshof's correspondence, with lengthy handwritten lists of comments and corrections to chapter drafts that Lyon preserved and deposited himself in the archives of the ULB.[11] Over the course of writing the Pirenne biography, Lyon submitted his own judgement to Ganshof's wherever the latter was proffered and accepted virtually all of his older colleague's edits. There is no other book in the writing of which Ganshof was involved in similar fashion. Yet, for all of their peculiarity, the specific features of this working relationship were inseparable from the development of the system of scholarly personae in the wider community of historical studies, during the period from the 1940s to the 1970s.

Status

The relationship between Lyon and Ganshof had been amicable and collegial ever since they first met in the 1950s. It became much more personal and was transformed into a close friendship only in the academic year 1963–64, for which Lyon had invited Ganshof to teach at the University of California, Berkeley, where he was a professor at the time. Ganshof had retired from Ghent in 1961. Their friendship also came to include their wives Mary Lyon (d. 2002) and Nell Ganshof (1898–1986). Mary Lyon was a classical philologist who collaborated with her husband on many research projects and for later publications regularly figured as co-author. Nell Ganshof's involvement in her husband's writing work was mostly limited to occasional help with English-language matters (the daughter of a Scottish expatriate, she had grown up in Brussels in an Anglo-French household). Scholarly personae populated an overwhelmingly male order of sociability; academic life was pitched against family life as the natural space for female presence. As Jo Tollebeek has shown for Paul Fredericq (1850–1920), Pirenne's close friend and colleague at Ghent, the symbolic significance of family life in scholarly work remained uneasy.[12] Family members, and especially female ones, contributed to the maintenance of working practice and often provided services as well as content to the putatively lone work of writing. There remained, then, an interval between the imagination of authorship as part of academic life and its reality as part of family life. The pressures of bridging this gap arguably provoked the spread of family metaphors into the description of working relationships between collaborators of different hierarchical rank, so that relations between professors and assistants or supervisees were frequently regarded as filial. For this reason, the easy inclusion of wives in the collegial relations between Lyon and Ganshof may be counted as a symptom of wider change over the course of the twentieth century. The all-male scholarly persona gradually had become unsustainable, and this change made a crucial contribution to upending the social norms previously governing these personae. Shifts in gender norms, then, provide a first, necessary though not sufficient, condition for the finitude of scholarly personae beyond smaller-scale institutional circumstances.

In the summer of 1963, suddenly and unexpectedly, during preparations for the Californian sojourn, Ganshof ran into an obstacle he felt was impossible to overcome. In order to obtain a visa, he – though not his wife – would have to submit to an official medical examination. Informed of this obligation, Ganshof solicited and obtained an appointment with the head of the department concerned at the US Embassy in Brussels. He argued his case, he wrote to Lyon on 24 June, with considerable urgency. It is worth quoting from the letter extensively as it offers a number of significant insights into patterns of speech that concerned the status of the scholarly persona:

> I told [the consular officials] that when in 1948–49 I went to the University of Chicago as a visiting professor for seven months, the American Consul general in Antwerp... gave me my visa without any medical examination, telling me this was not necessary for university professors. I told them also that I found

a medical examination an undeserved humiliation for a university professor, invited to teach by a great american *(sic)* university because they thought, rightly or wrongly, that it could be a good thing for their students (or at least some of them) to be trained by him. People going to the States for their business or for their pleasure have not to submit to a similar obligation. American professors whom we are lucky to invite in our universities have not got through this formality. Could I not be excused from it?

They told me it was completely impossible: it seems to be a clear-cut disposition in the law that foreigners coming on what they call the 'exchange scheme' for more than 122 days must have a *(sic)* I visa and have to be medically examined before...

I am indeed not ready to accept such a humiliation or rather to suffer such an affront. I quite understand that measures of security are taken about visitors in order to prevent dangerous people to enter the country. But this is not the case. I quite understand that a medical examination would be compulsory for people wishing to settle in the country such as refugees and immigrants. My case is a quite different one and I think it is unnecessary for me to comment about it. I would put discredit upon myself in my own eyes if I accepted to submit to that medical examination.

It is a great disillusion for me to be forecluded *(sic)* in this way from the stay and teaching in the University of California to which I was so much looking forward. I feel deeply distressed about it and I may add that what gives me the greatest sorrow is that I have to cancel an agreement that you and Mrs Lyon had prepared with so great care and kindness. To me (and I may say, to my wife) it is a great disappointment (this word is an understatement)...[13]

The medical examination was offensive, not because it was a superfluous bureaucratic procedure that invaded the privacy of anyone travelling to the United States, nor because it was an unfair treatment targeting Belgian citizens while American citizens were treated differently. The offence related to a far more limited category of relative equality than privacy or citizenship, namely the sheer status of 'university professors'. It was moreover a highly specific offence, namely that of a threat of 'humiliation' in private, in one's own eyes alone, neither in front of an audience of significant size, nor in the eyes of a group of peers. It may be added that, since World War I, Ganshof had been an officer in the Belgian army (of the reserve in peacetime). As such, he must have submitted to official medical examinations repeatedly. All the more startling is the fact that he so vehemently rejected undergoing a similar procedure at the behest of the US government, even though he could have regarded this as one of his duties as an (emeritus) professor and cadre of the Belgian state. Yet the situation of professors was 'different'; they formed a status group in their own right, distinct from, say, military officers. The professorial status group was marked by particular, implicit privileges and duties. Indeed, this is one of the most palpable senses in which one can encounter scholarly personae: as *academic* personae, constituted by norms and rights that set academics apart as an institutional status group. Academic privileges included for instance the use of the title 'professor'; the wearing of academic gowns; the right to march in a university parade (where such were still held); and rights to take part in faculty decisions and examinations. Status also subjected professors to certain perils of dishonour, such as e.g. the crimes of faulty or fraudulent scientific authorship, almost always non-issues for the criminal law, but often irreparably damaging in the sphere of learning. Requiring the professor to strip naked, too, would appear to have constituted a particular form of dishonour, as comparison to the military body indicates.

It appears that Ganshof's overall understanding of the status and the honour of a university professor was rooted in European university history. In transition to the late-modern period, when *ancien régime* forms of representation disappeared, the university ceased to exist as an estate, as defined by legally significant privileges. The particularity of academic status was subsequently translated into social norms without legal pertinence. These norms continued to apply and were certainly sufficient to generate a sense of academic personhood apart. The development of the discussion about scholarly personae has mainly focused on epistemic virtues and the performance of methodology. In contrast, the institutional and political implications of university history tend to have been somewhat neglected, although they were inseparably entwined with epistemological norms of demeanour. The scholarly persona – as a type, not merely as a token in the case of Ganshof – was co-constituted by categories of honour, and these categories may be interpreted as survivals of old-regime university history.

Lyon received Ganshof's letter in Switzerland where he was summering with his family after having spent the year on research work in Belgium and France. Clearly, he understood enough about the motifs of academic honour, but possessed enough distance from them, to know how to assuage Ganshof's wrath. The peculiarity of US university history, where especially in the so-called top tier mostly private institutions were (and are) constituted symbolically around alumnus and donor communities rather than around the professorial corps, may well have contributed to Lyon's more distanced outlook. On 28 June, he responded by pointing to other historians who to his knowledge had submitted to the medical examination in question in the years since 1951.[14] Then he pointed out:

> I agree with you completely that in certain cases this medical requirement seems pointless and unnecessary. I myself have experienced your same reaction. I want you to know that other countries have similar requirements. Let us take my case and your own country. In 1951–52, 1954–55, and this past year when my stay in Belgium exceeded 90 days I had to have a visa and in order to receive a visa from the Belgian government... not only I but also my wife and my two children had to pass medical examinations...

He went on to list other Belgian requirements, including copies of police records and proof of financial self-sufficiency. These conditions all applied to other Americans as well. Still, '[l]et me stress again that, like you, I consider all these requirements to be of little value and somewhat embarrassing. Evidently, however, the mysterious machinery of government has what it considers valid reasons and we are caught up in them.' So, on one hand Lyon insisted emphatically on the equality that actually prevailed within the status group of professors as they were subject to the intrusions of bureaucracy, a domain in which Belgium comported itself even worse than the United States. Yet on the other, he also ostentatiously deflated Ganshof's understanding of the privileges of the professoriate. The state, if it did not perhaps have overriding moral rights *vis-à-vis* its erstwhile academic estate, certainly enjoyed overriding power. Academics were left to appreciate the generally benign nature of the 'mysterious' workings of bureaucratic reason: the 'requirements' in question ultimately were no more than 'somewhat embarrassing'. Before the state, everybody was, and had to be, equal. The notion of a specific academic status or honour was, in 1963, illusory; the after-image of the old regime had finally faded.

This coupling of arguments sufficed to convince Ganshof to undergo the examination. He only protested mildly that his 'feelings' about the procedure remained 'unchanged', and he declared himself 'shocked' to learn about the Belgian visa requirements.[15] Yet, clearly, he himself felt a sense of relief that 'the very great pleasure of looking forward once more to our visit to California' could be recovered. If he had just been looking for a way to cancel the visit, he could easily have stood by his declared principles. Instead, he appears to have regarded Lyon's letter almost as liberation from the duty of upholding a form of honourable, if stuffy demeanour that had become cumbersome to a contrary desire.

This liberation, then, would seem to have moulded the subsequent development of their friendship. Shortly after arrival in California, the Ganshofs and the Lyons were on first-name terms, a unique development to the extent that the corpus of Ganshof's professional correspondence permits his academic friendships to be traced (apart from the Lyons, he was on first-name terms mostly just with those colleagues with whom he had studied around the time of World War I). Right until October 1963, Lyon had addressed his letters to 'Dear Professor Ganshof', while Ganshof had expressed his seniority by responding to 'My dear Lyon'. The language of subsequent letters, in particular after the return to Brussels, was easy-going, narrative and even chatty. Affection was displayed straightforwardly. 'I like the way Mary writes: it is life itself,' Ganshof asserted in his first letter after returning to Brussels.[16] Significantly, life itself was not the same thing as a scholarly persona tied to the honour of the status group of academia. The encounter with the Lyons provided a specific context for unburdening from the norms that had governed Ganshof's life in scholarship. This unburdening arguably extended into all areas of life. In a postscript written on the margins of one of her husband's letters, Nell Ganshof mentions their 'plans for improving our home, which seems grim after Berkeley'.[17] From other letters, it seems clear that the Ganshofs were taken with modern American contraptions such as the television and various kinds of household appliances. These features of everyday life, powerful as they were, no doubt impinged on the scholarly life, too. Still, for the latter, the ground had already started shifting before the American trip, with Bryce Lyon's letter from June 1963, which had signalled to Ganshof that punctilious maintenance of professorial 'honour' was no longer required. Although the institutional frames of historical research had not undergone pertinent change, the normative order behind the scholarly persona had, in a sense, come undone.

Precision and self-historicization

The friendship shaped in the 1960s informed a similarly atypical working relationship in the writing of the Pirenne biography and related historiographical works. As early as a 1965 article on Pirenne's correspondence with the Parisian medievalist Maurice Prou (1861–1930), Lyon had requested criticism and corrections. Ganshof was hard to outdo in matters of detail. The first comment he made on the Prou article indicates the manner in which the epistemic virtue of precision converged with institutional academic norms about the status of personae. Lyon had taken up a French marker of academic status, *confrère*, to characterize the relationship between Pirenne, Prou and their mutual, lifelong friend Abel Lefranc (1863–1952). Ganshof objects: 'p. 1: here "confrères" does not seem quite exact. The former students of the Ec[ole] des Chartes call one another "confrères": Prou & Lefranc were, Pirenne was not, because he was only an "auditeur libre" – "camarades" would be better.'[18] There is a blind spot in this comment, in the underlying assumption that Prou and Pirenne would have cared about the quasi-legal fine print of the meaning of academic status just as much as Ganshof did himself. Still, there is no doubt that the artificial distinctions imposed on students, between, say, *confrères* and mere *camarades*, mattered. Understanding one's own place in academic life was part of an induction into the virtue of precision that sustained historical and other scientific methods. As a twofold outsider – generationally and geographically – Lyon could be excused if he missed the finer meanings involved; but the printed text needed to be protected from error.

In the case of the Pirenne biography, the lists of corrections Ganshof appended to Lyon's first draft display a number of further traits that indicate interrelations between personae and historical 'facts'. In his edits, Ganshof frequently pointed out factual inaccuracies, especially as regarded the Belgian state as an institutional system and Belgian state universities as a section thereof. These notes testify to the depth and juridical exactitude of Ganshof's understanding of his own working environment. Judging from the misapprehensions he addressed, it seems unlikely that Lyon would have managed all on his own to achieve the level of accuracy the final version of the book displays. So for instance in Ganshof's explanation of the emergence of specialized training in history in Belgium:

> P. 38. 'For the first time... universities'. Here there is again a great confusion:
> All the seminars created in Belgian universities were 'free courses', not mentioned on programmes or on diplomas. So it is true that it was possible to get a training in history; but it was not possible to get 'a doctorate in history'. This was the object of a deeper reform which was a consequence of what had been realized unofficially since 1874. This reform, advocated by many professors and chiefly by Paul Thomas (professor first of ancient history, later of latin *(sic)* in Ghent), by Henri Pirenne & others, was realized by the law of 1890 'sur la collation des grades académiques'[.]
> In France nothing of the kind existed. You could get a good training in auxiliary sciences in the Ecole des Chartes, get seminar training in the Ecole Pratique des Hautes Etudes; but an organized technical training in history you could not get there before the early 20th century.[19]

The problem with the factual is, almost needless to say, that it is a category irreducibly tied up with judgement. Within a framework of disciplinary knowledge, such judgement is a matter of authority acquired through a working life that bears significant markers of institutional recognition. Ganshof's positions on the practical training of historians and its history were pronounced and refined, but also rather set in stone. What he tells Lyon in the quoted passage is exactly what he had taught in his introductory courses since the 1920s. His assertions are partly incontestable, but also partly coloured by personal opinion. For instance, his notions about the contrast between the French and Belgian systems are probably too stark, in the sense that he systematically overestimates the productivity and merits of the 'technical' training established piecemeal in Belgium, in 'imitation' (as he says elsewhere) exclusively of German models.[20] The knowledge Ganshof imparts is moreover deeply personal, a quality it gains simply by accumulation. None of the 'facts' mentioned in the quotation is, or could be, marked as Ganshof's original finding. Only by accumulation does the aggregation of facts cross an invisible threshold and then take the form of the epistemic virtue of erudition, a constituent of a scholarly persona.

Ganshof is entirely at ease with this crossing, so much so that he interweaves his account ostensibly with stories taken from his own memory, as for instance in the following anecdote about Pirenne's move from Liège to Ghent University:

> 74: there was also another man who had his part in orientating P[irenne] in the direction of Ghent. It was Eugène Hubert, then a young professor of modern history in Liège (who has produced important work both in the history of diplomacy and of Reformation; a pupil of Paul Fredericq). Pirenne has told me the story. He was washing his hands before going out for lunch, when Hubert dropped in telling him: 'W*o*uters est mort [Wouters is dead]'. Pirenne had understood 'W*a*uters' and thought it was the learned keeper of the Brussels town archives. Hubert corrected: 'Wouters, le professeur d'histoire du moyen âge de Gand [Wouters, the Ghent professor of medieval history]' (who had absolutely no reputation as a historian). Pirenne: 'un inconnu comme historien [an unknown as a historian]'. Hubert: 'oui, mon cher, mais il y a là un grand enseignement à reprendre, pensez y *(sic)* [yes, my friend, but there is a great teaching commission there to be taken over, think about it]'. There may be in the form a certain degree of inaccuracy, but on the whole the narrative is exact.[21]

Here Ganshof takes care to point to Pirenne himself as the oral source of the mildly amusing anecdote, and he insists on the degree of exactitude in his, Ganshof's, recollection and retelling, which also implicitly places Pirenne's recollection and retelling beyond doubt. Erudition is a matter, not merely of knowledge, but of life, and thus integrated into the scholarly persona. The history of historical writing, since it augments the self-knowledge of the discipline, is always open to the historiographer's self-historicization. It is attractive, as Ganshof does in this instance, to recur to one's own testimony. At the same time, such recourse reinstates older norms of witnessing that the methodological prioritization of archival documents, and especially the unintentionally preserved ones, had sought to overcome since the nineteenth century.[22] Those older norms of witnessing had asserted the epistemological priority of such knowledge as was derived from the proximity of an observer to the centre of a given historical event. Ganshof was a privileged witness as far as biographical knowledge about Pirenne was concerned; and Pirenne was the centre of the history of history writing in Belgium. Proximity to Pirenne defined the terms of a peculiar hierarchy that borrowed structures from the monarchical system, where social rank was symbolized through proximity to the sovereign. Ganshof ended the encyclopaedia article on his master with a quotation according to which Pirenne had been a 'prince' of scholarship.[23]

These clues indicate that Ganshof recognized a certain difference in method between the writing of history in general and the writing of historiography. This difference was embodied in the persona of Pirenne; and it was inextricably enmeshed with Ganshof's most basic methodological convictions. This is tangible for instance when he explains to Lyon Pirenne's attitude toward the famed *Introduction aux études historiques* (1898) by French historians Charles-Victor Langlois and Charles Seignobos, a key text for the modern understanding of historical method in the Francophone world (and, on account of various translations, beyond):

> 119: Langlois & Seignobos: Pirenne would say (and he said it to me as a first years *(sic)* student in october 1913): [']C'est un livre décourageant, car ce qu'un jeune étudiant doit normalement en conclure, c'est qu'il n'y a pas moyen de faire de l'histoire. Il ne faut lire cela qu'une fois formé par la pratique [It is a discouraging book, for, what a young student normally has to conclude from it is that there is no possible means of practising history. One must not read that until one has been formed by practice].' He knew Seignobos very little and did not like Langlois.[24]

This assessment of the 'discouraging' character of the most prominent available account of historical method – which was attributable especially to Seignobos's sceptical attitude towards how scientific historical writing could be – was part of Ganshof's own introductory teaching for decades. Judgement arguably gained in security by its entanglement with the master–student relationship. Lyon's readiness to follow Ganshof's corrections expressed a similar relationship, not only with Ganshof as a mentor, but also with Pirenne himself, *d'outre-tombe*, mediated by the latter's student. The writing of a historiographical biography was indeed an extraordinary context with special conditions. At one point, Ganshof explained to Lyon:

> t[ext] 20. Here there is a difficulty. You very exactly describe Pirenne's views in his [added above the line: 'important'] article of 1905. But Pirenne was wrong in calling the *castrum* 'bourg': *burgus* and 'bourg' in Flanders, as in northern France, had the same meaning as *portus*, merchant agglomeration (or any [originally] unfortified agglomeration). I may perhaps suggest a correction: 'From this merchant agglomeration in the *portus* or 'faubourg', nestled beside the *castrum* or *castellum* arose the town.' This has the advantage of correcting a fault made by Pirenne without calling the attention on it, and of dropping 'feudal' in front of 'bourg', as 'bourg' disappears.[25]

Curiously, then, Pirenne needed to be protected from having his errors pointed out. To be sure, historiography was bound up with commemorative duties; but there were also other aspects that reached further down into the discursive patterns of history writing itself.

The decision whether one should expose other scholars' errors belonged to the manner in which research work was represented in historical text;

and this was an order of representation apart from that of historical time, subject to a divergent method, in which witnessing still figured supreme, and that was marked as different by all kinds of graphic and narrative devices, e.g. footnotes or changes of tense.[26] Still, the genre of historiography, the history of historical writing, produced a blurring of established distinctions: the narrative temporality of accounting for past research came to coincide with historical time. It was therefore clear that historiography, as with methodology, had to be a secondary field to be practised only by historians already 'formed by practice'. For Ganshof – and he was representative of the discipline at large in this regard – history writing required both sides of this division. The truthful accounting for the historical past also demanded the representation, often in the form of rudimentary, episodic narrative in annotations, of the work of research. For this reason, although it carried particular normative standards – both of commemoration and of controlled transgression – the genre of historiographical biography stood in a continuum with historical writing. Scholarly personae, to the extent that their maintenance entailed at least the possibility of becoming the subject of such a biography, negotiated the suspension of the division. Therefore, being or performing a scholarly persona meant opening oneself to historicization. This was requisite for the integrity of historical text.

Finitude

So far, the context of the writing of Lyon's Pirenne biography might appear to supply only examples for the business-as-usual of the manner in which scholarly personae impinge on the production of historical knowledge. I will however propose two arguments – one medial, the other semantic in nature – that point to the manner in which the case actually speaks to the finitude of the system underpinning the persona.

Firstly, writing practice was more comprehensive than the mere jotting-down of ultimately published history text. In the Lyon–Ganshof correspondence, one cannot therefore ignore the subtle invasion of the genre of personal correspondence by patterns of correction alien to it. This process signals a rupture with previously stable models. The system by which letters are written, a fixture of scholarly practice since the early-modern period, had already begun to disintegrate. By 1970, it was disappearing slowly from the working lives of older scholars, and quickly from those of younger ones, who had never fully embraced it. Communication needs were more practically satisfied over the telephone. Letters had served for negotiating recognition of status within the social order of colleagues, while away from one another. Ganshof's archives contain countless letters of thanks that were written or received in response to sending offprints of publications. Indeed, publishing as such clearly had the function of establishing membership in the status group of the history discipline. In this way, recognition of status could move beyond the confines of the individual academic institution and settle on the discipline at large. A sociability of presence was transformed into one of absence.

When one takes into account their tremendous number, astonishingly few historians' letters of the first half of the twentieth century actually broach the substance of historical knowledge. Rather, the authors steered clear of argument and disagreement most of the time. The ritual functions of correspondence eclipsed the contribution letters could make to research. While it is hard to generalize from individual cases, the outlying pattern of Ganshof's letters correcting Lyon's Pirenne biography would seem to converge with the disappearance, not merely of the letter-writing system, but also of the normative order of sociability that was bound up with this system. This, then, would once again indicate that the order of norms around personae depended not merely on institutional factors, but also on given media techniques. Media change, such as from the letter to the telephone, would then co-determine change in personae and would figure among the preconditions for their finitude. This argument as to the change in mediatic forms in turn indicates why institutional change alone should not be deemed sufficient to explain why scholarly personae disappear.

Secondly, the case is marked by the presence of a subliminal semantic finitude that becomes accessible through the self-understanding palpable in Ganshof's edits of Lyon's manuscript. The corrections also had the purpose of transferring Ganshof's persona into the sphere of the historical, alongside Pirenne's. For decades, Pirenne's students had vested a particular sense of finitude in the persona of their master. The personal memories Ganshof inserted in the corrections signal his sense of elusive nostalgia for something that was already of the historical past; recollections, not merely of the life of the revered teacher, but of a world of scholarship whose representatives were mostly already deceased. Lyon's biography, no doubt in part under Ganshof's influence, came to embody perfectly the unity of commemorative and methodological norms that had been constructed around Pirenne. For Ganshof, the living memory of Pirenne was irreplaceable. Possession of such memory was also the only legitimate way to derive legitimacy for one's own work from the authority of the master. Given that for decades Pirenne had served as *the* model of the scholarly persona in the community of Belgian medieval studies, in Ganshof's understanding this model had its end written into it, which would by necessity arrive when no living memory of Pirenne was left.

The status group that had produced the sub-variant of the scholarly persona in the Pirenne circle that Ganshof embodied was a commemorative confraternity designed to make the transition from internal into external memory, from life into afterlife. Lyon's work did not merely illustrate that this transition was expected, but realized it. The biography marked the beginning of the afterlife of Pirenne's scholarly persona, in the memory of the wider discipline of history studies with no personal connection to the master. And since it was part of the exceptionality ascribed to Pirenne's persona that it enjoyed a defining and coordinating function for the – so to speak, apostolic – scholarly personae of his students, these other personae also made the transition into their own afterlife, even though some of their bearers were still alive in 1974. It would seem, then, that scholarly personae, even though arguably devoid of a 'psyche', can carry functions that amount to a variation of the Freudian death drive. The interplay between ordinary and historiographical historicization was an expression of this drive, a tool for establishing finitude, inasmuch as it was designed to destroy the essential methodological distinction between historical time and the time of scholarly work. All in all, this architecture of meanings was built as a necropolis. Once finished, it would be lived in no longer. In a sense, this was the core of scholarly personae: they were self-designed funerary monuments. Towards the beginning of the construction of the necropolis, its architects had counted on their successors to uphold the general funerary culture indefinitely; but by the time Lyon was writing his biography of Pirenne, it was clear that customs were changing more broadly. Still, the remaining builders of the necropolis, such as Ganshof, did not fight this change. Rather, they integrated it into the architecture, which became redefined as a monument to itself, a design that was to be abandoned and to fall into ruins, a symbol of the finitude even of symbols of finitude. This reflexive loop is, I would maintain, the most decisive constituent of the finitude of scholarly personae. The scholarly persona ended by bingeing on its finitude.

Conclusion

So why does the finitude of scholarly personae matter? In conclusion, I will attempt to indicate some of what I consider to be the wider explanatory force of the argument here outlined. To begin with, death drive was not good enough for one line of the critical reception of Ganshof's and Lyon's work on Pirenne. From these critics' perspective, the end of the scholarly persona was not to be left to its own devices. There was yet another development to be taken into account, the pattern of political mobilization that had already emerged in history writing during the interwar period. More precisely, the pattern was one of the assertion of political affiliations. Nineteenth-century patterns of liberal nationalism, which had by and large been dominant among 'positivist' or 'historicist' continental historians of the period, had usually maintained a tie to earlier constitutionalist movements. Since constitutional liberalism claimed to provide the legal foundations for all partisan strife, historians of this ilk, such as Pirenne, often felt that *their* partisan position transcended partisanship and enjoyed a privileged relationship to the virtue of objectivity. However, after 1914 the political landscape in which history was written underwent drastic changes, and the old order became unsustainable. Ganshof had found it necessary to stray from his master's positions in several crucial regards, for instance as concerned the necessity of accommodating the Flemish nationalist movement; and, especially after Pirenne's death, in his similarly accommodating stance towards German historians throughout the 1930s and 1940s. This latter stance, in particular, had troubled and offended a number of colleagues before World War II, both inside and outside Belgium. In the immediate postwar period, Ganshof had even been attacked as a collaborator in the Belgian press. The acrimony from this period continued to inform generational divides in the discipline of history in Belgium and fuelled several conflicts that marred the later phase of Ganshof's career at Ghent.

Still, from the mid-1940s onwards, Ganshof had withdrawn from visible political engagement into a frenzied activity of publishing 'pure' scholarship. This withdrawal sat uneasily with some younger colleagues who had adopted a critical mode of interpreting history writing that made visible scholars' underlying political commitments. In 1966, Ganshof's erstwhile student Jan Dhondt (1915–72), who since 1945 held the position of professor of contemporary history at Ghent, an appointment he regarded as an affront since he was a trained medievalist, harshly attacked the legacy of Pirenne.[27] As Adriaan Verhulst (1929–2002), one of Ganshof's younger students, remembered years later, Dhondt had openly admitted in conversation that his attack had been aimed at Ganshof and other students of Pirenne.[28] Dhondt argued that all of Pirenne's famed doctrines about the development of the medieval city and the urban bourgeoisie as the main carrier of European history merely expressed the biases of Pirenne's own social class. Significantly, Dhondt had committed to communism for a number of years from the mid-1930s onward, and in the postwar period was associated with socialist party politics. When Lyon, shortly after the publication of the biography, made an attempt to rebut Dhondt's views, he was in turn attacked by Wim Blockmans.[29]

In short, the politics of the persona of Pirenne, both in life and in afterlife, had become prominent. Dhondt's and Blockmans's points about the liberal-national bias behind the facade of 'epistemic virtues' were well made. Still, in a way, the very broadly Marxist current in academic history writing that had emerged since the 1930s, and to which Dhondt in particular belonged, offered a similar notion of privileged access to the very foundations of politics that had animated liberalism – only *these* foundations were to be located in class struggle instead of constitutionalism. Indeed, a view of who should have privileged access to the foundations of the political may well be part of any partisanship in twentieth-century Europe. The process one can observe in modern European universities was not one of politicizing something formerly unpolitical, but above all an adaptation to changes in social participation in politics and the landscape of parties. As universities became gradually more socially inclusive, history writing also came to display political orientations it had previously suppressed or marginalized. Since the old system of persona-building epistemic virtues could be characterized as disingenuous about its political biases, as Dhondt implied, it became caught up in the broader social change.

Still, it is hard to see why the old system should not have been able to adapt. There were even older models available for dealing with the partisanship of history writing. As has repeatedly been pointed out, the career of 'objectivity' (*pace* Daston and Galison) in historical methodology had been propelled precisely by a notion of multipartisan compromise that could pass as non-partisanship.[30] Assuming that this is not what happened in the 1960s, what then had come to stand in the way of recalibrating the system of scholarly personae along the traditional lines of multipartisan accommodationism? Arguably, it was precisely the inbuilt death drive in symbolic academic selves such as Ganshof's that explains the manner in which the political shifts in the university became hooked up with the problem of the finitude of the scholarly persona. The year the Ganshofs spent in Berkeley was the one that preceded the emergence of the Free Speech Movement and the escalation of US military engagement in Vietnam. The resulting upheavals to academic life in California prompted Lyon to resign and move to Brown University abruptly, in the summer of 1965.[31]

In both American and Western European universities during this period, broader social change became entangled with a realignment of some important cultural frames concerning selfhood. The academic world was central to this shift. Radical theories of the disappearance of the self, at least in its modern European guise, were formulated in various places. Practices of questioning the norms of social selfhood pervaded academic milieus. Anti-humanism – often with recourse to Nietzsche, whose philosophy could be read as one enormous attempt to rid himself of his scholarly persona – alternative pedagogies, various emancipatory movements and theories, psychotherapeutic discourse and the chemical manipulation of consciousness had the reshaping of the category of selfhood as a common denominator. Arguably, one of the causes of this development lay precisely in the simultaneous decline of the scholarly persona, not just in the natural sciences, but also in those disciplines of the humanities and social sciences that were particularly concerned with the domains of theory in question. The student culture may have been far more under the influence of professorial culture than it cared, or dared, to admit. The tremendous flurry of deconstructions of subjectivity, selfhood and sovereignty that continues to mark theoretical debate may have originated in the shared participation of academic generations in the consumption of the finitude of scholarly personae.

Notes

1 See Lorraine Daston and Otto Sibum, 'Introduction: scientific personae and their histories', *Science in Context*, 16 (2003), 1–8.
2 As developed in more detail in Lorraine Daston and Peter Galison, *Objectivity* (New York: Zone Books, 2007).
3 Steven Shapin, *The Scientific Life: A Moral History of a Late Modern Vocation* (Chicago: University of Chicago Press, 2008).
4 I have pursued an argument to this effect in 'Dispersed personae: subject-matter of scholarly biography in nineteenth-century oriental philology', *Asiatische Studien*, 67:4 (2013), 1325–60.
5 Pierre Bourdieu, *Homo academicus* (Paris: Minuit, 1984).
6 See for instance Hélène Mialet, *Hawking Incorporated: Stephen Hawking and the Anthropology of the Knowing Subject* (Chicago: University of Chicago Press, 2012).
7 Bryce Lyon, *Henri Pirenne: A Biographical and Intellectual Study* (Ghent: Story-Scientia, 1974).
8 See e.g. the short remarks by Walter Prevenier, 'Bryce Lyon and the Royal Historical Commission of Belgium', in David Nicholas, Bernard S. Bachrach and James M. Murray (eds), *Comparative Perspectives on History and Historians: Essays in Memory of Bryce Lyon (1920–2007)* (Kalamazoo, MI: Western Michigan University, 2012), pp 13–18.
9 François Louis Ganshof, 'Pirenne (Henri)', *Biographie Nationale de Belgique*, vol. 30 (Brussels: Bruylant, 1959), 671–723.
10 Bibliotheek Universiteit Gent, nalatenschap François Louis Ganshof, HS III 86. For an analysis of the forms of correspondence in this archive, see Henning Trüper, *Topography of a Method: François Louis Ganshof and the Writing of History* (Tübingen: Mohr, 2014), part III. I refrain from referring to the book more extensively, though in the following, for biographical context, I frequently draw on research presented there.
11 Archives Université Libre de Bruxelles, correspondence donated by Bryce Lyon (seen before inventorying).
12 Jo Tollebeek, *Fredericq & Zonen: Een antropologie van de moderne geschiedwetenschap* (Amsterdam: Bakker, 2008). Daniela Saxer has arrived at similar results in her *Die Schärfung des Quellenblicks: Forschungspraktiken in der Geschichtswissenschaft 1840–1914* (Munich: Oldenbourg: 2014), pp 173–220.
13 Ganshof to Lyon, 24 June 1963, Archives ULB, Correspondences Lyon, envelope

'Correspondance avec Professeur Ganshof and [!] aussi sa femme' (also subsequent correspondence unless stated otherwise).
14 Bryce Lyon to Ganshof, 28 June 1963.
15 Ganshof to Lyon, 2 July 1963.
16 Ganshof to Lyon, 21 June 1964.
17 Ganshof to Lyon, 1 July 1964.
18 Notes, labelled by Lyon: 'Ganshof's comments on article on Maurice Prou for *Le Moyen Age* (1965)', p. 1.
19 Ganshof, Manuscript corrections of Lyon's works on historiography, Notes on chapter II, p. 8f.
20 This notion of the 'imitation' of German scholarship is mentioned, for instance, in Ganshof's notes on chapter I, p. 8. On the historical limits of such imitative processes, see Gabriele Lingelbach, *Klio macht Karriere: Die Institutionalisierung der Geschichtswissenschaft in Frankreich und den USA in der zweiten Hälfte des 19. Jahrhunderts* (Göttingen: Vandenhoeck & Ruprecht, 2003).
21 Notes on chapter II, p. 1f.
22 Kasper Eskildsen has indicated some important aspects of this shift in 'Inventing the archive: testimony and virtue in modern historiography', *History of the Human Sciences*, 26:4 (2013), 8–26.
23 Ganshof, 'Pirenne', 723. See further Sarah Keymeulen, 'Henri Pirenne: historian and man of the world', *Low Countries Historical Review*, 131:4 (2016), 71–92.
24 Notes on chapter II, p. 13.
25 Notes on chapter V, p. 3 (NB square brackets in italics are not in the original).
26 See Trüper, *Topography*, pp 113–49.
27 Jan Dhondt, 'Henri Pirenne: historien des institutions urbaines' [1966], in *Machten en Mensen: De belangrijkste studies van Jan Dhondt over de geschiedenis van de 19e en 20e eeuw* (Ghent: Jan Dhondt Stichting, 1976), pp 63–119.
28 As Verhulst explained in a letter to Susan Reynolds, 28 August 1987, Bibliotheek Universiteit Gent, nalatenschap Adriaan Verhulst, HS III 108, doos 5.
29 Wim Blockmans, 'Mandarijnenhulde en wetenschapsgeschiedenis', *Handelingen van de Maatschappij voor Geschiedenis en Oudheidkunde te Gent*, 29 (1975), 27–38.
30 Following Peter Novick, *That Noble Dream: The 'Objectivity Question' and the American Historical Profession* (Cambridge: Cambridge University Press, 1988) and Jo Tollebeek, *De toga van Fruin: denken over geschiedenis in Nederland sinds 1860* (Amsterdam: Werelbibliotheek, 1990).
31 As referred to in Ganshof to Lyon, 13 March 1965.

Index

Ade-Ajayi, J. F. 184
Albert, Prince Consort of the United Kingdom 97, 98, 101
Albuquerque Mourao, F.A. 186
Alemany, Joseph S. 62
Algazi, Gadi 42, 43, 56, 57, 89
Ameal, João 140–2
Arnot, R. Page 152
Azevedo, Rui de 133

Baiao, António 132
Bancroft, Hubert Howe 12, 53–7, 59–64, 66, 67
Bartók, Béla 172
Bauer, Bruno 19
Bayle, Pierre 117
Beirão, Caetano 137
Bell, Kenneth 153
Bernheim, Ernst 11
Berr, Henri 72
Berthelot, Marcellin 78
Bezold, Friedrich von 45
Bierce, Ambrose 54, 55
Billias, George Athan 10
Bloch, Marc 73, 76, 79, 81–3, 165
Blockmans, Wim 215, 216
Boahen, Adu 186, 188–90, 193–5
Boddice, Rob 94
Borel, Emile 80
Bosch, Mineke 3
Bourdieu, Pierre 202
Braudel, Fernand 9
Bremner, G. A. 90
Brito, Saint João de 140
Bryce, James 93, 94

Caetano, Marcelo 132
Capern, Amanda 91
Carlyle, Thomas 57, 58
Chanaiwa, David 186
Church, Dean 90
Collini, Stefan 92
Columbus, Christopher 11
Confucius 109, 117, 118, 124
Conlin, Jonathan 90
Cook, James 11
Cornforth, Maurice 150
Craik, George 97
Creighton, Mandell 94
Cromwell, Oliver 154, 158
Cubitt, Geoffrey 92
Curie, Pierre and Marie 80

Dahlmann, Friedrich Christoph 45
Dantas, Júlio 132, 133
Daston, Lorraine 3–6, 8, 84, 131, 134, 146, 147, 216
Daub, Karl 19
Deák, István 167, 168, 174, 180
Devisse, Jean 186
Dewey, John 119, 121
Dhondt, Jan 215, 216
Diagne, Pathé 189
Diekamp, Wilhelm 44
Dilthey, Wilhelm 40, 41
Diop, Cheikh Anta 189
Dirlik, Arif 127
Dobb, Maurice 146, 148, 149, 151–3, 155–8, 160
Doran, John 90
Droysen, Johann Gustav 45

INDEX

Du Bois, W. E. B. 197
Du Cange, Charles 75
Durkheim, Emile 82
Dutt, R. Palme 154

Eichhorn, Johann Albrecht 19
Engels, Friedrich 149, 154, 155, 157, 159, 180
Erdmannsdörffer, Bernhard 43–5
Ermisch, Hubert 44
Eskildsen, Kasper Risbjerg 38

Fanon, Frantz 197
Febvre, Lucien 72–4, 76–9, 82–4
Fichte, Johann Gottlieb 25
Firth, Charles Harding 155, 156
Fontoura da Costa, Abel 132
Franklin, Benjamin 176
Fredericq, Paul 204, 210
Freeman, Edward A. 8, 9, 89–102
Freud, Sigmund 172
Froude, James Anthony 8, 53, 54
Fustel de Coulanges, Numa Denis 82

Galbraith, Vivian Hunter 153
Galison, Peter 5, 6, 134, 216
Gans, Eduard 19
Ganshof, François Louis 202–16
Ganshof, Nell 204
Gardiner, Samuel Rawson 155, 156
Garman, Douglas 155, 157, 158
Gervinus, Georg Gottfried 40, 44
Glélé, Maurice 193
Godinho, Magalhães 142
Goethe, Johann Wolfgang von 41
Goffman, Erving 3, 201
Grauert, Hermann 46
Green, John Richard 90, 93, 96–100
Greenblatt, Stephen 3
Grob, Gerald 10
Guanghan, Liu (a.k.a. Shipei, Liu) 114
Guizot, François 174

Habermas, Jürgen 11
Halphen, Louis 72
Hanák, Péter 164–80
Hasan, Yusuf 192, 193
Hasse, F. C. A. 39
Häusser, Ludwig 45
Hegel, G. W. F. 15, 16, 18–25, 27–9, 32

Hempel, Carl G. 132
Hesketh, Ian 92, 96
Higham, John 5
Hill, Christopher 146, 147, 149, 151–60
Hillebrand, Joseph 36, 37
Hinrichs, Hermann 19, 21
Hobsbawm, Eric 151, 153, 178
Hoffmanstahl, Hugo von 172
Howsam, Leslie 91, 98, 103
Hrbek, Ivan 187, 189, 198
Hubert, Eugène 210
Hüffer, Georg 44
Hung-chien, Fang 107, 127
Hutt, Allen 156

Iggers, Georg and Wilma 24

Jameson, J. Franklin 55, 63
Janssen, Johannes 44, 46
Jászi, Oszkár 173
Jefferson, Thomas 176
Jiegang, Gu 120, 121, 123, 124, 126
Jirô, Shirakawa 117
João V, King of Portugal 135

Kafka, Franz 172
Kan, Huang 124
Kant, Immanuel 18, 19
Keynes, John Maynard 152
Khrushchev, Nikita 149
Kiernan, Victor 151
Kimambo, Isaria 186
Ki-Zerbo, Joseph 188, 189, 190, 192
Klimt, Gustav 172
Klugmann, James 160
Kocka, Jürgen 171
Koestler, Arthur 175
Kokoschka, Oskar 172
Konaré, Adame Ba 189
Kraus, Karl 172
Kriegk, Georg Ludwig 38
Kuczynski, Jürgen 154–60
Kundera, Milan 177
Kurz, Heinrich 40
Kyuichi, Endô 117

Lachmann, Karl 19
Lamprecht, Karl 45
Langlois, Charles-Victor 73, 79
Lasch, Christopher 5, 10
Laya, Dioulé 195

INDEX

Lefranc, Abel 208
Lenin, Vladimir 159
Lenz, Max 44
Leo, Heinrich 19, 23, 27, 30
Lerner, Gerda 2, 4, 7
Lesueur, Monique 190
Lindau, Paul 36, 37, 39–41, 46, 47
Löbell, Johann Wilhelm 40
Lopes, David 141
Lukács, George 172
Lyon, Bryce Dale 202–4, 206–9, 211, 214, 216
Lyon, Mary 204, 205

M'Bow, Amadou-Mahtar 193
Mabillon, Jean 75
Macartney, George 110
Macaulay, Thomas 174
Macmillan, Alexander 96–8
Macmillan, Frederick 101
Mannheim, Karl 173
Marheineke, Philipp 19
Marques, Oliveira 142
Marx, Karl 149, 155–7, 159, 180
Matos, Gastão de 132
Mazrui, Ali 188, 190, 191, 194, 195, 197
Melville, Herman 59
Mencius 117, 119, 120
Merêa, Paulo 132, 139, 140, 142
Michelet, Jules 73, 76–8, 84
Milosz, Czeslaw 177
Monod, Gabriel 72–9, 85
Morton, A. L. 146, 149–51, 153, 155
Mosley, Oswald 151
Mudimbe, Valentin 184, 197
Múrias, Manuel 132
Musil, Robert 172, 173
Mutibwa, Phares M. 193–5

Napoleon Bonaparte 20
Naudé, Alfred 45
Niane, Djibril Tamsir 187
Niang, Mangoné 189
Niansun, Wang 120
Niebuhr, Barthold 19, 75
Nipperdey, Thomas 11
Niskanen, Kirsti 3
Noorden, Carl von 40
Norgate, Kate 94, 99, 100, 102
Novick, Peter 1

Oak, Henry 54, 60–2, 66
Ogot, Bethwell 192–4
Oncken, Wilhelm 36

Paul, Herman 85, 102, 108, 131, 138, 147, 196
Peres, Damião 132, 134, 136, 141
Pimenta, Alfredo 132, 133, 136, 137
Pirenne, Henri 202–4, 208–15
Pirenne, Jacques 203
Plekhanov, Georgi 155
Poe, Edgar Allan 59
Pokrovsky, Mikhail 155, 158–60
Polányi, Karl 173
Pollitt, Harry 149, 154, 160
Prou, Maurice 208

Qian, Sima 123
Qianlong, Emperor of China 110
Qichao, Liang 111–19, 121–5

Ranke, Leopold von 7, 11, 15–17, 19, 20, 23–7, 32, 39, 40–4, 46, 75
Rau, Virgínia 139, 140, 142
Rawlings, Jerry John 190
Renda, Francesco 178
Ritter, Heinrich 19
Ross, Travis 12
Rothe, Richard 29
Rühl, Franz 43, 44

Salazar, António de Oliveira 9, 136
Sánchez-Albornoz, Claudio 139
Savage, Thomas 60, 62
Savigny, Friedrich von 19, 20
Schiller, Friedrich 41
Schleiermacher, Friedrich Daniel 19, 20, 22
Schlosser, Friedrich Christoph 23, 36–44, 46, 47
Schoenbrun, David 191
Schönberg, Arnold 172
Schorske, Carl 171–3
Seignobos, Charles 73, 79–83, 85, 211
Serrão, Joel 134
Seton-Watson, R.W. 174
Shapin, Steven 38, 201
Shi, Deng 114
Shi, Hu 119–24
Sibum, H. Otto 3–6, 8, 84, 131, 146, 147
Simon, Ernst 15

Sinian, Fu 120, 124–6
Slater, Henry 186
Southard, Robert 45
Stalin, Joseph 152, 156, 159
Stephen, Leslie 91
Stephens, W. R. W. 94, 95
Stephenson, Carl 203
Stopford Green, Alice 94
Sybel, Heinrich von 36, 40, 43, 45

Taiyan, Zhang 111–13, 115–21, 124, 125
Tawney, R. H. 155, 156
Thierry, Augustin 174
Thomas, Paul 209
Thompson, Dorothy 150
Thompson, Edith 89–92, 94–102
Thompson, Edward Palmer 150, 151
Tollebeek, Jo 204
Torgal, Luís Reis 131
Torr, Dona 146, 149–51, 153, 155, 157–60
Treitschke, Heinrich von 7, 11, 36, 39, 44, 45

Unger, Irwin 2

Vansina, Jan 188, 190–2, 194, 195, 198
Vasconcelos, Father Garcia de 132, 135
Verhulst, Adriaan 215
Victor, Frances Fuller 60, 62
Victoria, Queen of the United Kingdom 98, 101
Vlugt, Willem van der 80

Wagner, Michele 191
Waitz, Georg 7, 44–7, 74, 75
Washington, George 176
Weber, Georg 41
Wehler, Hans-Ulrich 11
Weiland, Ludwig 45
Weiner, Jonathan 4
Weinstein, James 10
White, Hayden 2, 4, 24, 108
Williams, Raymond 151
Wils, Kaat 3
Wittgenstein, Ludwig 172
Wouters, Pierre Jean 210

Xi, Zhu 112
Xuantong, Qian 121
Xunzi (Xun Kuang) 117–21

Yat-sen, Sun 116
Yinzhi, Wang 120
Yirang, Sun 120
Youwei, Kang 112, 113, 115, 116
Yuanpei, Cai 121
Yue, Yu 112, 115, 120
Yukichi, Fukuzawa 114, 115

Zedong, Mao 119
Zhongshu, Qian 107, 127
Zinn, Howard 1, 2, 4–6
Zizhen, Gong 110, 111
Zöllner, Erich 170
Zumpt, Karl Gottlob 19

EU authorised representative for GPSR:
Easy Access System Europe, Mustamäe tee 50,
10621 Tallinn, Estonia
gpsr.requests@easproject.com

www.ingramcontent.com/pod-product-compliance
Lightning Source LLC
Chambersburg PA
CBHW021353300426
44114CB00012B/1211